The Concept of
Ideology and
Political Analysis

Contributions in Philosophy

The Concept of Ideology and Political Analysis

A Critical Examination of Its Usage By Marx, Lenin, and Mannheim

Walter Carlsnaes

Contributions in Philosophy, Number 17

GREENWOOD PRESS
Westport, Connecticut • London, England

Library of Congress Cataloging in Publication Data

Carlsnaes, Walter.
　　The concept of ideology and political analysis.

　　(Contributions in philosophy; no. 17 ISSN
0084-926X)
　　Bibliography: p.
　　Includes index.
　　1.　Marx, Karl, 1818-1883.　2.　Lenin, Vladimir
Il'ich, 1870-1924.　3.　Mannheim, Karl, 1893-1947.
4.　Ideology—History.　I.　Title.
B823.3.C37　　　306'.4　　　　　80-1202
ISBN 0-313-22267-3

Library of Congress Catalog Card Number: 80-1202
ISBN: 0-313-22267-3
ISSN: 0084-926X

First published in 1981

Greenwood Press
A division of Congressional Information Service, Inc.
88 Post Road West, Westport, Connecticut 06881

Printed in the United States of America

10　9　8　7　6　5　4　3　2　1

To Ingela
who contributed little
but has given so much

Wherever primitive man put up a word, he
believed he had made a discovery. How utterly
mistaken he really was! He had touched upon
a problem, and while supposing he had solved
it, he had created an obstacle to its solution.
Now, with every new knowledge we stumble over
flint-like and petrified words and, in so doing,
break a leg sooner than a word.

H. Friedrich Nietzsche

Q. What learning is most useful to all men?
A. Christian learning.
Q. Why?
A. Because it leads us to God, to everlasting
salvation, or, in other words, to everlasting happiness.
Q. How can we draw near to God?
A. By thought, wish and deed.

The Shorter Catechism,
revised and approved by
the Most Governing Synod
of the Russian Orthodox
Church (1845)

CONTENTS

PREFACE

The subject matter of this study is explained in the introductory chapter and can also be gauged to some extent from the table of contents. Hence I need not go into it here. What I should make clear at the outset, however, is that although my central concern in this analysis is with the meaning of the concept of ideology, I will not offer a definition or conceptualization of my own. Instead, what will emerge is merely an indication of what, in my view, should constitute the basic elements or contours of such a conceptualization. Hence the reader who seeks for anything like a definitive statement on this question will probably be disappointed. He should, however, be cognizant of the fact that what has been lacking in the literature are not stipulations as to what "ideology" means or signifies, but critical discussions of the explanatory significance—or rather, lack of such significance—of the almost endless variety of meanings of the term littering the pages of the literature. Thus it is not timidity which prompts my reticence on this point, but the fact that the overriding aim of this study has been critical and abstersive rather than directly remedial or corrective.

Since its beginning this study has both physically and metaphorically followed a somewhat tortuous path. Hence acknowledgments and thanks are owed to a number of individuals and institutions. First of all, general thanks are due to all who gave me the rare opportunity to go my own way with little interference or interruption. Such independence is indeed something to be grateful for, and in this respect I have been most fortunate. This of course absolves everybody except myself from the mistakes and errors of interpretation, judgment, and misunderstanding which undoubtedly are to be found in this study.But this is a small price to pay for the freedom that I have enjoyed, especially for the luxury of being able to err freely. For freedom from gross financial strain—a necessary concomitant of intellectual freedom—I wish to acknowledge my thanks to the following institutions: Princeton University, for giving me a doctoral fellowship for a sufficient number of years to allow me to get my bearings as a graduate student; the University of Uppsala, for subsequently taking over this financial role for an extensive period of time; the Swedish Kennedy Foundation, for making possible my stay at Harvard University as a visiting research fellow; and the Fellows of The Queen's College, for awarding me a Florey European student-ship, facilitating my stay at Oxford. I also wish to thank the U.S. Office of Education for its award of a Fulbright-Hays research fellowship, which allowed me to go to Africa, where I first became perplexed about the meaning of ideology. Gratitude is also due to the various bodies that underwrote my attendance at various international conferences.

For their interest, help, and inspiration I also wish to thank Nils Elvander and Leif Lewin, both of the Department of Government at the University of Uppsala, where I was first introduced to the strange world of the political science confraternity. My stay at Oxford was deeply enriched by my two supervisors there: the late John Plamenatz, whose last doctoral student I was before his sudden, untimely, and tragic death; and Sir Isaiah Berlin, who despite the immense pressures on his time was kind enough to take over the supervision of my work. His sympathetic guidance and great wit will always remain a very pleasant memory asso-ciated with Oxford. However, my deepest feelings of appreciation go to Nina, Sann, and Micke, and in particular to Ingela, none of whom ever kept silent when around, and all of whom have made this effort worthwhile. Their lack of interest in the concept of ideology has been not only profound but also sound, well-founded, and salutary.

ACKNOWLEDGMENTS

For permission to reproduce materials, we are indebted to the following:

From "Marx and the Intellectuals," Shlomo Avineri, *Journal of the History of Ideas*, Vol. 28, No. 2 (April-June 1967): 270, 276, 278, Temple University, Philadelphia, Pa. Reprinted with the permission of the publisher.

From Z. A. Jordan, *The Evolution of Dialectical Materialism*, 1967, St. Martin's Press, Inc. New York, and Macmillan & Co. Ltd., London. Excerpts from pages 152, 212, 214, 216, 220, 221, 238, 327, 353, 355 reprinted with the permission of St. Martin's Press Inc. for use in the United States and of Macmillan & Co. Ltd., London, for use in the rest of the world.

From *Ideology and Utopica* by Karl Mannheim, published first in 1936 by Routledge & Kegan Paul Ltd., London. Reprinted for use throughout the world excluding the United States by permission of Routledge & Kegan and for use in the United States by permission of Harcourt Brace Jovanovich, Inc., New York.

From *The Poverty of Historicism* by Karl Popper. First published in Economica, 1944 and 1945; first published in book form in English by Routledge Kegan Paul Ltd., London, 1957; 10/1979. Also published by Basic Books and by Harper and Row, New York. Passages from pages vii, viif, 3, 76, and 78 from the 1961 edition of Harper Torchbooks have been reprinted with the kind permission of Sir Karl Popper.

From *Ideology of Politics* by Martin Seliger, pp. 13, 14, 15, 16, 17, 18, 26, 87, 103f, 119f, 135, published 1976 by George Allen & Unwin (Publishers) Ltd., London. Reprinted for use throughout the world excluding the United States by permission of George Allen & Unwin (Publishers) Ltd., and for use in the United States by permission of The Free Press, a Division of Macmillan Publishing Co., New York.

Every reasonable effort has been made to trace the owners of copyright materials in this book, but in some instances this has proven impossible. The publishers will be glad to receive information leading to more complete acknowledgments in subsequent printings of this book, and in the meantime extend their apologies for any omissions.

The Concept of
Ideology and
Political Analysis

1

'IDEOLOGY' IN POLITICAL ANALYSIS: A SHORT INTRODUCTION

The word *ideology* enjoys an undisputed popularity today, both in the scholarly community and in everyday discourse. Indeed, within the social sciences it has become one of the more salient terms in the contemporary literature, where it has reached such eminence that the *International Encyclopedia of the Social Sciences*, published in 1968 and constituting as authoritative an arbiter of terminological respectability as we are to find anywhere in the Western world, gives us, under the heading *ideology*, not one but two articles (and nearly twenty two-column pages), both by leading scholars in the field. However, it is also a fact, and a somewhat more surprising one, that this is a relatively recent terminological development, even though the word itself was first used as long ago as the end of the eighteenth century. Thus if we consult the predecessor of the above work of reference, the *Encyclopaedia of the Social Sciences*, published in the early 1930s, we will search in vain even for a rubric bearing the name of the concept. It is thus only in little over one generation that *ideology* has moved from being a nonterm to its present two-star status in the vocabulary of the social sciences.[1]

There are undoubtedly various reasons for this somewhat sudden upsurge in the usage of the term in social and political analysis. The growth and defeat of fascism and nazism clearly played an important role, as did the subsequent cold war atmosphere with its division of the world—or at least parts of it—into two antagonistic, so-called 'ideological' camps. It is important to note, furthermore, that this growth in popularity of the term has also been coeval, in the main, with the political awakening and emergence of the Third World, particularly that of the African continent. This awakening itself has often been portrayed as being foremost 'ideological' in nature, at least in the sense that it is viewed as a political movement—or a series of movements— primarily guided and inspired by ideas and ideals, particularly those associated with liberty and equality as expressed in the principle of self-determination. However, it is not only with reference to these various developments in twentieth-century history that the term is utilized today. One can indeed submit with confidence that few and far between are the contemporary social scientists who have not used it at one time or another, for purposes ranging from the most insignificant to the most momentous.

But it is also a fact, and one which is more noteworthy and less felicitous, that this popularization of the term and the proliferation of its usage along the whole spectrum of sociopolitical studies appear not to have been paralleled by its refinement as an analytic tool. Instead, this increasing visibility of "ideology" in scholarly discourse seems to be coupled with a growing obscurity and elusiveness in meaning. Arne Naess, more than twenty years ago, obviously anticipated this regression in semantic clarity when he felt compelled (in one of the first major studies of the term) to raise the conjecture that

the movement of the term "ideology" into social science, social psychology and political science will, within a generation, be followed by a movement in the other direction. It will continue to be used in headlines, in summaries and popularizations, but scarcely in statements intended to express . . . theories, hypotheses or classifications of observations.[2]

Despite the obvious ex post facto invalidity of this prediction, the underlying contention and injunction expressed above cannot be evaded. Indeed, we are more than ever impelled to raise and to pursue the question whether there remains much if any utility in retaining the term "ideology" for explanatory purposes, that is, if it constitutes a *substantive* and *significant* tool in the analysis of politics. It is the aim of this study to do precisely this.

The first query hinges on a distinction made by Abraham Kaplan between what he calls 'notational' and 'substantive' terms. The former are, essentially, interchangeable with other terms without any loss in descriptive content, while the latter are distinctive in the sense that no other term (or set of terms) adequately reflects the substantive content subsumed by it. In a scientific inquiry a term is deemed necessary insofar as its absence would entail a reduction in analytic scope with reference to the empirical or theoretical subject matter at hand. Conversely, a term is not strictly necessary (though it may be stylistically or otherwise useful) if it is simply utilized as a synonym or shorthand for another term or set of terms.[3] In other words, this distinction pertains to the cognitive equivalence or nonequivalence of terms or expressions.[4]

If, however, it can be shown that a term is not superfluous in the above sense, we are still left with the question if its usage is significant or fruitful for purposes of scientific inquiry. To answer this it is necessary, first of all, to make an elementary distinction between "terms" and "concepts."[5] The former are linguistic expressions, words or sets of words, as when we speak of a "tree" or "to be a nincompoop"; and we understand their meaning through their established usage or usages, which often vary but which nevertheless are tied together by such interrelating or classifying features as are attributable to the given expression (it is in this sense that Wittgenstein speaks of a "family of meanings"). Terms (or expressions) are the products of linguistic needs and habits, and almost willy-nilly acquire their meaning or meanings as they are used in the various universes of discourse which mark man's eloquence (or his lack of it, which may be considerable even among scholars). Concepts, on the other hand, are not linguistic expressions or classifications but abstract constructions pointed to or symbolized by terms or expressions.[6] For example (to use Carl Hempel's lucid illustration) the expression "soluble in alcohol" conveys the concept of 'solubility in alcohol,' that is, an abstract property shared by some substances but not by others.[7]

Although concepts are abstract constructions, this should not, however, lead us to assume that the meanings of terms—or their 'conceptions,' as they also have been called—are simply psychological events while concepts are logical or abstract entities floating around in the more abstruse regions of Platonic and timeless splendor. Rather, concepts are invariably rooted in conceptions (Kaplan, echoing Wittgenstein, speaks of the former as "families of conceptions"), so that as the conceptions change which enter into the abstract constructions, so will the constructions—that is, the concepts—themselves. The process of conceptualization is one in which terms and concepts constantly interact with each other, giving meaning not only to isolated phenomena but also to the relationships connecting them.[8]

Given these considerations, a term can be said to be scientifically significant or fruitful in at least two senses. We may, first of all, refer to the descriptive or semantic adequacy of a term, to its ability to describe the things or events that are the subject matter of investigation. We seek terms that possess a cognitively clear meaning and an optimum of emotive neutrality.[9] For terms may prima facie be substantive in nature but may also have acquired connotations which have become so ambiguous or emotively loaded that they no longer serve a fruitful semantic purpose as conveyors of descriptive meaning (for this reason it has sometimes been questioned if terms like "intelligence" or "instinct" today serve a positive function in the behavioral sciences).[10] Since cognitive clarity and emotive neutrality suffer, above all, in proportion to the vagueness and/or ambiguity of a term, it is clear that fruitfulness in this first sense will depend not only on the semantic clarity of a term but also, and more particularly, on a clear indication of thresholds or borderlines of meaning. That this latter requirement is particularly pertinent follows from the fact that meaning is never definite, permanent, or universal but is continually in a state of 'openness,' a condition reflecting both the nature of our conceptions—which vary not only over time but also in terms of the context and purpose of their usage at a particular moment—and what has been referred to as the 'indefiniteness of fact,' that is, the impossibility, inherent in the nature of things, of achieving a complete set of factual discriminations.[11]

The second and more important measure of terminological significance is not concerned with terms as linguistic expressions but with their conceptual scope or, as Hempel calls it, their systemic import or value. What is meant here is the capacity of a scientific term to generate true or valid statements about its subject matter other than those which state the meaning of the term itself. Strictly speaking, we are here dealing with the significance of concepts rather than terms; but since, as we have seen, concepts are rooted in the conceptions from which they acquire their import, it follows that if a term expresses a fruitless or insignificant concept, it is the term rather than the concept which is the immediate referent of inadequacy. A term may be clear but symbolize a sterile or artificial concept, which is the case when, as it has been said, we cannot do more with it than we first intended—a conceptual anemia which is readily apparent in so many of the classificatory schemas or typologies of social and especially political science. [12] A term which avoids this pitfall is sometimes referred to as expressing a 'natural' classification, its naturalness consisting "in this, that the attributes it chooses as the basis of classification are significantly related to the attributes conceptualized elsewhere in our thinking." [13] From this it follows that conceptual significance in the above sense cannot be achieved simply by attaching a semantic or lexical meaning (however precisely or stipulatively) to empirical phenomena; for the scientific endeavor owes its rationale to the generation of valid propositions, to the explanation of phenomena and not simply to their description. [14] It is with regard to this point that the interdependence between concept formation and theory formation is most clearly perceived. For if it is true to say that the "concepts in terms of which we pose our scientific questions limit the range of admissible answers," it is equally true that this range is codetermined by prior and subsequent judgments and inferences and that we therefore continue to conceptualize anew because we are not satisfied with the answers as they stand. [15]

In the light of these basic desiderata for a scientific vocabulary we can turn next to a more specific if as yet preliminary analysis of ideology both as term and concept. Despite the skepticism adumbrated above, it appears indubitable that at least the concept is indispensable for political analysis; and I also feel that the term itself is worth saving. [16]

'IDEOLOGY' AS A SUBSTANTIVE TERM

When we seek to inquire if a given term is substantive, our purpose is not to establish what such a term means, but rather whether its usage indicates a conceptual content not sufficiently or completely covered by another, allied term. It is possible to take at least two methodological positions in determining such cognitive nonequivalence: we can either proceed axiomatically (availing ourselves of the 'awaiting-contrary-proof' clause) by simply assuming the nonequivalence of closely associated terms with the particular term at hand until contrary proof has been proffered; or we can indicate that equivalence does not hold by demonstrating that none of these other terms is a synonym for it. The first procedure is obviously more elegant and parsimonious, since it places the burden of proof on others; but I shall follow the second, if only to illustrate briefly the variety of definitions which in fact have been given to "ideology." In doing so there is no need, however, to supply an exhaustive or even a sketchy, though representative, list of such definitions; this is not only unnecessary for my purposes but has been adequately done by others. [17]

"Ideology" is most often qualified in terms of "ideas," "beliefs," "doctrines," "theories," "philosophies," "*Weltanschauungen*," "values," "opinions," "myths," "utopias," and other associated and derivative words. It is of course this rich endowment of intermingling notions that makes the word such an omnibus and thus 'usable' term, since it is often believed that the various phenomena for which these and similar terms stand are somehow related to one another as a consequence of their 'ideological' nature. One often reads that ideology is a set of ideas, beliefs, doctrines, or that philosophies, myths, and so forth, are ideological manifestations of one kind or another.

It is apparent that if we give these terms a cursory examination, they readily (if only intuitively) fall into two broad categories. All except "myth" and "utopia" are what we can call open-ended terms, since they are rather vague and wide in meaning and have in common the fact that almost all human beings can be said to have some kind of relationship to what they signify (indeed they can be considered in a certain sense to signify man's peculiarly human intellective capacities). The last two, however, are more circumscribed and closed and can be classified as special cases of the former. Also, the first group consists of relatively neutral terms, while "myth" and "utopia" have acquired either hortatory or pejorative associations or connotations, depending on the context and function of their usage.

If we turn to the former group first, it is clear that as long as "ideology" is qualified in terms of a set of ideas, beliefs, opinions, doctrines, values, or as a theory, *Weltanschauung*, or philosophy, held by an individual, a group, or society, then as a term it has no substantive content beyond these notations, which remain to be explained with regard to their own particular references in each case. This judgment would apply, for example, to Harold Lasswell and his conception of ideology as "the thoughts, feelings, and conduct of human beings,"[18] or to the notion that ideology is every "pattern of thought, every philosophical or other cultural product, which belongs to the specific social group with which it originated and with whose existence it is bound up."[19] To define the term in this manner is simply to pave the way for tautologous and thus nonfalsifiable statements, since it tells us nothing beyond the fact that these notations are interchangeable and therefore preclude, a priori, "ideology" as a term which in any way qualifies or predicates the nature of these other notations.[20] Given such a conception of the term, its use rather than that of the other terms or expressions is simply a question of arbitrary or stylistic preference; and if we accept the rule of terminological parsimony, its use can be said to be superfluous for scholarly purposes, except perhaps as a convenient shorthand, that is, as a notational device economizing the use of words or phrases.

It is clear, however, that more often "ideology" is used as a term in its own right and not simply to abridge more extensive notations. We read that ideologies are "the integrated assertions, theories, and aims that constitute a sociopolitical program,"[21] or that an ideology "is a pattern of beliefs and concepts (both factual and normative) which purport to explain complex social phenomena with a view to directing and simplifying sociopolitical choices facing individuals and groups."[22] In these two conceptions "ideology" becomes a subclass or qualification of a general set of ideas or beliefs defined in terms both of its systemic characteristics and sociopolitical function. A further common view is that ideology pertains to the espousal of notions that are characterized by their selective distortion (conscious or not) of reality in the defense or rationalization of social or class privileges. On the whole, this is usually taken to be the Marxian—or at least Marxist—formulation of its meaning. It is also often defined as "an extremist sociopolitical program or philosophy constructed wholly or in part on fictitious or hypothetical ideational bases" (this was probably the typical cold war conception in the West).[23] It is undoubtedly this usage that Daniel Bell had in mind when he defined an ideological writer as one running down the street crying: "I've got an answer, who's got a question?"[24] From these examples of usage and definition—and I have noted but a few—it becomes obvious that "ideology" is often given a more ambitious function in scholarly discourse than signifying merely any set of ideas, doctrines, and so on. It is viewed as expressing aspects of reality which are not adequately subsumed by other terms.[25]

If "ideology" cannot simply be substituted by the above notations, what about the more circumscribed ideational notions of "myth" and "utopia"? To answer this question we have to ask ourselves not only if all utopias and/or myths are to be conceived of as 'ideological,' but also if ideology is necessarily 'utopian' or 'mythical' in nature.[26] At least in terms of classical conceptions of these two terms, affirming either of these two questions would seem very willful and arbitrary. This is clear, for example, in two such radically different thinkers as Sorel and Mannheim, who, although they do not agree with each other with regard to their definitions, are explicit about the fact that these three terms should be clearly differentiated.[27] Mannheim distinguished myth from ideology as an irrational as opposed to a rational cultural form, and utopia from ideology as a dynamic, subjective idea as opposed to an essentially static and conservative force rationalizing the status quo.[28] Sorel, on the other hand, conceived of myth as the dynamic expression of the 'will to action,' while utopia is an 'intellectual product' without any dynamic social significance. To ideology he gives a twofold if inconsistent meaning, the one close to Mannheim's notion of a static rationalization of the social order, the other allied to myth as its intellectualized form, a "trainer of thought" creating the "ideological unity" required for effective political action.[29]

Such a differentiation has also been argued for on the basis of historical considerations, in the sense that ideology is viewed as a distinctly modern phenomenon, while both myths and utopias—and particularly the former—can be said to have existed ever since homo sapiens first started cogitating about the past, present, and future. Reinhard Bendix writes that the term "ideology" is "not properly applicable to Western civilization prior to the seventeenth and eighteenth centuries, somewhat in the way that terms like 'economy' or 'society' or 'intellectuals' do not fit the premodern period either"; and that it is only "when human reason and the ends of action are questioned that 'ideology' comes into its own."[30] Mannheim seemed to have suggested something similar when he noted that "the capacity to grasp an idea as ideological is unthinkable prior to a certain time in history."[31] Most commonly this historical threshold is viewed in terms of the line which divides the modern age and that of the ancien régime.[32]

In summary, I think it is quite clear that "ideology," however much it has been used only 'notationally' by careless scholars, is a 'substantive' term in its own right. This fact, however, provides us only with a baseline from which to tackle a much more important and difficult question, namely, the question of the conceptual significance of the term.

'IDEOLOGY' AS A SIGNIFICANT TERM

I need hardly emphasize that "ideology"is not particularly blessed with a consistently applied and generally accepted meaning either in intellectual history in general or in the more circumscribed annals of social and political science. Indeed, the semantic prowess of this term since it was first coined more than a century and a half ago is quite astounding; therefore, it is understandable why it has sometimes received short shrift in the hands of some exasperated scholars, while others have made it the theme of numerous and often verbose professorial efforts. As a result, heated and even acrimonious altercations regarding its meaning have been both numerous and unavoidable, involving not only social critics, polemicists, and pamphleteers in general, but also such members of the more detached scholarly confraternity as social scientists, historians, philosophers, and even professors of literature. When we consider the fact that some of the more prominent (if not always outstanding) of these disputations have centered around the delightful argument that the proffered definitions of "ideology" are unacceptable because of their 'ideological' nature, then it becomes all the more evident that we are dealing either with the mythical tail-eating reptile in semantic garb—in which case we should forthwith direct our attention elsewhere— or with a concept of some considerable complexity and importance.

Words are not just words, and therefore definitional contentions should not, as is often done, be slighted in a simpleminded manner as being just meaningless exercises in semantic nitpicking. Rather, "semantical differences are usually symptoms of differences which reach into the core of the matter."[33] Or as Richard Rudner has put it,

> There is . . . a view as widespread as it is curious (celebrated in the indiscriminate use of the phrase "merely verbal") that to be concerned with linguistic analyses or with logical analyses of any discourse, or with linguistic problems at all, is to overspecialize, or even trivialize, one's concerns. No doubt this disparaging view of linguistic concerns has its genesis in the conviction that very few real and pressing problems can be construed as "merely matters of language." But, whatever the genesis of such a view may be, it is surely mistaken.[34]

These remarks are, I believe, especially pertinent to the war of words surrounding the term "ideology." However, just as the difference between terms and concepts is a crucial if elementary one in the logic of inquiry, so is the difference between terminological and conceptual disputes—between what I have earlier referred to as the question of semantic adequacy and that of conceptual scope. Unfortunately, this has not always been recognized in the literature on the subject matter, to the detriment of both clear thinking and fruitful discussion.

A dispute is strictly terminological when there is a prima facie agreement on the meaning of a concept but not on what name to

apply to it. Such is the case, for example, when there is disagreement over the use of a specific word because of the associations,
eulogistic or dyslogistic, which it has acquired in the vernacular
and which consequently may lead to misinterpretations of the
concept to which it refers. (Neologisms often owe their incipience
to this associative factor in human discourse; but, as it has been
emphasized by more than one scholar, even they easily lose their
purely 'technical' meaning and acquire associations—not the least
of which is that of being 'technical' and ipso facto 'value-free'
without in fact being so.) In other words, such disputes are essentially semantic in nature and concern themselves with the problem of communication and especially the problem of emotive bias
affecting the clear meaning of words.[35] It is with reference to this
factor that John Plamenatz, in his short but incisive book on the
concept of ideology, suggested that this "concept is indispensable,
though we may use it under a different name."[36] Conceptual
disputes, however, are over the extensions of a given term—over
what phenomena it classifies and does not classify, over which
denotations are to be regarded as basic to the concept, and so
forth. Such disputes are over conceptualization—not language,
lexical norms, or semantic consistency. It is apparent that the
dispute regarding the meaning of "ideology" is primarily conceptual, although it includes certain terminological ramifications
which are not unimportant and which therefore have to be considered.

Unlike poetics, for which the associative richness of words or
language is a mainspring, scientific inquiry can be fruitful only
insofar as its concepts are useful. Consequently, disputes over
conceptualization are inherently more fundamental and important
to analysis than terminological disputes. Ever since Kant we have
come to recognize that in forming concepts the scientist is engaged
in the very essence of his particular calling—that of organizing or
structuring a seemingly chaotic reality in order to answer the
questions it raises within his mind. That is, scientific concepts
acquire meaning only because scientists give them meaning for a
certain explanatory purpose; as a result, a given conceptualization
is useful only insofar as this purpose is being served—when its
usage indeed affords a resolution of the problem or problems that

occasioned it. Of course, usefulness is not the only consideration, since one also has to take into account the additional, method-ological aspect, that of scientific validity, which is determined by the question whether things conceptualized in a given manner will in fact lend themselves to the use previsioned.[37]

Unfortunately, scientists do not always ask the same questions, nor do they always bring similar conceptions of how reality is structured (or is believed to be structured) to their analysis of it. This is particularly true within the behavioral sciences, in which questions often are posed from dissimilar perspectives regarding the constitution and functioning of societies or of social and politi-cal interaction, which as a result 'color' the results of inquiry and indeed the analytic effort as a whole, including the conceptual underpinnings involved.

An illuminating example of just how fundamental this factor can be for analysis is provided by the dispute concerning 'power' in political inquiry and the ensuing debate between the 'elitist' theory as developed most prominently by C. Wright Mills, and the 'pluralist' theory as represented preeminently by Robert Dahl.[38] William E. Connolly has shown that owing to different conceptions or assumptions of how American society functions, and particularly of how power relations are operative within it, "strategic decisions [are made by Mills and Dahl] which reflect the perspective brought to the inquiry and which in cumulative effect push the outcomes of inquiry in the preferred direction," with the consequence that "their resulting analyses are in large part self-fulfilling."[39] Without in any way delving into the particulars and intricacies of this germane example from political inquiry, it is clear that what it does illustrate is how differing meanings allotted to "power"—a zero-sum conception, on the one hand, and the conception of it as the collective product of societal cooperation, on the other—ineluctibly lead to different lines of inquiry and consequently to different answers to the questions at hand.[40] The lesson to be learned from this is clear, namely, the importance of conceptualization to analysis, and hence the nontrivial nature of conceptual disputes.

Perhaps the dispassionate observer of such conceptual disputes may wonder why different terms or words are not applied to the overlapping phenomena subsumed by a single, seemingly broad concept such as 'power' or 'ideology,' each of which can then be used selectively, either singly or in some conjunctive pattern, as dictated by the given political subject matter at hand, thereby dissipating the disputational character surrounding the various definitions proffered for the single, overarching concept. Such a suggestion misses the central point that such disputes are unavoidable precisely because there is no general agreement (or 'general theory') on how to structure political reality for explanatory purposes. As has been noted in this matter (with particular reference to 'power'), the "conceptual disputes exist because we have found no adequate means of deciding which concepts best fit the decision-making process in contemporary politics."[41] This is particularly true for such apparently central concepts as 'power' and 'ideology,' which, in part at least, have gained their widespread utilization from the belief that they are constructions of central and pervasive empirical aspects of the political system and its operation. It is a naive assumption that the disaggregation of the characteristics or components subsumed by such concepts into separate, more discrete concepts will lead to the demise of disputes over their significance in explanatory endeavors. Again, we have to face the problem head-on.

Furthermore, such a disaggregative procedure toward more and more discrete or circumscribed concepts counteracts one of the primary purposes of conceptualization, to wit, the construction of conceptual classes under which as great a variety as possible of independent but interrelated observations can be subsumed. That is, we should always aim at *increasing* conceptual scope or import rather than decreasing it (without, of course, falling prey to what Giovanni Sartori so aptly has called 'conceptual stretching'), for herein lies one of the most important criteria of the fruitfulness of concepts.[42] With regard to this, Naess has indicated the direction and therefore danger of the disintegrative process, when he writes that the "zero of fruitfulness according to this criterion is realized if nothing can be inferred except what has already been said about the things by mentioning the conceptual characteristics of the concept class."[43] This is always a danger in the definition of concepts: that they are unable to tell us anything more—or very little more—than what is true by definition.

Both terminological and conceptual disputes owe much of their quarrelsomeness and disputatious thrust to the historical roots of words, and to their subsequent profluence within what we generally call the history of ideas. This is particularly true with regard to a term such as "ideology," which is closely tied to some of the major political and especially intellectual upheavals of the past century or so, and which as a consequence is burdened with a rich if not always venerable historical ballast. It is this factor that gives a term like "ideology" its causal effectiveness *qua* word in human discourse, an efficacy which, although it is patently emotive in nature and thus has to be differentiated from the function of a term as a technical designation in political analysis, nevertheless cannot be ignored or evaded simply by stipulative fiat. It is a fact, on the one hand, that statements "that this or that is an ideology or more general characterizations of something in terms of 'ideology' appreciably affects attitudes towards the things thus characterized."[44] On the other hand, we cannot hope to defuse or neutralize such emotive associations by merely positing an arbitrary and purportedly value-free definition of "ideology." Such a procedure, based on the assumption, as Hannah Arendt has written, that we have "the right to retreat into our own worlds of meaning, and demand only that each of us remain consistent within his own private terminology," only contributes further to the problem of conceptualization instead of offering a viable solution.[45] It involves the imposition of willful intellectual constructions on a reality—the historical reality of words and concepts—which is simply not amenable to such a highhanded and essentially myopic resolution of the problem at hand.

This being the case, and given the present unsatisfactory state of affairs with regard to the various definitions and usages of the term, a critical inquiry into past meanings of "ideology" and into the conceptual and philosophical frameworks which have sustained these past meanings, as well as into the relationship—or lack of relationship—between these meanings and the contemporary usages of the term "ideology," acquires a not inconsiderable importance for political analysis. It is my belief that only such a sustained analysis of the term will yield a fruitful and significant conceptualization of "ideology" for present-day explanatory purposes within political science. In pursuing such an inquiry my aim is not to add yet another footnote to the historiography of ideas. Rather, by critically analyzing some of the major uses and functions of the term in the past, and by identifying some of the salient continuities and discontinuities in the history of its usage, I hope not only to clarify (to some degree at least) the issues involved in the disputes over 'ideology' but also to indicate why most of these usages—past and present—will have to be rejected as unsound on methodological and philosophical grounds.

Before proceeding with this task, however, a few additional remarks need to be made on the scope and purpose of the chapters to follow. First of all, I have chosen to treat in some detail only what I consider to be significant and influential usages of the term "ideology" since it was first invented. That is to say, this will not be an exhaustive historical or classificatory analysis of the word, but only of what I consider to be formulations which have proved to be germane, seminal, and lasting in the history of social commentary and analysis. In my view there are three such major usages to be noted in the relevant literature: the Marxian, the Leninist, and that of Mannheim and the 'sociology of knowledge.' Each of these will receive treatment in a full chapter, in the same chronological order as mentioned above.

Secondly, it is my belief that the philosophical roots of the different conceptions are of significant importance for a proper appreciation of them since they are in almost all cases closely related to the larger framework in which the usages function. Therefore I have found it necessary to engage in some detailed philosophical explorations in each case, with the purpose of delineating the underlying assumptions on the basis of which the concept has been put forward as deserving our attention. It is obvious that if these philosophical underpinnings are such that there are legitimate and compelling reasons for rejecting them, then this will have to reflect on the acceptability of the particular conception of the term itself and on whatever conceptual or explanatory purposes it is made to serve.

Finally, it should be emphasized once again that although the major part of this study is critical in nature, its prime objective is nevertheless an attempt to pave the way for a methodologically acceptable and fruitful conceptualization of "ideology." H. L. A. Hart, quoting one of his late colleagues, once wrote that "in searching for and finding . . . definitions 'we are looking not merely at words . . . but also at the realities we use words to talk about. We are using a sharpened awareness of words to sharpen our perception of the phenomenon'."[46] What I hope the critical chapters on the various usages and conceptions of "ideology" will produce is precisely such a sharpened awareness not only of the term itself but also of the phenomenon of ideology. In the short concluding chapter I will attempt to intimate, in barest outline, what seem to me to constitute the conceptual consequences of such a perception.

NOTES

1. The comparison of encyclopedic coverage is made by Giovanni Sartori in his excellent "Politics, Ideology, and Belief Systems," *American Political Science Review* 63 (1969): 398 fn. In a British series on "Key Concepts in Political Science" it is interesting to note that the contribution on *Ideology* (London, 1970), the short but very stimulating and subtly argued book by John Plamenatz, is one of the very first in a long list; indeed, it takes precedence over such traditional concepts as 'power,' 'representation,' 'legitimacy,' 'liberty,' 'tradition and authority,' 'consent and consensus,' and other hallowed notions of the social science canon.

2. Arne Naess, *Democracy, Ideology and Objectivity—Studies in the Semantics and Cognitive Analysis of Ideological Controversy* (Oslo, 1956), p. 171. (Hereafter referred to as *Democracy, Ideology and Objectivity*). As to the growing obscurity of the term, it suffices to give only a few quotations from more recent articles on the topic. "The word ideology points to a black box. As a philosopher puts it, ideology 'signifies at the same time truth and error, universality and particularity, wisdom and ignorance.' Likewise, for the political scientist the term ideology points to a cluster concept, i.e., belongs to the concepts that bracket a variety of complex phenomena about which one tries to generalize; and the growing popularity of the term has been matched, if anything, by its growing obscurity. All in all, one is entitled to wonder whether there is any point in using 'ideology' for scholarly purposes." Sartori, op. cit., p. 398. Another student of the concept has more recently noted that the ambiguity "in the concept is reflected from author to author in a wide variety of definitions, explicit or implicit, and a lack of agreement regarding even the basic properties of ideology. If the concept of ideology is worth saving for political analysis . . . then the conceptual and terminological confusion surrounding it must be dispelled." Willard A. Mullins, "On the Concept of Ideology in Political Science," *American Political Science Review* 66(1972): 498.

3. *See* Abraham Kaplan, *The Conduct of Inquiry* (San Francisco, 1964), pp. 49ff and Arne Naess, *Communication and Argument* (Oslo, 1966), pp. 9ff.

4. *See* Naess, *Communication and Argument*, pp. 16ff.

5. The distinction between double and single quotation marks is a common one in philosophy and semantics, serving the function of distinguishing between terms and expressions, on the one hand, and the phenomena, statements, or concepts they refer to, on the other. In what follows, I shall use this notational device systematically when dealing with semantic issue.

6. Incidentally, although we are informed by St. John that in the beginning was the word, this is reputedly not true for concepts, the discovery of which—according to Max Weber—we owe to the Greeks. See W. G. Runciman, *Social Science and Political Theory* (Cambridge, 1963), p. 165.

7. *See* Carl Hempel. *Aspects of Scientific Explanation* (New York, 1965), pp. 46ff.

8. *See* Kaplan, op. cit., pp. 48ff.

9. For an analysis of emotive meaning and persuasive definitions, *see* the classic statement by Charles L. Stevenson, *Ethics and Language* (New Haven, 1944), pp. 206ff.

10. "Science aims at knowledge that is objective in the sense of being inter-subjectively certifiable, independently of individual opinion or preference, on the basis of the data obtainable by suitable experiments or observations. This requires that the terms used in formulating scientific statements have clearly specified meanings and be understood in the same sense by all those who use the term." Hempel, op. cit., p. 141. As to the emotive use of language, I. A. Richards made the following succinct juxtaposition: "A statement may be used for the sake of *reference*, true or false, which it causes. This is the *scientific* use of language. But it may also be used for the sake of the effects in emotion and attitude produced by the reference it occasions. This is the emotive use of language." *Principles of Literary Criticism* (London, 1924), p. 267. For an example, both illuminative and depressing, of the emotive meaning which a putatively 'scientific' term can acquire—in this case "intelligence"—*see* H. J. Eysenck's article, "The Dangers of the New Zealots," *Encounter* 39, no. 6 (December 1972): 79ff, and the whole debate ensuing upon Arthur Jensen's famous monograph in the *Harvard Educational Review*, part of which is described by Eysenck.

11. *See* Kaplan, op. cit., p. 50, and Hempel, op. cit., 146f., 156ff.

12. Kaplan, op. cit., p. 51. It can of course be maintained that such anemia is not due to terminological deficiencies but resides, rather, in our thinking. There is some truth to this, but only in the sense that bad thinking is possible despite the employment of good terms and concepts; the converse, however, appears highly improbable, except in short bursts of illuminating grace and unearned serendipity.

13. Ibid., p. 50. Hempel notes of such concepts that "those characteristics of the elements which serve as criteria of membership in a given class are associated, universally or with a high probability, with more or less extensive clusters of other characteristics." Hempel, op. cit., p. 146f. *See also* his *Philosophy of Natural Science* (Englewood Cliffs, N.J., 1966), pp. 91ff., and Naess, *Democracy, Ideology and Objectivity*, p. 146.

14. Hempel notes, however, that a scientific discipline often proceeds from an "initial 'natural history' stage, which primarily seeks to describe the phenomena

under study and to establish simple empirical generalizations concerning them," only to arrive at a more scientific level at a later historical stage in its development. *Aspects of Scientific Explanation*, pp. 139f.

15. Kaplan, op. cit., p. 53.

16. This point is made not only by Plamenatz, as we shall see below, but by almost all recent writers on ideology. Where they differ is *how* to conceptualize a term which willy-nilly is here to stay.

17. *See*, for example, the following: Naess, *Democracy, Ideology and Objectivity*, pp. 141ff; Norman Birnbaum, "The Sociological Study of Ideology: 1940-1960: A Trend Report and Bibliography," *Current Sociology* (Oxford, 1962); Kurt Lenk, "Bibliographische Einfuerung" in *Ideologie, Ideologiekritik und Wissenssoziologie* (Neuwied, 1961); Robert E. Lane, "The Meaning of Ideology" in Calvin J. Larson and Philo C. Wasburn, eds., *Power, Participation and Ideology* (New York, 1969), pp. 321ff.; Samuel H. Barnes, "Ideology and the Organization of Conflict: On the Relationship Between Political Thought and Behavior," *Journal of Politics* 28 (1966): 513ff.; David W. Minar, "Ideology and Political Behavior," *Midwest Journal of Political Science* 5, no. 4 (1961): 317ff; and for a more recent list, unfortunately in Swedish, Robert Heeger, "Vad är en ideologi?" *Statsvetenskaplig Tidskrift*, no. 3 (1972): 307ff.

18. Quoted by Richard V. Burks, "A Conception of Ideology for Historians," *Journal of the History of Ideas* 10 (1949): 183.

19. Joseph S. Roucek, "A History of the Concept of Ideology," *Journal of the History of Ideas* 5 (1944): 479. For additional examples of such comprehensive and thus ultimately self-defeating definitions, *see* Mullins, op. cit., pp. 500ff.

20. On the nature and function of 'precization' *see* Naess, *Communication and Argument*, pp. 38ff.

21. Definition in *Webster's Third International Dictionary*, quoted by Harry M. Johnson in the *International Encyclopedia of the Social Sciences*, (New York, 1968), vol. 7, p. 76.

22. Julius Gould, as quoted in ibid.

23. Also from *Webster's*, as quoted in ibid.

24. Ibid.

25. For further discussions of the various substantive meanings given to "ideology," *see* inter alia, David E. Apter, ed., *Ideology and Discontent* (New York, 1960); Daniel Bell, *The End of Ideology* (New York, 1960); idem., "Ideology and Soviet Politics," *Slavic Review* 24 (1965): 591ff.; Gustav Bergmann, "Ideology," *Ethics* 61 (1951): 205-18; Richard H. Cox, ed., *Ideology, Politics, and Political Theory* (Belmont, 1969), pp. 1ff.; Leon Dion, "Political Ideology as a Tool of Functional Analysis in Socio-Political Dynamics: An Hypothesis," *Canadian Journal of Economic and Political Science* 25 (1959) pp. 47ff; George Lichtheim, "The Concept of Ideology," in *The Concept of Ideology and Other Essays* (New York, 1967), pp. 4ff; and Mostafa Rejai, "Ideology," in Philip P. Wiener, ed., *Dictionary of the History of Ideas* (New York, 1973), pp. 552ff. There are of course many more references that can be given here; however, I shall have occasion to

refer to many of these in the course of this study and, furthermore, the reader will have the benefit of an extensive bibliography.

26. Cf. Burks, op. cit., p. 185, and Daniel Bell, *The End of Ideology*, pp. 275ff., 393ff. Note also the nature of Raymond Aron's polemics in *The Opium of the Intellectuals* (New York, 1962).

27. *See* Ben Halpern, " 'Myth' and 'Ideology' in Modern Usage," *History and Theory* (1960), 1: 137ff. *See also* Henry Tudor, *Political Myth* (London, 1972), pp. 121ff.

28. *See* Karl Mannheim, *Ideology and Utopia* (London, 1972), pp. 173ff., and Halpern, op. cit.

29. *See* Halpern, op. cit., pp. 135-49.

30. Reinhard Bendix in David Apter, ed., op. cit., pp. 295, 296. *See also* Halpern, op. cit., p. 135 and Tudor, op. cit., pp. 121ff.

31. Quoted in Kurt H. Wolff, ed., *From Karl Mannheim* (New York, 1971), p. liii.

32. *See*, e.g., Mullins's article, op. cit., pp. 501ff.

33. Stanislav Ossowski, as quoted by William E. Connolly, *Political Science and Ideology* (New York, 1967), p. 18.

34. Richard S. Rudner, *Philosophy of Social Science* (Englewood Cliffs, N.J., 1966), p. 8.

35. This associative characteristic of language should be distinguished from the attraction—apparently aesthetic but decidedly unworthy—which some words seem to have for some academics. This phenomenon is sometimes called jargonism, and of it Naess has the following to say: "A term may have no delimited cognitive meaning, but nevertheless be accepted in the social sciences if the term somehow elicits agreeable associations. Technical terms may dominate discussion independently of their ability or inability to communicate knowledge or working hypotheses. Groups of sentences labeled theories or doctrines tend to be accepted or rejected for reasons which, on closer scrutiny, might prove to be concerned with terminological likes or dislikes rather than with cognitive meaning." Naess, *Democracy, Ideology and Objectivity*, p. 146.

36. Plamenatz, op. cit., p. 45.

37. *See* Kaplan, op. cit., pp. 46ff.

38. For the main statements of these two interpretations of political power in American society, *see*, respectively, C. Wright Mills, *The Power Elite* (New York, 1959), and Robert Dahl, *A Preface to Democratic Theory* (Chicago, 1956); idem., "A Critique of the Ruling Elite Model," *American Political Science Review* 52 (1958): pp. 463ff., and idem., *Who Governs?* (New Haven, 1961).

39. Connolly, op. cit., pp. 49, 50.

40. *See* ibid., pp. 49ff. *See also* Leif Lewin, *Folket och Eliterna* (Stockholm, 1970) for a more recent discussion of these issues.

41. Connolly, op. cit., p. 18.

42. *See* Giovanni Sartori, "Concept Misformation in Comparative Politics," *American Political Science Review* 64, no. 4 (1970): 1034ff.

43. Naess, *Democracy, Ideology and Objectivity*, p. 146. Naess continues by saying: "Fruitfulness shows itself by answers such as: Because if you have ascertained that the thing is an ideology, then you may expect—with varying degrees of certainty—that the thing will exhibit the following important relationships to other things which interest you:————". See also Note 11 above.

44. Ibid., p. 147.

45. Quoted by Mullins, op. cit., p. 498.

46. H. L. A. Hart, *The Concept of Law* (Oxford, 1961), p. 14.

2
MARX AND THE CONCEPT OF IDEOLOGY

EXPLICATION OF THE MARXIAN CONCEPT OF IDEOLOGY

INTRODUCTION

The importance of Marx in the history of the concept of ideology cannot be overemphasized. Indeed, were it not for the fact that he, early in his scholarly life, appropriated it for a scathing critique of certain ideas and particularly of certain notions about their function in society, there might today be no such history to appeal to; or at the very least, this history would undoubtedly be quite different from what it is. For it was he above anybody else who introduced "ideology" into the mainstream of intellectual debate and political analysis, and in so doing gave it a currency which, whatever its denomination may have been since then, has lost none of its bartering power in the marketplace of ideas and beliefs.

But it was not Marx who invented the term. In order to do it full justice and to indicate how and why "ideology" entered into the Marxian vocabulary we will have to go back a step or two before attempting an explication of what Marx intended to say when using the term and its derivatives. This is particularly necessary in view of the fact that in his hands the word became something quite different from what it had been when first coined—a deliberate transformation which he posited in reaction to its original meaning and usage. Marx did not pick the word at random or out of the blue; rather, he used it as a foil for attacking precisely that which the word was originally meant to say, and for this reason it is not wholly unimportant to enquire into the origins of the term, however small the influence of its initial meaning on its subsequent history.

It is generally acknowledged that Antoine Destutt, a French philosophe, was the first to use the word "ideology," although it is not altogether clear what he meant to express when inventing it in 1796. For our purposes it can be said that the word served to designate a doctrine of ideas—what he later would present in some detail as a "Science des idées"—in which the meaning of "ideas" is closely associated with the philosophy developed by Locke, Condillac, and other representatives of the empiricist school of thought fashionable at that time. [1] What attracted him to these philosophers was his belief—justified or not—that they had laid down the cornerstone for a "natural history of ideas," that is, an epistemological system which, as an amalgam of rationalism and a naturalistic approach, had successfully expunged a super-sensible reality from the realm of inquiry, instead limiting the legitimate pursuit of knowledge to an analysis of individuals and how their sensations and notions (idées) are formed. [2]

The scientific analysis of the formation of ideas was considered important for at least two reasons. First, it was believed to be of methodological significance in the most fundamental sense, or, as we would say today, as a necessary exercise in metascience or metatheory. The method of the natural sciences as it had developed during the Enlightenment came to be viewed as the only legitimate model for the acquisition of knowledge and truth, and applying it to an analysis of the procedures of mind itself was seen as its application to the most basic and inclusive level of the scientific enterprise. In the words of Canabis, one of Destutt's most illustrious colleagues, this methodology is the only and "true metaphysics," for it alone encases

the knowledge of the procedures of the human mind, the enunciation of the rules that man must follow in the search for truth. . . . It is equally applicable to the physical and moral sciences, and to the arts. . . . True metaphysics is, in a word, the science of methods, which it bases upon knowledge of the faculties of men, and which it applies to the nature of the different objects of the world. [3]

Secondly, it was held that scientific knowledge is possible to obtain only by "the deliberate, systematic reduction of every idea pertaining to every phenomenon into its simplest, irreducible elements, followed by a synthesis of those elements."[4] It is with regard to this aspect that Destutt could maintain that 'ideology' is part of the study of 'zoology'—that is, of the natural world, with no regard for religion, normative considerations, or traditional metaphysics in general; for these latter realms are, as he once wrote derisively, "destined not to instruct but merely to please us."[5] In other words, the term or designation "idéologie," and with it the "idéologues"—the eminent groups of savants and philosophes which formed itself around Destutt in the newly created Institut de France (established in 1795)—became identified with an optimistic philosophical doctrine or set of beliefs which can be loosely characterized as rationalistic, naturalistic, reductionist, antimetaphysical, and generally 'scientific' in nature.[6] It is also clear that these aspects of their scientific faith are a legacy of Lockean sensationalism and Cartesian rationalism and that as a credo it is therefore not particularly original.

A second main purpose of 'idéologie' as a science and methodology was to enquire into the cognitive processes in order to lay bare, and thereby to divest the mind of, the many influences on it of bias, prejudice, and the other so-called affections. In other words, the positive, salubrious program of establishing the real and fundamental nature of ideas is accompanied by the more abstersive ambition of eliminating those accretions and influences on the mind and its ideas which are a function mainly of noncognitive factors. Here we find, once again, a theme which obviously predates the idéologues but which they were able and willing to appropriate for their own particular purposes. It builds on an epistemological notion which is clearly pre-Revolutionary in origin: the proposition that within the realm of cognition the various affective categories tend to obstruct a clear apperception of true knowledge.[7] As an idea it is already present, if only in embryonic form, in Plato's ancient distinction between illusion and reality, between opinion and truth, *doxa* and *episteme*, and in his elitist conception of how the "light of truth" is to be acquired.[8] Francis Bacon, in his theory of the 'idols,' similarly indicated how knowledge of truth is hampered by socially conditioned and thus faulty reasoning: "[N]umberless . . . are the ways, and sometimes imperceptible, in which the affections colour and infect understanding," he thus wrote.[9] And Bacon's *idola* became the *préjugés* found not only in Condillac and Holbach but also in Helvetius, who made the claim (rendering him one of the forefathers of twentieth-century sociology of knowledge) that our ideas are bound to our social environment, and to the passions and ignorance, all of which are patent sources of error and false judgment: a claim which was later to endear him to both Marx and Nietzsche, though obviously for different reasons.[10]

However, the most important and interesting fact about the idéologues and their conception of ideology lies in neither of these epistemological themes; these are, as we have seen, on the whole derivative and consequently possess little that is new or particularly noteworthy. What is worth noticing, rather, is the incipient 'political sociology' which the idéologues took to be an outflow of this epistemology, and on the basis of which they proposed to act in almost the contemporary sense of an activist 'policy science.' Thus, as Hans Barth has noted in his excellent study of the concept of ideology, "ideology not only possesses a theoretical but has, since the very beginning, had a practical meaning; for it alone furnishes the foundation for the practical, moral and pedagogical sciences."[11] Similarly George Lichtheim noted that

the "Science des idées" is to yield true knowledge of human nature, and therewith the means for defining the general laws of sociability. The reduction of individual "ideas" to generally held notions is intended to lay bare the common ground of human needs and aspirations, thus providing the lawgiver with the means of furthering the common good. What is "natural" is also "social." Once human nature is properly understood, society will at last be able to arrange itself in a harmonious fashion. As with Condorcet, Destutt's aim is pedagogical: it is to lay bare the guiding principles of republican citizenship. . . . Reason progressively discloses a true picture of humanity which constitutes the foundation of civic virtue.[12]

In other words, the idéologues believed that from their epistemological conception of 'idéologie' *qua* science they could deduce the optimum patterns of sociopolitical interaction, that is, the basis for an activist program of societal reform and political reconstitution. Another way of putting this—an admittedly fuzzy one—is to make a distinction in terms of "ideas" and "ideals." That is to say, the idéologues can be said to have been 'ideological' in the twofold sense of being concerned not only with a doctrine of ideas but also with certain ideal aims which they perceived to follow from this doctrine, and on the basis of which they were prepared to act. [13] As we shall have occasion to see below, both of these strands in the original formulations of "ideology"—the philosophical and socio-political, or the scientific and the prescriptive or programmatic— are important to bear in mind, since they will run through the subsequent history of the term like a red thread, although perhaps never again with the same harmonious pattern.

The result was the emergence of a pedagogical zeal which was well suited to the historical situation in which the concept of ideology first came to be rooted. It was also due to this zeal of Destutt's political pedagogics rather than to his "Science des idées" that the word "idéologie" gained entrance into the French language, from which it spread concentrically into the vernacular of the other major European countries. But it did not do so as intended by him and his associates: as a technical term with more or less well-defined cognitive parameters. It is clear that the term, and especially the idéologues, soon became known to the larger public for reasons which had little to do with an appreciation of the role of the "new science" in either philosophy or politics. Rather, "idéologie" almost immediately acquired a derogatory meaning, one which was attached to it by none less than Napoleon, who, though he at first had had the support of the idéologues, soon found himself opposed by them, with the consequence that he showed them an increasing anti-intellectual contempt and scorn. [14] Indeed, by 1812 this contempt on the part of the man of action for men of ideas had blossomed into a full-grown and petulant animosity. Napoleon, in a speech to the Conseil d'État upon his return from the disastrous Russian campaign, thus put the blame for this military catastrophe on none other than the idéologues and the doctrines disseminated by them. [15]

The reasons for this souring of relations between the idéologues and the emperor are not difficult to unearth. As we have already seen, the former were not simply 'intellectuals' for whom the political situation was a given fact or a factor to be ignored without peril to what they perceived to be their mission. On the contrary, they felt themselves very much part of the new dispensation which had shaken France to its roots, and they intended to play a significant role in building up a new France, based on their faith in rational progress, their conception of the good society, and their dedication to the public virtues of republican citizenship. Indeed, as Robert Nisbet has written, their interest was in "power, which they saw as the indispensable means of exterminating the social order around them and then bringing into being, as Tocqueville has put it, 'an imaginary ideal society in which all was simple, uniform, coherent, equitable, and rational in the full sense of the term'."[16] Napoleon and those around him—especially Chateaubriand—were quite aware of these visionary ambitions of a small but influential group of academicians: ambitions which were clearly at variance with those of an increasingly autocratic regime which had made its peace with the Church and other traditional forces, all of which were anathema to the idéologues and their followers.

However, although the words "idéologie" and "idéologue" as a result of this open political animosity became dyslogisms and derogatory designations in political (and some intellectual) circles, as interpreted by a generally pro-Bonapartist public, Arne Naess notes that no new cognitive meaning seems to have been attached to "ideology" as such.[17] Despite the quality of derogation that the Napoleonic regime was able to impart to it, the term apparently did not become a concept which included a connotation representing a negative value.[18] This distinction is important, since it pertains to the difference, discussed in the first chapter, between terminological and conceptual characteristics of a word. In short, although Napoleon was the first to give the *term* (and those connected with it) a derogatory association, this feature was not incorporated as a characteristic into the *concept* in the form of a negative evaluation. The derogatory association belongs to the Marxian usage, although it is fair to surmise that the pejorative use of it by Napoleon and his followers contributed to the Marxian development.[19]

The introduction of "ideology" into the language of philosophic and intellectual discourse thus almost immediately led to its reception into the political arena, and that in two senses: as an ostensibly neutral though prescriptive term and as a derogatory battle-ax in the form of a political profanity. This identification of ideology with politics will become even more pronounced as we enter into a period in Western history—one fundamentally influenced by the French Revolution—that became increasingly characterized by the politics of turbulence, disquietude, and opposition, with revolutionary and reactionary ideas playing a prominent role. It is also a period which saw the emergence of the towering figure of Marx and through him the development of a whole new language of political discourse.

If, as Lichtheim writes, the idéologues were above all concerned with "the growth of rationality and the imposition of conscious control upon 'natural' chaos . . . by making an appeal to man's 'nature,' " then it can be said of Karl Marx that although, or because, he never faltered from his original faith in reason, he was not overly concerned about chaos of any kind; and that his ultimate appeal was not so much to the saving grace of man's given nature per se as to the objective, universal logic of the historical process.[20] This is not to say that he was unconcerned about the nature of man or about man himself—although some critics have echoed a Rousseauian charge in maintaining that his concern for mankind was greater than that for the individual.[21] Rather, his rationalist appeal to history as the only viable universal rather than to 'nature' —human or not—is an appeal based upon the proposition that only through a critical, philosophical reflection upon the totality of the historical process, and acting upon this consideration, will man be enabled to perceive his real and true nature, his generic nature as species-being, and thus transform himself in and through it. This transformation can only be accomplished by bringing the external world into harmony with man's essential humanity through the 'subjectification' of the 'objective rationality' of history that only such a reflection can provide.[22]

The apperception of the fact that man is not simply a feature of temporal, historical situations, an actor unconsciously realizing a purpose hidden to his mind, or a transitory, passive instrument of an ineluctable fate—this cognizance of man's true and self-creative destiny is, furthermore, in the Marxian analysis, foreclosed to empirical perception. It is debarred for the simple reason that the empirical mode of analysis is limited to an understanding of isolated aspects of the world that man inhabits: a limitation compounded by empiricism in taking these isolated aspects to be permanent features of the world rather than transitory elements of a dialectical process of historical development. In other words, in order to understand himself and to realize his own true nature, man has to rise above himself and the limitations imposed by his circumscribed, individual existence. And this he cannot do, as the idéologues had contended, by simply tracing the 'natural' history of ideas. For this history merely exhibits instances of the forms of consciousness which are relative to changing historical situations and conditions and thus is devoid of permanence and true knowledge: it merely provides a cognizance of reality and the self in which "men and their circumstances appear upside-down as in a *camera obscura*. . . ."[23] It is probably for this reason that Marx specifically appropriated the word "ideology" and its derivatives; and it is because he was fundamentally opposed to the whole philosophical stance taken by the idéologues (and their followers, amongst whom Comte was included) that he proceeded with a *critique* of 'ideology,' which, however, in the process came to stand for something more than simply the notions associated with this group. 'Ideology' became a negative epithet not only for what Marx perceived to be a philosophically erroneous conception of the nature of knowledge, but also for any faith in the pedagogical and political efficacy of Enlightenment principles, as well as for ideas associated with its ideals of societal progress.

To understand this attack on 'ideology'—and Marx conducted it with great, almost excessive vehemence, in the tradition of the searing polemic riposte—it is necessary, however briefly and superficially, to place 'ideology' within the context of that monumental edifice known as German idealism, an imposing philosophical heritage on which Marx the budding philosopher was reared and without which, as Lichtheim notes, "the 'materialist conception of history' would never have come about."[24] John Plamenatz emphasized the necessity of making this philosophical connection in order for us to understand fully the concept of ideology per se and the issues revolving around or raised by it. For these derive

from German philosophy or, rather, from a marriage of philosophy with history, consummated in Germany. That is to say, the concept of ideology in the broadest sense was born of that marriage, and so too were the narrower concepts. This whole family of concepts derives from the attempts by German philosophers to explain what knowledge is and how it arises.[25]

Insofar as 'ideology' is taken to deal with the nature and formation of ideas and knowledge in one form or another, it therefore becomes imperative that we place it within the context that gave the concept prominence, namely, that philosophical perspective which has epistemology, on the one hand, and the philosophy of history, on the other, as its prime loci. In the history of ideas German idealism as a philosophical tradition and system is this perspective ne plus ultra.

THE PHILOSOPHICAL ROOTS OF MARX'S CONCEPTION OF IDEOLOGY

German philosophy in general, and particularly the epistemological notions associated with it, owes most of its greatness to Kant. He is also the founding father of German idealism, which is a concerted attempt to counteract the philosophical doctrines of British empiricism as developed by Locke, Berkeley, and Hume, and which as a school of thought was dominant in both Britain and France during much of the eighteenth century (we have already noted the intimate connection between it and the idéologues). Of these philosophers David Hume is undoubtedly the most important, if only because of his consistent and fearless adamancy in carrying to its logical conclusion the premises of empiricist philosophy.[26] This conclusion leads to a thoroughgoing skepticism with regard to knowledge and belief, since it states, in effect, that mind does not exist in itself as an active agent of cogitation but merely as the passive receptacle of sense impressions and as a container of the memories of such impressions. Thus all reasoning regarding cause and effect is, according to Hume, based merely on associations between past and present impressions on the mind, that is, on habit or custom; whatever 'ideas' we have are consequently the product solely of antecedent impressions and their relationships as associated within the mind.[27] 'Ideas' are formed only as a result of the fact that experiences of frequent conjunction of external objects are frequently conjoined with the habit of associating these conjunctions within the mind.[28] Since there is, in Humean terms, no reason to believe that external objects 'cause' impressions on the mind, knowledge becomes purely subjective and disconnected from things external to ourselves; with the result that pure empiricism, when carried to its logical conclusion, must result in the view, as Bertrand Russell has written, that man is "shut up in a solipsistic world, and ignorant of everything except his own mental states and their relations."[29] This is obviously a dead end in philosophy.

And yet, according to Kant's own testimony, it was precisely this epistemological cul-de-sac of pure empiricism which woke him from his "dogmatic slumbers" and stimulated that 'idealist' rebuttal of Hume which has as its basic proposition the assertion that knowledge is inconceivable without the *active* use of certain cognitive or ideational categories, which are not given to us inductively through experience (sensations, habits, and expectations) and which therefore must be logically antecedent in the cognitive process, even though they are active in experience itself.[30] Knowledge does not consist in passive perception but, rather, in mind's necessary activity in the process of ratiocination.

Moreover, although Kant accepted sense impressions as a function of the outer, empirical world—and in this sense he did not reject empiricism for pure idealism but instead attempted to fuse the empirical with the rational—he also made a further fundamental assertion: that the source of these sensations, what he spoke of as *das Ding-an-sich* ("reality in itself") is unknowable to the mind. We can only have knowledge of the *phenomenal* but not the *noumenal* world, since the latter lies beyond time and space, has no substance, and therefore cannot be acted upon or described by any of the concepts which form the basic categories of the intellective self.[31] The reason for this follows from the above: the mind can interact only with and synthesize *perceptions* of the objective, outside world, but not with that world in and of itself. However, Kant agreed with Hume that the principles of understanding are 'natural,' and therefore our perceptions of the world are constant from epoch to epoch and from society to society; what we perceive in knowledge "is the world as it appears to men in all places and at all times."[32] Without such constancy, knowledge would be incommunicable and thus inconceivable.

Kant does not explain the genesis of these intellective categories or "basic ideas," as he also called them. His purpose was, above all, to demonstrate that a critical analysis of knowledge will reveal that these basic ideas are both epistemologically necessary and a priori, because it "is only by using them that we acquire a coherent experience, an awareness of an ordered world and of ourselves as enduring persons inside it," as Plamenatz writes.[33] It has been pointed out that Kant's primary concern was not with knowledge itself but with the epistemological link between an abstract mind and empirical objects—in short, with the question how human minds are able to have knowledge of the world, or in Peter Winch's words, how the mind can have contact with reality in order to make it intelligible.[34] Kant's answer lies in the proposition (and hence the 'idealist' designation of his philosophy) that this is possible only if we posit mind and its 'categories' as in a fundamental and necessary sense logically prior to the outside world of empirical objects. Only in this way are the objects of our perceptions, as a consequence of being 'ordered' or 'formed' in terms of the synthesizing categories of the active mind, made comprehensible and intelligible to the intellect.[35]

Hegel not only accepted Kant's proposition that knowledge is active and not passive but extended it to its limits, with the result that he went beyond Kant's idealism in several significant and novel ways.[36] First of all, he rejected the Kantian distinction between *phenomenon* and *noumenon* (of which only the former is knowable) as an absurdity, since to him it made sense "to distinguish the apparent from the real only if the real is knowable, for we cannot recognize the merely apparent for what it is unless we can account for its being as it is."[37] That is to say, if something is not real, then we can only speak of it as unreal if we can explain why and in which way it is not real; and in order to do that we have to have knowledge of that which *is* real as our point of departure. Thus, according to Hegel's point of view, our perception of the 'real' and the 'apparent' must be an apperception within the same cognitive realm. As a consequence, one of the main philosophic tasks—neglected by Kant—consists in establishing and explaining the reality of the relationship between the two.[38] This Hegel proceeded to do by insisting that knowledge is not simply a product of the single, intellective subject at a moment in time but rather of the activity of a plurality of minds, dynamically interacting with one another through time and space. With this thesis we come to one of Hegel's paramount themes and one which, although couched in a language somewhat obscured by his penchant for the grand style of philosophic disputation, also shows how far in fact he departs from Kant.

The rationalist belief, shared by Kant, that concepts are of universal application, that the world of objects is experienced in the same way by all human minds, is only viable, according to Hegel, if we accept the additional proposition that "finite minds are differentiations of a universal mind"—that is, the conception that Reason, or Mind, or Spirit (the German word is *Geist*), is a 'concrete universal.'[39] This Kant failed—or rather, adamantly refused—to do, and therefore he "remained in a halfway position between empiricism and true universalism."[40] Kant had "no philosophy of Nature, only a philosophy of natural science."[41] Hegel, however, never lacking in the gift of boldness, took this step in what Karl Popper has referred to as his philosophy of identity, of identifying nature or matter with mind.[42] In response to the problem of epistemology posed by Kant, how our minds can grasp the outer, objective world, Hegel did not simply say that this is possible because mind *forms* matter. Rather, going even beyond Fichte, who maintained that mind *creates* the world, he went the whole way by positing the no-nonsense claim that mind *is* this objective world.[43] One of Hegel's purposes was to justify the ways of God to men in an age which had started to unshackle itself from the hold of theology; he did this by stating, although in a somewhat different form, the old 'argument from design' by which theologians had for so long sought to prove the existence of God. His philosophy of identity states that we can comprehend the workings of the objective world because this world was created by divine intelligence: the same intelligence which exhibits itself in the minds of men. Hegel's solution to how ideas can encompass and comprehend the world—to the mind/body problem—was to assert that there is no material or objective world as commonly conceived, no 'body,' but that everything is 'mind.' Therefore mind is both the object and subject of cognition. If Kant restored the primacy of mind over matter (to use Lichtheim's felicitous phrase), it can be said of Hegel that he extended this notion to the far grander affirmation that mind is not only superior to matter but that it is the incarnation of all of reality: that, to quote that most famous of tautological equations, "what is rational is real and what is real is rational."

Knowledge, as we have already seen, was regarded by Hegel not as an instance of individual cogitation but as a function of the active, dynamic *process* of Reason as it manifests itself in many minds through time and space.[44] This epistemological notion brings us to Hegel's philosophy of history, which, although it should be distinguished from his theory of knowledge and especially from the identity principle, is not only fundamentally intertwined with both but is in itself one of the mainstays of Hegelian thought.[45] Hegel's idealistic conception of the identity of mind and matter is tied to his further claim that history is the embodiment of universal Reason, both as a concrete universal and as its differentiation into the discrete cognitive acts of human beings. The doctrine of concrete or objective idealism (as expressed in the identity principle), and the doctrine of knowledge as a dynamic process of Mind (the activist epistemological principle) are conjoined with the concept of History because Reason is still in a state of unfolding itself, of moving, in and through men and their cognitive processes, toward absolute or perfect knowledge—a *telos* which is contained within Reason but which is still to be attained by man. What Hegel is saying is that although the truth of the proposition that matter is an epiphenomenon of mind—that the conceptual, idealistic realm is all of reality—is an incontrovertible verity supported and substantiated in and by Reason, this truth is still not fully established concretely in the self-consciousness of men, who persist in their acceptance of the dichotomy between object and subject. As long as the tension between these two apperceptive forms remains unresolved, 'alienation' will continue to characterize the collective consciousness of mankind and thus also Spirit itself. Since the growth of knowledge consists in the coming together of object and subject in the panlogistic activity of Mind, absolute knowledge—the cognitive state when the tension between appearance and reality, between object and subject, no longer alienates consciousness—is in the process of being attained. This process of the resolution of alienation is what History is all about.

History as the unfolding of absolute Reason in human self-consciousness is propelled by a further concept fundamental to the Hegelian system: Hegel's conception of the dialectical logic. Kant had tried to refute pure rationalism by showing that knowledge is not possible if it is not grounded in the interaction between mind *and* the experiential world. In his discussion of the 'Transcendental Dialectic' (in *Critique of Pure Reason*) he attempted to demonstrate that an epistemology based on pure reason alone can never establish a standpoint which cannot also, in the same rationalist terms, be contradicted. He tried to show that a philosophical system based on pure reason can lead to two equally plausible but contradictory arguments. Or, as Popper has paraphrased Kant, "reason is bound to argue against itself and to contradict itself, if used to go beyond possible experience."[46] Hegel's identity principle is a rebuttal of this Kantian refutation of pure rationalism; his logic of the dialectic contains, among other things, an unruffled acceptance of contradiction as part of reality and, therefore, of Mind or Reason. Insofar as the history of mankind is demonstrably riddled with contradictions and negations, and since this history is the process of Mind moving toward fuller and fuller self-knowledge, Reason as it manifests itself in an incomplete form in the progressive phases of human history must also necessarily be filled with contradiction, which, therefore, instead of being inimical is natural to it as a universal process. In trying to show that reality as a whole is knowable, Hegel claims that it is not at all what it appears to be to empirical perception, Kantian epistemology, or traditional logic. Instead, reality can only be revealed through the kind of philosophic reflection within which the categories of formal, Aristotelian logic—"these dead bones," as he once called it—are discarded for a dialectical apperception by means of which the content of philosophical inquiry is seen to coincide, *qua* dialectical process, with its method of analysis.[47]

As a result, although the progress of Spirit in human history is to be found in the self-consciousness of men, it is also bound to be an activity of Mind through which it "uses" men for its own, higher purposes. As long as Reason is still in the process of realizing itself, mankind will necessarily be partaking in illusions about nature, society, and itself. To Hegel, these illusions, as reflections of Mind's alienation, are necessary and unavoidable adjuncts of the historical process. In [Hegel's] "view individuals, and even entire nations, are instruments of history, executors of a process whose meaning is concealed from them, and which becomes self-conscious only *post festum* in the philosopher who sums up the sense of the epoch."[48] History has an ontological and teleological logic of its own transcending that which at any particular instance can be comprehended by individuals—except, of course, by the philosopher summing up an epoch: but even that understanding is bound to be incomplete until History has run its full course and Spirit therefore no longer is self-alienated in human consciousness. This is a harsh doctrine, but one which Hegel apparently accepted with equanamity, perhaps because he considered his own philosophy to be the culmination of the unveiling of Reason in History, and thus himself as its High Priest.[49]

MARX'S FORMULATION AND EXPLICATION OF THE CONCEPT OF IDEOLOGY

Marx inherited Kant's activist epistemology, but like Hegel he could not accept the Kantian dictum that knowledge can only be predicated on the appearance of things but not on their reality. Instead, following Hegel, he subscribed not only to the principle that reality itself is knowable on the basis of reason, but also to Hegel's dialectical doctrine that object and subject are both active as a process in knowledge.[50] Furthermore, as we have already noted, Marx believed that history is logical, that it "makes sense," and that mankind is increasingly made aware of things as it partakes in the progressive development of the logic of history.[51]

However, and this was the first step Marx took away from Hegel, he could not accept Hegel's justification for the "cunning of reason" in human affairs, by which the "individual's fate was swallowed up in the dialectic of the process" of Spirit realizing itself.[52] Hegel's conception of history

presupposes an Abstract or Absolute Spirit which develops in such a way that mankind is a mere mass that bears the Spirit with a varying degree of consciousness or unconsciousness. Within empirical, exoteric history, therefore, Hegel makes a speculative, esoteric history develop. The history of mankind becomes the history of the Abstract Spirit of mankind, hence a spirit far removed from the real man.[53]

And "That is why history, like truth, becomes a person apart, a metaphysical subject. . . . "[54] Marx was above all concerned with transforming concrete reality, and in Hegel he found almost the opposite motive—the reconciliation of idea and reality—which to him smacked strongly of political conservatism, Christian-Lutheran theology and an elitist sanctification of the status quo (and he had much right to feel this).[55] All of this seemed to show little regard for the welfare of human beings, that is, for the praxis involved in the actual struggle by ordinary men to subdue nature to their own purposes and to develop their innate powers as species-beings different from animals.[56] Hence his call in the eleventh and last of the *Theses on Feuerbach*, often repeated but seldom heeded: "The philosophers have only *interpreted* the world, in various ways; the point is to change it."[57]

The principal result of this deep dissatisfaction with the normative thrust of Hegel's thought was the 'naturalist' inversion of Hegelian idealism into the 'materialist conception of history.' Marx was able to accomplish this philosophic volte-face in the early 1840s through the immense influence on his thinking of Feuerbach's disclaimer of Hegelianism from a secular (or anthropomorphic) rather than a metaphysical religious standpoint. So important was Feuerbach's influence on Marx that Robert Tucker has suggested that "Marxism might perhaps be epitomized as Hegelianism mediated by Feuerbach's critique of Hegel."[58] In essence, and in Feuerbach's words, what this disclaimer involved was the following transubstantiation of Hegel's metaphysics: "The real relation of thought to being is as follows: *Being is subject, thought is predicate.* Thought proceeds from being, not being from thought."[59] And 'being' for Feuerbach is 'man,' who is the 'subject' and of whose thought-processes Spirit is a predicate or attribute. Spirit (Feuerbach's anthropomorphized God) is an expression of man's ideas (or rather, idealizations) and not the other way round, as Hegel would have it.[60] In a sense, therefore, what the philosopher Feuerbach accomplished was a theological equivalent of the epistemological postulate of George Berkeley, bishop of Cloyne. Just as Berkeley had contended that things or matter cannot exist unless perceived by some mind, so Feuerbach claimed that God (or Hegel's Spirit) cannot exist except as the cognitive extension of man as the primary being. Hegel's objective idealism became, in Feuerbach's hands, the doctrine of subjective materialism. In so doing Feuerbach had, in Marx's view, effected the reduction of "the metaphysical absolute spirit to 'real man on the foundation of nature' "; and this reduction would continue to remain the baseline for Marx's subsequent thinking, however much he later would disagree with his erstwhile "intellectual liberator."[61] "In direct contrast to German philosophy," Marx proclaims, "which descends from heaven to earth, here we ascend from earth to heaven."[62]

The result of this rejection of Hegelian idealism is evident, first of all, in Marx's epistemology, which, while it retains the Hegelian dialectic, pulls it "down to earth" in no uncertain terms. This transformation is in essence a rejection of a reality which is not that of human beings as active agents; for while Marx accepted Hegel's proposition that (as Shlomo Avineri has written) "reality is not mere objective datum, external to man, but shaped by him through consciousness," he insisted that this reality is not a product of Spirit but of the "sensuous" praxis of *man*, since there is and cannot be any other reality than that which is made conscious in man *qua* species-being.[63] Thus Hegel's 'heavenly' reality becomes a 'sensuous' reality in the hands of Marx; and it is man rather than

Spirit who holds the key to reality and therefore to knowledge.[64] This is, of course, what Feuerbach had stated, when he turned Hegel's otherworldly but as yet self-alienated Spirit into a secularized and self-alienated human being; and in whose view history, rather than being the process of Spirit's transcendental attaining to full self-knowledge in human consciousness, becomes the locus within which man attains self-consciousness and thus self-realization in this world.

But Marx went one step further than Feuerbach. He notes in the first of his famous theses on Feuerbach that the

chief defect of all hitherto existing materialism (that of Feuerbach included) is that the thing, reality, sensuousness, is conceived only in the form of the *object or of contemplation*, but not as *sensuous human activity, practice*, not subjectively. Hence, in contradistinction to materialism, the *active* side was not developed abstractly by idealism—which, of course, does not know real, sensuous activity as such. Feuerbach wants sensuous objects, really distinct from the thought objects, but he does not conceive human activity itself as *objective* activity.[65]

In short, Marx insists that the active nature of human consciousness—and thus epistemology—cannot be limited to cognitive action; on the contrary, it must be extended to the shaping and changing of reality, since 'knowing' extends beyond mere reflective theory and must become a means for molding, shaping, and reconstituting the world given to mankind. As C. E. M. Joad has written, Marx insists that there "is no such thing . . . as knowing which is a mere contemplation of the outside world. . . . Knowledge cannot be understood, nor does it occur independently of its relation to action, the object of which is to change what is known."[66] Knowledge involves a constant interaction between man and his environment and is therefore never static since it affects, through praxis, the world around it. Reality is thus both object and subject of knowledge; because the process of knowing involves a continuous transformation of what is known, reality itself is never static.

And yet, despite this fundamentally different conception of epistemology, it is noteworthy how close Marx still remains to his Hegelian roots. For just like Feuerbach, he did not desert Hegelianism; what both hung on to was, rather, a "naturalised Hegelianism."[67] The formula or equation remained the same, however much they reinterpreted the original symbols, pushed them around, or introduced new ones.[68] Or as E. H. Carr has written of this beholdenness, "Herzen's description of Hegel's doctrines as the 'algebra of Revolution' was signally apt. Hegel provided the notation, but gave it no practical content. It was left for Marx to write the arithmetic into Hegel's algebraical equations."[69] Marx does not really challenge the Hegelian *method*, only its purpose and the content of some of its categories. And as we shall see shortly, this is true with reference to not only Marx's dialectical epistemology, but also to some of the more specific Hegelian concepts as previously adumbrated.

For our purposes, the most important of these categories is Hegel's notion of 'alienation.' Here, again, Marx follows in Feuerbach's footsteps only to overtake him and to go beyond his 'naturalization' of the Hegelian system. He cannot accept Feuerbach's anthropomorphization of the notion of self-alienation, since he feels that Feuerbach, just like Hegel before him, had accepted reality as given and only wanted to establish a 'correct consciousness' without any fundamental changes in the world surrounding man.[70] Instead of an inward, quietistic, and 'spiritual' resolution of self-alienation, Marx declares that the "demand to renounce illusions about one's situation is a demand to renounce a situation that required illusions."[71] Marx contends that the only solution to the problem of self-alienation is to turn *outwards* toward the world and thus to an assault on the structures of the existing state and society, since these are fundamentally responsible for man's life-situation and thus for existing human self-alienation. This, and nothing else, is the revolutionary task of philosophy—the "realization of philosophy"—and forms the basis of what has been called Marx's 'original' theory.[72]

It is within this context of an outward, activist resolution of 'alienation' that Marx's conception of 'ideology' begins to achieve its first contours. But he goes beyond Feuerbach in his condemnation of the latter's concern solely with an 'inner' solution to the problem, and a rather abstract, otherwordly one at that.[73] In addition Marx insists that there is not—contrary to Feuerbach's Hegelian view—a single, universally applicable touchstone which can serve as the criterion for determining the nature of the self-alienation of man. Feuerbach had shown that man is religiously alienated from himself because of the projections of ideal human attributes which stand in contrast to, or are in existential conflict with, the actual and unsatisfying conditions and existence of his daily life. To Marx, the conception of alienation is broader and more differentiated and (in his view) truly materialistic, in contrast to Feuerbach's 'old' or mechanistic materialism: for to Marx man is truly himself—unalienated—only insofar as he is able to recognize himself in the man-made world which surrounds him and of which he is both member and creator. The reason man finds himself alienated from his environment and from his fellowmen lies in man's alienation from himself as *homo faber*, that is, in his alien relationship to the goods produced by his own hands.[74] This is the same notion of alienation that Marx later develops into his conception of the 'division of labor,' which becomes the source of social as distinguished from individual alienation.[75] Or rather, in his later thought he "interpreted the division of labour as the social expression of self-alienation."[76] Instead of Feuerbach's universal, religious standpoint, "there are only particular human standpoints, corresponding to forms of society which arise from the interplay of material conditions and (more or less) conscious attempts to organize the 'productive forces'."[77] Feuerbach's position was regarded as incomplete, since his analysis of man's religious self-alienation was merely an analysis in terms of a 'theoretical' form of alienation without any particular *historical* reference. For Marx it was more important, indeed imperative, to proceed rapidly to the 'practical' aspects of alienation as evidenced in specific sociohistorical situations, since only these deal directly with men and their concrete existence. "Now," Marx thus exclaims, "that the *holy family* of human self-alienation has been exposed, the next task for philosophy in the service of history is to expose self-alienation in its *unholy forms*. The *criticism of heaven* thus turns into the *criticism of earth*, the *criticism of religion* into the *criticism of law*, the *criticism of theology* into the *criticism of politics*."[78]

According to Marx, social alienation occurs when man's freedom over what he has created for his own enjoyment is taken away from him, when he is dispossessed of his own creation in the form of products or objects, when what he has externalized of himself is prevented from being internalized again as an object for subjective needs and their fulfillment.[79] This is 'social' alienation because only society—the outside, pervasive force—can impose its will against the appropriation of his own product by the individual producer. "In tearing away from man the object of his production . . . estranged labour tears him from his generic existence . . . and transforms his advantage into the disadvantage that his inorganic body, nature, is taken from him. Similarly, in degrading spontaneous activity, free activity, into a means, alienated labour transforms man's generic existence into an instrument for his physical existence."[80] From this conception of alienated labor— as labor which no longer is 'generic'—Marx extrapolates the concept of the 'division of labor' as the fundamental alienative characteristic of modern society. For as he writes in the manuscripts of 1844, "the *division of labour* is the political-economical expression of the sociality of labour within alienation. Or, since labour is only an expression of life as externalization of life, *division of labour* is nothing other than the *alienated, externalized* positing of human activity as a real species-activity or activity of man as species-being."[81]

It is within this framework, that of social alienation as the product of the division of labor, that Marx's conceptualization of "ideology" has to be placed if it is to be correctly and fully appreciated. For just as the division of labor permanently 'objectifies' the products of man's labor—by denying him all rights to the goods produced by him—so man is also led by society, on the basis of the same productive, alienative structure, to 'reify' *consciousness* and *thought* itself. From the moment

when a division of material and mental labour appears . . . consciousness *can* really flatter itself that it is something other than consciousness of existing practice, that it *really* represents something without representing something real; from now on consciousness is in a position to emancipate itself from the world and to proceed to the formation of 'pure' theory, theology, philosophy, ethics, etc.[82]

It is, in other words, the division of labor that lies at the heart of "[m]orality, religion, metaphysics, all the rest of ideology";[83] and furthermore, Marx here has in mind this principle in its most mature and developed form, since the "[d]ivision of labour only becomes truly such from the moment when a division of material and mental labour appears."[84] 'Ideological' manifestations are, therefore, the ideational products of societies constituted on the basis of the division of labor, and particularly on the division between material and mental work. The 'ideologicalness' of this body of ideas, that is, of 'consciousness,' consists in the illusion that it belongs to a separate, real, and independent sphere 'beyond' or 'above' the world of human praxis—a realm which, in addition, is endowed with causal and autonomous efficacy vis-à-vis the concrete, historical situation in which man is a participant.

Although 'social alienation' is not to be equated with 'ideology' as *reified* or *objectified consciousness*, the latter concept would be meaningless if not placed within the broader context provided by the former.[85] 'Ideology' is, in fact, a special case of social alienation, namely, that form of alienation that is a function of the division between material and mental labor. It thus follows directly from Marx's materialist epistemology and historiographical standpoint. Marx never did in a fundamental sense distinguish between material and intellectual activity, since he regarded both as aspects of the same praxis by which man molds the world and himself in and through history. Later, Engels would also speak about 'ideology' as 'false consciousness'—a consciousness which is 'false' in the sense that any form of consciousness which attributes to itself a position superior to or independent of praxis does not and cannot conform to the 'true' nature of man as species-being. As Marx emphasized time and again, such an arrogation is built on illusions about the relationship between man, society, and consciousness—illusions which have their genesis and roots in the 'unnatural' division between material and mental activity.

Therefore, although Marx's vocabulary and ideas concerning alienation and consciousness have obvious and transparent Hegelian roots, they deviate from them in significant ways, even though they cannot be apprehended except in terms of them.[86] First of all, Hegel's conception of alienation "was a state of consciousness that could only be received through self-consciousness,"[87] while Marx emphatically rejects this contemplative mode of resolution

—indeed, any resolution resting upon the primacy of mind and thus consciousness—as wholly inimical to the nature of the problem. This problem is a function not of 'consciousness' but of the concrete historical and socioeconomic framework within which man has become but a contingent factor of the productive structure and its socially divisive strictures. This rejection is, of course, a corollary of Marx's rejection of Hegel's idealist epistemology. Secondly, Hegel equates alienation with the concept of objectification (as laid down in his theory of knowledge, that is, in terms of the subject-object dichotomy in the sense that the *epistemological* object was identified with what was 'alien'), and as a consequence proposes that Spirit's negation or resolution of this alienation-cum-objectification is possible only by recognizing that 'objects' which appear to be 'outside' are merely phenomenal expressions of consciousness. Marx, on the other hand, clearly rejects this conceptualization, this definition, and this solution of the problem of alienation in terms of objective idealism.[88] From Marx's "point of view the Hegelian transcendental idealism becomes a mystification in that the only manner of de-reification is thought, in that the dialectic is only truly realized in knowledge."[89] To Marx the whole question is 'concrete' and 'practical' rather than 'theoretical' or 'philosophical.' The result is that he, contrary to Hegel, "distinguishes between objectification, the premise of material existence, and alienation, a state of consciousness resulting from a specific method of relationship between men and objects."[90] That is to say, Marx does not in any way decry the fact of material production, 'materiality,' or 'objectification' in the Hegelian sense; indeed, as he succinctly put it, an object-less being is a non-being.[91] Instead, Marx reverses the alienative relationship by pointing to *man* rather than to *object* as the subject matter of alienation.[92] He does this by positing man as an essentially creative, productive species-being bent on subjecting to himself the concrete world which he confronts—but who is forced to be a noncreative slave, producing objects (or products) over which he, a mere contingent productive entity, has no say and which therefore become reifications in that they are alienated from him. Hegel's conception of 'object' as a *phenomenal* aspect of 'subject' thus becomes hypostatized by Marx into being the concrete 'object' of labor. While Hegel viewed 'object' as "alienated, reified consciousness,"[93] Marx accepts the produced object as a natural extension of the generic essence of man, but objurgates the fact that this extension has been abrogated by a social system based on the division of labor and the resultant 'fetishism of commodities.'[94]

The problem of 'ideology' as 'false consciousness,' as a reified consciousness disassociated from the material world and the praxis which is its human hallmark, is further highlighted by Marx in terms of another fundamental distinction. He not only differentiates between modal characteristics of *labor* as determinative of the problem but also points to the significant difference and relationship between 'consciousness' (*Bewusstsein*) and 'being' (*Sein*). Adhering to his Hegelian roots, he defines the former as "from the very beginning a social product, and remains so as long as men exist at all."[95] The latter concept, however, he conceives in terms of the actual situation—and the conditions defining it—within which man acts in his capacity as a producer of goods. As a consequence, the substance or contents of 'consciousness' "can never be anything else than conscious existence";[96] or, as he would maintain later, it is not human consciousness which determines man's being, but rather his social being which determines his consciousness.[97] This adds a further dimension to the link between man's social condition and the nature of 'ideology' as conceived by Marx. For what he is essentially saying here is not only that the reified existence of man *qua* alienated *homo faber* produces the reification of 'consciousness'—or of the realm of thought as a whole—but also that this is a product of the fact that 'consciousness' is *determined* by man's material conditions: by the structure of his socioeconomic (or productive) situation. It follows that not only will the reified existence of man (his *Sein*) be reflected in his consciousness—thereby extending the reificatory nature of the division of labor to thought itself—but that this is necessarily so because 'consciousness' is basically determined by man's material conditions, that is, by the structure of his socioeconomic (or productive) situation.

An 'ideological' consciousness is 'false' not only in the reified sense of being a 'consciousness' which posits a realm of ideas 'above' or 'beyond' man's praxis, but is also necessarily false since such an imputation rests on the assumption that 'ideas' are not determined by man's material conditions. Marx has given us both a definition, or description, of what constitutes 'ideology' *qua* 'false consciousness' (that is, a reified consciousness, a consciousness resting on the illusory supposition that 'ideas' belong to an indepedent ontological realm), as well as an explanation of how such an imputation can arise in the first place. It arises because man's ideas are determined by his material existence, and as long as this existence—his "social existence"—is reified, so also will his consciousness of it be. If the division between material and mental labor defines the alienation of the latter from the former, the doctrine that consciousness is determined by man's material conditions gives us the causal explanation for why an alienated 'being' is accompanied by an 'ideological' consciousness. The former provides criteria for determining the nature and structure of 'ideology,' while the latter explains its emergence. Or as Marx writes in *The German Ideology*:

> The production of ideas, of conceptions, of consciousness, is at first directly interwoven with the material activity and the material intercourse of men, the language of real life. Conceiving, thinking, the mental intercourse of men, appear at this stage as the direct efflux of their material behaviour. The same applies to mental production as expressed in the language of politics, laws, morality, religion, metaphysics, etc., of a people. . . . In direct contrast to German philosophy which descends from heaven to earth, here we ascend from earth to heaven. . . . We set out from real, active men, and on the basis of their real life-process we demonstrate the development of the ideological reflexes and echoes of this life-process.[98]

Marx is not content with merely showing us the inauthentic nature of man as viewed with reference to his species-being, on the one hand, and the 'division of labor,' on the other. He also provides us with a statement of how man's 'ideological reflexes' in reality are tied to his material conditions and how these manifest themselves in the multiform aspects structuring his 'real life processes.'

This brings us to a further and crucial aspect of Marx's conceptualization and usage of the term "ideology," one which is sociological rather than philosophical and which is more explicitly stated in his (and Engels's) later writings. Only when we come to this utilization of 'ideology' does the concept of 'class' enter into his analysis; and it does so not in terms of the *nature* of 'ideology' but of its function, which he has described as follows: "The ideas of the ruling class are in every epoch the ruling ideas: i.e., the class which is the ruling *material* force of society, is at the same time its ruling *intellectual* force"; and furthermore (tying this statement to his philosophical premises), these "ruling ideas are nothing more than the ideal expression of the dominant material relationships grasped as ideas; hence of the relationships which make the one class the ruling one, therefore, the ideas of its dominance."[99] These 'ruling ideas'—or, as he would later call them, the 'ideological superstructure', viz., "morality, religion, metaphysics, all the rest of ideology"—are merely "sublimates" of the "material life-process, which is empirically verifiable and bound to [the] material premises" of the ruling class *qua* ruling class.[100] As the "ideological reflexes and echoes" of the material conditions for the 'ruling power' of this class they serve to entrench, perpetuate, and rationalize its power without in reality possessing even a "semblance of independence."[101] It is this conception of the functional nature of ideology which Lenin would take over and develop into a clear-cut form of 'class ideology,' or rather, into his doctrine of two mutually exclusive ideologies: the 'bourgeois' and the 'socialist.' It is also a notion which is still very much alive today, albeit in many different varieties and often in forms bearing little resemblance to Marx's original statements.

It should be emphasized, however, that it is not the 'superstructural' nature of 'ideology' which distinguishes this functional conception but the fact that it is tied to Marx's notion of a 'ruling class'; that is, to the social conditions of man's existence in a system consisting of a class of laborers and a class of rulers. The 'superstructural' characteristic is already embodied in the notion that the material conditions of life 'structure' or 'determine' the ideational realm, while here Marx has extrapolated from this philosophical statement to a sociological proposition regarding the political function of 'ideology' as defined in the above terms. He is here speaking in terms of a different realm of analysis, and we therefore have to distinguish clearly between two different if interrelated senses in which Marx defined and used the concept of ideology.

First of all there is a conception of ideology in Marxian thought which rests upon its epistemology and the view of the 'nature of man' which is intimately aligned with it. For the sake of convenience we can call this conception Marx's definition of ideology in terms of his *epistemological anthropology*. A second conception occurs more often than the first in Marx's later writings and (mainly through Engels's influence) has become by far the more popular—to the extent, almost, that often it is believed that Marx used "ideology" only in this second sense. This second concept defines ideology functionally in terms of the basis-superstructure model: the conception of ideology as the ideational efflux of *class-societies*. Again, for convenience, we can call this the Marxian conception of ideology as defined with reference to his *materialist sociology*. Both instances of 'ideology' are predictable in terms of 'false consciousness.' In Marx's first conception of ideology this state of consciousness is defined in terms of, and is used to analyze, the alienation of *man* with regard to his authentic species-being. The second conception refers to 'false consciousness' as the dynamic but illusory ideological superstructure existing in all class-societies (because they are based on the 'division of labor') which, consciously or not, is 'used' by the *ruling class* to rationalize and thereby reinforce the material substructure from which it draws its ruling power. [102] It should be noted in passing that this distinction has certain clear affinities with the earlier distinction made with regard to "ideology" as used by the idéologues. In both cases the former category refers to a more general, epistemological or philosophical conception of the term, while the latter points to a meaning and usage which is closely identifiable with more specific sociopolitical and empirical aspects of social reality. [103] What Marx has given us is a forceful rejoinder to the Enlightenment principles which he saw embodied in the idéologues' dual conception of the nature and function of 'ideas' and thus of their conceptualization of 'idéologie.'

A CRITIQUE OF THE MARXIAN CONCEPTUALIZATION OF IDEOLOGY

INTRODUCTION

Before turning to a critical analysis of Marx's conceptualization of "ideology," a few words on the question of how to read and to interpret his thought are not only in order but are indeed called for; and this also holds for the concomitant problem of what constitutes a relevant or meaningful critique of his writings.

As for the interpretative question, Marxian studies have in the past decades—ever since his youthful works were first published in the 1930s—been deeply involved with the problem of an 'early' and a 'mature' Marx and with the issue regarding the nature of the linkages between these two periods. In my discussion I have followed the current trend, characteristic of most Marxist and non-Marxist scholarship in the West, of interpreting Marxian thought as a continuous if changing whole rather than as separate ideational entities.[104] It is also partially for this reason that I have concentrated mainly on *The German Ideology*. In it we find both the idea of 'alienated consciousness' (flowing from his preoccupations in the so-called *1844 Manuscripts*) as well as the idea of the 'superstructure' of class-societies, which is the reigning conception in his later and more substantive 'economic' and 'scientific' works (the clearest example being in the *Foreword*). As I have tried to show, there is no real incompatibility between these two conceptions; although they address themselves to different universes of analysis, they follow the intertwined pattern which most contemporary scholars have found in the Marxian oeuvre. Nor do I believe that Marx in any significant sense changed his mind about using "ideology" as signifying 'false consciousness' in the different senses explicated above, although it is true that he spoke less about either as he became increasingly engrossed in his economic analyses of capitalism. This is a further reason why *The German Ideology* has received major attention in this study.[105]

A different and more knotty—if perhaps not an equally disputed —question is that of Marxian semantics. Bertell Ollman in his excellent contribution to the literature on 'alienation' has admonished us that the "most formidable hurdle facing all readers of Marx is his 'peculiar' use of words. . . . Vilfredo Pareto provides us with the classic statement of this problem when he asserts that Marx's words are like bats: one can see in them both birds and mice."[106] It is sometimes alleged that it is precisely because of Marx's 'peculiar' use of words that he has been misinterpreted and thus unfairly criticized; and there is probably much truth to this charge. However, the real problem is not so much his novel use of words—much of recent scholarship on Marx has, after all, gone into diminishing if not entirely eliminating this hurdle—as the fact that his terminology is often inconsistent, as Engels admitted quite frankly. However, instead of apologizing, Engels defended this practice on the basis that it was inevitable and in fact necessary in order to establish the completely new understanding of societies—viewed as being in continual flux—which Marx (according to Engels) perceived to be his main objective. In such an endeavor, Engels writes, we should not expect to find

fixed, cut-to-measure, once and for all applicable definitions in Marx's works. It is self-evident that where things and their interrelations are conceived, not as fixed, but as changing, their mental images, the ideas, are likewise subject to change and transformation, and they are not encapsulated in rigid definitions, but are developed in their historical or logical process of formulation.[107]

In Ollman's eyes, this is an acceptable apology for Marx's terminological inconsistency and thus, according to him, the only way to avoid misinterpreting Marx is to follow the path "which leads from Marx's terminology to the picture of the world he was trying to convey."[108] In other words, we are advised to submit to what has been termed an 'immanent' interpretation (and critique) of Marx's terms and his conceptualization of reality. Similarly, if not entirely for the same reason, Lichtheim has maintained the immanent standpoint when he explains, in the introduction to his exemplary analysis of the development of Marxism, that "it is the thesis of this study that Marxism is to be understood as an historical phenomenon, as against the now standard analysis of Marxian theory in terms of its compatibility with modern thought."[109] Herbert

Marcuse, in his analysis of Soviet Marxism, takes a similar stand in favor of an 'immanent critique' (his own words); for

a critique which merely applies the traditional criteria of philosophical truth to Soviet Marxism does not, in a strict sense, reach its objective. Such a critique, no matter how strong and well founded it may be, is easily blunted by the argument that its conceptual foundations have been undermined by the Marxist transition into a different area of historical and theoretical verification. The Marxist dimension itself thus seems to remain intact because it remains *outside* the argument.[110]

To my mind there are, however, some strong objections to be made against the kind of interpretative stance which is here defended.

The first problem with the immanent approach to Marxian thought (and to Marxism in general) is that it tends to support and thus to perpetuate the state of mutual neglect, relative incomprehension, and indeed animosity which to a large extent has characterized most of the relations between Marxist and non-Marxist scholars and thought since at least the early days of this century. This foreclosing of at least a 'dialogue' between Marxist and other modes of social thought and analysis is something which, I am sure, is neither beneficial to nor ought in principle to be desired by either group.[111] Of course, if one is persuaded by the arguments offered by T. S. Kuhn and especially P. K. Feyerabend— that there exists neither a generally valid scientific methodology nor a neutral or objective observational language, and that the terminology and concepts of different and opposing 'paradigms' or 'theories' consequently are incommensurable and therefore neither compatible nor comparable—then little can be done since someone else's different conception of reality cannot be understood or explained except as a consequence of a process of conversion.[112] However, if this is a defensible position, then it is difficult to understand how science in any meaningful sense can be said to have had, and continues to have, a comprehensible history of its own. More to the point, one then must question the very existence of scientific development and science itself.

The fact is, of course, that Marxists themselves, especially in the West, on the whole tend to deny the immanent thesis, if for no other reason than that not to do so is to submit to the charge, commonly heard and often resented, that Marxism is neither scientifically nor philosophically a viable standpoint. Maurice Cornforth, for example, is quite explicit in his nonimmanentalist acceptance of the truth of Marxism. "For my part," he writes after having stressed his adherence to Popper's falsifiability criterion of methodological validity, "I am a Marxist because I have not yet found any logical or scientific argument that refutes Marxism, though there are plenty that contribute to its development, whereas I have always found that arguments which claim to refute Marxism are neither logical nor scientific."[113] It is, indeed, on this basis, on that of a commonly understood terminology and mutually accepted concepts—"in accordance with the canons of rational scientific discussion and in no other way," as Cornforth introduces his book-length reply to Popper's critique of Marx—that most Marxist thinkers have inveighed against their non-Marxist counterparts.[114] In these altercations we find many charges of misunderstanding and willful or unconscious obtuseness, but little reference to a specialized terminology comprehensible only to the 'converted' Marxist. That many Marxian and Marxist concepts have proved to be unacceptable to Western philosophers and scholars, that they, as Charles Taylor writes of Marxism with specific reference to England, have proved to be "obstacles to its naturalization into the British republic of letters," is one thing; it is something quite different, however, to maintain that the language which Marx bequeathed to posterity cannot in principle be understood by those who have not followed in his philosophical footsteps.[115]

Lastly, the argument offered by Engels (and apparently accepted by Ollman), that Marx's definitions of his terms necessarily had to vary because they expressed the conception of "things and their interrelations . . . not as fixed, but as changing," is dubious at best: things, especially historical things, are surely not all that fickle or variable, as undoubtedly Marx's own studies of historical epochs and epochal change must have made clear to him. Indeed, were we to draw Engels's 'dialectical' argument to its logical conclusion we would arrive at the position of Plato's first teacher, Cratylus of Athens, who, we are told, was so overwhelmed by his apperception of the constant transmutation of reality that he could not assume the stability of words long enough even to sustain a single conversation. That a thinker throughout his lifetime—or even in a single work or essay—uses a changing or inconsistent terminology is, in fact, not a peculiarly Marxian (or Marxist) trait; nor do we have to appeal to dialectics in order to explain the common occurrence of such unfortunate semantic obfuscation in the annals of scholarship and creative thought.

In the critique that follows I will adhere to the nonimmanentalist practice of regarding the works of Marx as amenable to the "rational scientific discussion" which Cornforth has called for. I will do so because it seems evident to me that this is both possible and meaningful; more to the point, this is called for by the very nature of the attempt in this study of arriving, by means of considering various terminological usages, at a fruitful and significant conceptualization of "ideology." The Marxian usage, like that of any other, will thus by necessity have to submit to the strictures of this primary objective. I should like to add that the negative criticisms that follow are not to be interpreted as a negative evaluation of Marx's *historical* contribution to the social sciences and to the study of ideology. They constitute, instead, a contemporary judgment of some of his *methodological* contributions —predications which, it should be added, were made without the benefit of the insights available to us today, almost a hundred years after Marx's death.

CRITIQUE OF MARX'S PHILOSOPHICAL CONCEPTION OF IDEOLOGY

To Marx, as to Hegel, knowledge is both historical and dialectical; and insofar as Marx insists that knowledge cannot be separated from the human praxis contained in social reality—which provides it with both its form and content—it seems to follow that knowledge is nothing but a reflection or an epiphenomenon of this reality. At least this is what Marx appears to be saying (among other things) when he claims that consciousness "can never be anything else than conscious existence," or when he insists that social existence determines consciousness but is not determined by it. "The question," he furthermore enjoins in his second *Theses on Feuerbach*, "whether objective truth can be attributed to human thinking is not a question of theory but is a *practical* question. Man must prove the truth, that is, the reality and power, the this-sidedness of his thinking in practice. The dispute over the reality or non-reality of thinking which is isolated from practice is a purely *scholastic* question."[116] Another way of saying this is that 'ideas' as such have no truth value, a proposition which (as R. G. Collingwood has written) "commits Marx to the paradox that if certain people held, for example, certain philosophical views, they had no philosophical reasons for holding them, but economic reasons" (or, if we interpret Marx's economic materialism less strictly, only material reasons).[117]

Obviously this epistemological standpoint is fraught with problems; and although it is not my intention here to submit it to a critique of any depth or scope, some issues have to be raised inasmuch as they pertain to the concept of ideology and its usage. What we have here, in short, is Marx's critique of 'ideas,' and hence the link that he draws between epistemology, ideas, society and ideology. Since this linkage ostensibly is, in a very fundamental sense, the prime locus of 'ideology', and since Marx, above anybody else, has influenced the use of this concept in social and intellectual analysis, his contribution to its meaning deserves close attention.

The distinction which Marx draws between 'consciousness' and 'social being' or 'social existence,' and particularly the asymmetrical relationship which he posits between the two, is far from unequivocal. Although metaphorically his thesis may conceivably be justified as a heuristic conception, it is far from being obviously tenable in the logico-philosophical terms familiar to, and utilized by, Marx himself. Hegel, for example, had distinguished between what he called 'Objective' and 'Subjective Spirit'—between conventional modes of behavior and institutions, on the one hand, and beliefs, sentiments and attitudes, on the other—and to some extent this corresponds to the distinction which Marx insisted upon. But Hegel applied the concept of Spirit to both groups of phenomena which he contrasts with each other, since in his view Spirit manifests itself both in social institutions and in the cognitive and affective processes of men. Thus, as Plamenatz has argued, although the "line he [Hegel] draws between these two aspects of Spirit is not precisely drawn . . . he does at least, by the very terms he uses, make it clear that every kind of social activity involves 'consciousness'; that is to say, a kind of thinking possible to beings that use ideas."[118] Marx, however, by his positing of the distinction between 'consciousness' and 'social existence' seems to imply that the latter does not involve the use of thought, or at least not conscious thought. In other words, Marx seems to say that "there are forms of social activity that do not involve the use of ideas."[119] Now it is not at all clear that this is what Marx really did intend to say, or that he denied that the use of ideas is essential for social activity and existence.[120] But he did say that consciousness is determined by social existence, but does not determine it.

Obviously the crucial predication here is not that consciousness is a function of social existence, since this statement is so undifferentiated in its use of terms as to be either an unobjectionable truism or a tautology (it is quite feasible to argue that 'consciousness' is subsumed by 'social being,' especially in view of Marx's earlier dictum that 'consciousness' is 'conscious existence').[121] What is problematic is the other half of the above statement: that consciousness does not determine social existence. Either this statement is also tautological, given Marx's definition of 'consciousness' as 'conscious existence,' or it expresses a far-reaching materialist determinism, namely, the assertion that 'ideas' as distinct entities have no efficacy in social action: that is to say, ideas are solely confined to a passive, epiphenomenal, and 'reflective' domain or 'superstructure' (one French Marxist philosopher has indeed asserted that ideas "can only be accounted for by a sort of ontological fate that compels consciousness to differ from being").[122] This seems, in fact, to be Marx's position when he writes, in the Afterword to the second German edition of *Das Kapital*, that the "ideal is nothing else than the material world reflected by the human mind and translated into form of thought"; or in his quintessentially 'materialistic' and more pithy statement, that "Milton produced 'Paradise Lost' for the same reason that a silkworm produces silk."[123] But he did not consistently adhere to this extreme position. For example, in a passage that deals with the role of ideas in revolutionary movements, he seems to submit that ideas do figure and indeed play an active, determining role in social existence. For, although he first asserts that the "existence of revolutionary ideas in a particular period presupposes the existence of a revolutionary class," he continues:

For each new class which puts itself in the place of one ruling before it, is compelled, merely in order to carry through its aims, to represent its interest as the common interest of all the members of society, that is, expressed in its ideal form: it has to give its ideas the form of universality, and represent them as the only rational, universally valid ones.[124]

However, given this submittal, it obviously becomes difficult to continue to insist upon both the clear distinction and asymmetrical relationship between 'consciousness' and 'social existence' which constitutes such a central aspect of Marx's analysis and usage of 'ideology.' So he must either claim the rather strange notion that the social existence of man as producer does not involve the active use of ideas and therefore is a purely instinctive process of production of the Miltonian kind referred to above; or he must water down his dictum and especially the asymmetrical relationship contained in it. As to the former option, Raymond Aron has argued that

it must be recognized that the idea of an immediate apprehension of objects, of an authentic reality, is itself an illusion which would only apply to a type of life mechanically adapted to its environment, either by instinct or omniscience. Man, who is neither animal nor God, and who also conceives of real objects and values, can only interpret the world in terms of the meaning he attributes to his own existence.[125]

As to the latter choice, it poses for Marx the difficult task of differentiating between ideas which are either 'within' or 'outside' of social existence, some of which are reifications and thus 'ideological,' while others are not.[126] In addition, it involves the different problem of explaining why and how some forms of ideas are determined by social existence while others are presumably part of or even affect its contents. But this Marx refrained from doing, perhaps because of the obvious difficulties it would entail, given the larger framework within which he was operating.

This framework is that of the active, dialectical determination of both consciousness and social reality and a similar dialectical development of the relationship between the two. Now if this is the case, it is difficult, without falling prey to confusion, to draw a clear line between the two in terms of asymmetrical causality (as Max Weber was to point out later).[127] What Marx actually attempted to suggest, it seems to me, was that consciousness and social existence—however defined—are *interdependent* rather than asymmetrically determined. But when one is dealing with the interdependency of two variables, it is notoriously difficult if not impossible to engage in causal analysis as distinguished from correlative predications. The problem, therefore, to which Marx did not sufficiently address himself, is that if consciousness is determined, so too is the social reality which putatively determines it (this latter proposition is, after all, a cornerstone of the Marxian system of the dialectic of history *qua* process). Now, if this is the case, and if the determination of social reality is a determination in terms of *human* praxis, that is, the praxis which distinguishes the animal world from that of the human, then this activity is either a conscious one, and therefore consciousness and ideas play an active, determining role of some kind in history, or it is instinctive, in which case there is no sense in differentiating between man and animal. In short, Marx appears either to have created a problem for himself while assuming that he had proffered a solution, or he was not certain in his own mind (or expressed himself in a confusing manner) about the relationship which he dealt with.[128]

There is, of course, an even more fundamental problem involved in Marx's conception of ideology in terms of the doctrine of false or reified consciousness. If 'ideas' are merely the reflected epiphenomena of alienated existence, then it seems that Marx is bound to subscribe to epistemological relativism, in which case his own doctrine *qua* idea cannot but be yet another example of the phenomenon of ideology which he is attacking and therefore by his definition be an illusory product of the intellect. For Marx obviously endorsed ideas, some pedestrian and some very grand (though hardly any mediocre ones).[129] Equally obviously, however, Marx did not believe that he himself was falling prey to illusion or false consciousness; nor was he, despite certain evidence in his writings to the contrary, an adherent of radical or epistemological relativism, since he insisted upon the fact that there is also a 'true' consciousness, which consists in the understanding by man of his authentic nature as species-being, and of his role in a universal, historical process which will culminate in the final dissolution of the societal chains which bind men to productive inauthenticity. Insofar as the rationality contained in history is universal, its apperception by man (and here Hegel's influence is, once again, unmistakable) must necessarily be the apperception of absolute truth—the truth contained in history as the vehicle of man's emancipation.

But there is obviously a true dilemma involved here, not simply a logical one; and Marx appears to have refused either to recognize or to acknowledge it. As Mannheim was later to chide, Marx was clearly claiming for his own theory or doctrine a privilege which he denied others. Consequently, either his attribution of 'falsity' to a given body of ideas is a value judgment rather than a proposition claiming truth-value; or, insofar as he posits a distinction between 'true' and 'false' ideas (or 'true' and 'false' consciousness), he must also have a criterion of truth and illusion which is applicable, within the same frame of reference, to all forms of consciousness. Marx clerly rejected the former, normative attribution, since he maintained that the "the premises from which we begin are ... verified in a purely empirical way."[130] As to the latter, we are at pains to know where Marx found his criterion of truth. Surely it cannot be an epiphenomenon or product of social existence or being, since we then would be saddled with the further task of establishing criteria for differentiating between (socially determined) true and false criteria, and so forth, ad infinitum. And yet, according to Marx, all our ideas are determined by our social existence. So where are we to find a basis for judging the truth-value of 'consciousness' which is not itself a function of social or material determination?

Klaus Hartmann, in a substantial philosophical treatise on *The Marxian Theory*, has shown that Marx's critique of ideology is an attempt to be both "ideologically relevant" (i.e. possessing analytic as well as critical applicability in the study of ideological phenomena) and at the same time "ideologically exempt"—a critical contribution which itself cannot be charged with 'ideological' coloration.[131] Both of these claims, Hartmann argues, are spurious and merely highlight the paradox which lies at the center of Marx's theory of ideology. With regard to the first claim—that pertaining to ideological relevance—Marx's basic materialist and epistemological premise is (according to Hartmann) that 'knowledge' and therefore 'truth' can never be anything but an epiphenomenon of the 'material base,' that is, a translation of this base into ideas, as Helmut Dahm has paraphrased it.[132] On this account,

it seems that every epiphenomenon is true with reference to its base. But the opposite is in fact meant, since thought is understood as something which has alienated itself from its base. Inasmuch as this is the case, thought is a negation of the material base, and thus the reality represented by thought is false with reference to this base and true only with reference to itself *qua* epiphenomenon.[133]

However, if this is what Marx meant to say, then he cannot escape the fact that, as Dahm writes, he makes "thought *in toto* . . . a negation of the material base." And inasmuch as this follows from the above, "Marx's thought itself is shown to be . . . ideological. . . . "[134] Or as Hartmann puts it, "as long as the materialist thrust of the Marxian theory is maintained, the pejorative conception of ideology applies to Marx's own thought as well, for if this were not the case, the critique of ideology as an enterprise would itself be meaningless."[135] The result, Hartmann concludes, is that far from being a theory with 'critical relevance,' Marx's theory of ideology can have relevance only as a theory of 'praxis,' as a "committed theory of praxis"; and as such it allows "no criticism but only justification, i.e., justification with regard to its own aims."[136] In other words, if Marx, as Kurt Lenk has written appreciatively, "viewed the critique of ideology as a practical-revolutionary undertaking, as part of 'revolutionizing historical praxis'," his theory, as long as it remains simply an appeal to this praxis, is (as Hartman notes) "not falsifiable, since the fulfilment of the aims posited by the theory remain in the future."[137] And this inevitably leads to the ideologicalization of theory itself, despite all contrary claims.[138] In short, if this analysis and criticism of Marx's theory is correct, then all that he can claim for it is that it offers a justification for a *particular* form of 'ideology' but not a relevant or applicable critique of the phenomenon of ideology as such.

Marx's claim that his critique of ideology is *exempt* from the charge of itself being 'ideological' rests upon the metatheoretical foundation of his transcendental method as practiced not only in his analysis of 'ideology' itself but also in his critique of the philosophy of his day. Although Marx rejects 'philosophy'—that is, all philosophizing—as being 'ideological,' it is clear that the essence of his method is philosophical to the core, albeit that the philosophical elements which characterize his method are strictly negative (in the sense that he denied that 'philosophizing' would lead to the truth, since a 'true' consciousness could only be achieved through praxis). But, as Hartmann has argued, Marx cannot claim that his own theory is nonideological while all of philosophy is ideological, if he at the same time uses a preeminently philosophical method in order to justify this claim.[139] Here, again, Marx seems to have wanted it both ways in his attempt to 'revolutionize' philosophy in the name of historical materialism.

Mannheim, who to a certain extent accepted Marx's critique of ideology, tried to escape this impasse by assigning to 'intellectuals' as a group the privilege of not being determined (at least not decisively) by social or class interests—of being an "unanchored and *relatively* classless stratum"—and thus of constituting the only possible or legitimate source for thought which transcends particular points of view or the 'ideological' orthodoxy of a given historical period.[140] Shlomo Avineri has attempted to apply this solution to Marx and to the problems surrounding his obvious ambivalence regarding the "role of the intellectual within the framework of his social epistemology." Thus Avineri contends that

The intellectual's 'social being,' as determined by bourgeois society, is, according to Marx, coeval with the very fact of his being an intellectual, i.e., a person who moves from ideas to facts, from the universal to the particular.... Thanks to his position, itself formed by society, the intellectual is placed in a unique situation: his 'social position' is tantamount to offering him the possibility of choice, a possibility obviously denied to the generality of workers and the capitalists alike, whose actual 'social being' is formed by socio-economic determination. . . . His consciousness is indeed formed by his 'social being,' it is just formed to be free. The *content* of his consciousness, *qua* intellectual, gives him the possibility of choice. . . . There is no *a priori* determination, as in the case of the capitalist or the worker. Choice is the very embodiment of the intellectual's determined 'social being.'[141]

On the face of it, this is an attractive solution to the problem; but the fact is that it will simply not hold water. First of all, as we have already noted in some detail, Marx did not accept as in any way conducive to 'true' or 'unideological' consciousness the moving "from ideas to facts, from the universal to the particular." Indeed, as a basic philosophical principle his position was the exact reverse: he opposed his fellow intellectuals precisely because of their failure to grasp the fact that one ought to "rise from earth to heaven" rather than the other way round. This was the very stick which he used to beat Hegel on his idealistic knuckles. Secondly, as Marx had already made very plain in his preface to *The German Ideology*, he did not in any way believe that intellectuals (at least not those of his time in Germany) were offered the possibility of *choice* with regard to their ideas and beliefs. Rather, speaking sarcastically of them as 'philosophic heroes,' he wrote:

The first volume of the present publication has the aim of uncloaking these sheep, who take themselves and are taken for wolves; of showing how their bleating merely imitates in a philosophic form the conceptions of the German middle class; how the boasting of these philosophic commentators only mirrors the wretchedness of the real conditions in Germany.[142]

Indeed, the intellectuals, being products of the division between mental and physical labor, are par excellence the ideologues whom Marx is attacking with such apparent relish. This attack gains particular vehemence when he indicts them for their belief in their emancipation from the materially determinative world, in being creators of ostensibly " 'pure' theory, theology, philosophy, ethics, etc."[143] If, as Avineri claims, the content of the intellectual's consciousness is such that it gives him the opportunity of choice, Marx's emphatic reply is that this is a plain *illusion* on the part of the intellectual: an illusion fostered by his failure to recognize that the "phantoms formed in the human brain are also, necessarily, sublimates of their material life-process, which is empirically verifiable and bound to material premises."[144] It was Marx's declared position that not the *fact* but the *illusion* of choice "is the very embodiment of the intellectual's determined 'social being'."[145] But even if Avineri's interpretation were correct, it would still not—as we shall see when discussing Mannheim in a subsequent chapter—solve the underlying problem relating to Marx's concept of ideology and the question of objective truth. It would merely bring us back to the issue of how to explain and prove the validity of a criterion of truth based on social (or material) determination.

How, then, does Marx justify the untainted truthfulness of his own predications? Does he have a criterion which (contrary to Mannheim's later insistence) is itself not relative to his own historical epoch and social position? He submits that he does, since he asserts that his doctrine is true because it reflects not an epoch but the logic of history as a *whole*. Obviously this is a metaphysical claim of the first order, despite his many and fiery antimetaphysical disclaimers. As such it is a product of, and can only be justified with reference to, German idealism in its Hegelian transposition and culmination. Tucker rightly points out, in tracing the influence of Feuerbach on Marx that "his immensely exciting message . . . was that *Hegelianism has truth-value*. If one has only to turn speculative philosophy 'upside down' in order to reach the truth in its 'unconcealed, pure, manifest form,' it follows that Hegelianism is the truth, albeit in concealed, inverted or mystified form. Here, indeed, was a revolutionary idea for Marx, quite dazzling in its implications."[146] What, perhaps above everything else, characterizes Marx's immense debt and intellectual attachment to Hegel is his wholehearted acceptance of the latter's *totalistic* view of history as the dialectical unfolding of reason, which is both its essence and motive force. The belief, therefore, that his system contains and expresses this fact—that it is a reflection of the "avator of reason in human history"—is the basis for his submission of it as the absolute truth about man, nature, history, society, and the relationships which mediate between these aspects of the totality which is human history.

The notion that something is more than merely the sum of its parts is usually referred to as being an expression of 'holism' or 'holistic' thinking. It is found both in everyday and more sophisticated contexts—in judgments about the character of ordinary people and events, as well as in lengthy discussions of art, poetry, the novel, philosophy, and so forth. In the social sciences this notion has acquired respectability above all in Gestalt psychology, which as a method of experimental investigation is utilized to examine the nature of human perception, on the assumption that it involves something more than simply the aggregation of discretely perceived clues: that, to cite a fairly common example, a melody is more than just a sequence of musical sounds. However, as has been emphasized especially by Popper, there is another, more conceptive and metatheoretical rather than perceptive form of holism, which consequently is much broader in scope and total in judgment. For the term "whole" is also used to denote the "totality of all the properties or aspects of a thing, and especially of all the relations holding between its constituent parts."[147] Consequently, it is different from the former type of holism for the reason that it rests on the postulate, or is at least based on the assumption, that the *totality* of something is amenable to predication. While a Gestalt analysis of a melody would limit itself to certain selective aspects of the perceived total sequence (the rhythm of a melody is, for apparent reasons, considered apart from its relative pitch), a 'whole' of the second type does not constitute a selective aspect of a given phenomenon but resolutely embraces all aspects and their relationships within and to the 'whole.' This distinction is perhaps best indicated by pointing out that while the latter form of holism is essentially based on epistemological principles, the former is primarily a method and subject matter within psychology, having the Kantian principle of selection as a prime modus operandi. For reasons of lexical economy, I shall hereafter refer only to the epistemological form as 'holism.'

'Holism' as defined above has certain grave shortcomings, both as an epistemological principle and as an explanatory concept. As a principle in the theory of knowledge it rests upon the further notion of *essentialism*; as an explanatory concept it can only lead to *reductionism*. By essentialism I mean the epistemological postulate that knowledge is concerned with the 'essence' of things, which is universal and the only proper object of knowledge. Aristotle was the founding father of this tenet. Since his time it has, in one form or another, remained a constant bone of contention and a baseline for many and almost endless arguments, which have abated only because of the onslaught (starting with the Enlightenment) of scientific thought and the collapse of many of the old metaphysical mainstays of epistemology.[148] Today it is generally acknowledged that the study of, for example, the state is not the study of the 'essence' of the 'state' but rather of the state as an empirical, variable, and institutional phenomenon of social organization. The term "state" stands for a concept of the 'state,' which is an abstraction from empirical reality, and which in addition can be defined differently, depending on the scope and purpose of analysis. (The fact that the 'state' or 'nation' is sometimes still referred to as something sacred or transcendental in no way changes the matter: for that too is an empirical fact of the political—a phenomenon closely associated with what I. A. Richards was the first to call the 'emotive' use of language.) In short, therefore, it is an almost universally held principle that any form of essentialism is incompatible with scientific analysis.

Reductionism is closely tied to essentialism; that is to say, with some qualifications it can be held that essentialism as an epistemological principle requires reductionism as a methodological tenet. It is obvious that the urge to reduce explanation to as few principles or laws as possible is in itself not a shortcoming but indeed a prime scientific goal. Reductionism is sometimes referred to as the principle or criterion of parsimony; or as Marion Levy has expressed it, "the ideal of the great architect, Mies van der Rohe, 'the less is more' is certainly that of science."[149] However, the term "reductionism" is usually reserved for a type of explanation which is regarded as fallacious, but not because of a parsimonious capacity for explaining a plethora of phenomena by means of a minimum of principles or generalizations. Instead, it is a fallacy because it purports to explain a complex phenomenon by reducing the explanation to an aspect contained within the phenomenon, rather than by giving an explication in terms of one or more independent variables, that is, variables not defined in terms of the phenomenon in question. In other words, the reduction consists in the positing of a constituent, abstracted feature of the phenomenon to be explained as the necessary and sufficient factor for explaining the phenomenon itself as a whole. "Show me the palm of your hand and I will tell you who you are" is the quintessential superstitution of this fallacy; or to use William James's more telling but equally profane example, as a type of explanation it is based on an assumption such as that "a Beethoven string quartet is truly . . . a scraping of horses' tails on cats' bowels, and may be exhaustively described in such terms. . . . "[150] Insofar as the ideal form of reductionism as a principle of explanation is monism, that is, an explanation containing only one variable, this principle also tends to suffer from the afflictive barrenness which is a characteristic of monism, namely, of being either true but meaningless or meaningful but false.[151]

Holism reduces a thing to an inherent essence contained within it, which is then defined as constituting the totality of the thing; this is why holistic thinking is a true brainchild of essentialists and an example of the reductionist tendency par excellence. Insofar as Marx reduced the nature of man to his function as *homo faber*, and thus the essence and totality of history to man's "production and reproduction of real life" (to use Engels's characterization), he represents a holistic thinker ne plus ultra (if we for a moment are allowed to disregard Hegel's omnipresent spirit).[152] As a consequence his conceptualization of 'ideology' as human self-alienation in false consciousness is a conception with roots deeply embedded in a soil which is inimical to scientific but not to metaphysical nurture. "The doctrine," Popper writes in his decisive refutation of this manner of thought, "that we can obtain a kind of concrete knowledge of 'reality itself' is well known as part of what can be technically described as *mysticism*; and so is the clamour for 'wholes'."[153]

Furthermore, the use of holistic categories and especially of the reductionist mode of analysis inherent in holism, leads Marx to additional methodological errors of major importance. Although he has defined his epistemology and his sociohistorical terms with reference to the essential, concrete nature of man, his conception of man—despite his disclaimers—never really leaves the realm of the abstract. It is apparent that man's *productive* nature as species-being is not the nature of man as he appears in concrete reality, but is merely an abstraction of an *aspect* of man as flesh and blood. Marx, in his use of holistic categories, first identifies this aspect with the *whole* which constitutes human nature (thereby paving the way for the massive—if now abated—Marxist opposition to Freudianism and other forms of nonbehavioristic psychological theories of this century). Marx then goes one step further and identifies this abstraction with man's *concrete* nature, thereby committing with vengeance what Whitehead has called the 'fallacy of misplaced concreteness,' that is, the failure to distinguish between analytic and concrete structures. This error is also sometimes referred to as the 'fallacy of reification'—a charge against Marx which carries obvious ironic overtones.

Despite the numerous references to Marx's interest solely in the praxis of 'real' men in 'real' history, as against Hegel's concern for the transcendental Spirit in History, there is little doubt that we have in his writings clear instances of the reification of man as species-being and of human consciousness as 'alienated, false consciousness.' Since this leads him to impute human instrumentality to 'productive relations,' to the inauthentic (or inauthenticating) 'social structure,' to 'social existence' and 'history,' all of which are said 'to do' this or that, it is fair to indict Marx for committing the 'pathetic fallacy' as well, that is, the attribution of human traits to analytic or abstract structures. "In science this leads to errors; in morality it leads to self-pity; in governance it leads to irresponsibility."[154] It is on the basis of this error that Marx apparently could maintain that 'ideology' *qua* 'false consciousness' is 'caused' by the division of labor between mental and physical labor, that is, by 'society.' Therefore man's consciousness cannot but be a function of this abstract motive force over which man as an individual has no power. The difference between this materialist conception of history and Hegel's transcendental Spirit as the process of History realizing itself is minimal; in both cases we have an abstraction hypostatized as a volitional agency of unrelenting omnipotence. It is not without interest to note that Max Weber—who constantly kept Marx's contributions to sociology before him—was very conscious of the danger of both of the above methodological fallacies. Hence he purposely avoided, whenever possible, the use of nouns for collectivities or other social aggregates. [155]

The conception of knowledge which led Marx to his patently metaphysical accounts of reality, and consequently to their fundamental errors, is of course inextricably embedded in the logic of the dialectic, of which he lovingly spoke in his doctoral dissertation, as "the inner, simple light, the penetrating eyes of love, the inner soul . . . the vehicle of life." [156] Hegel, as we know, presented the logic of the dialectic less romantically, while forging it into an ingenious ontology which obliterates the distinction between logic as an instrument of analysis and reality as the subject matter of inquiry. Although Marx rejected idealism by inverting it into materialism, he still retained Hegel's conception of the dialectic intact, thereby also retaining the rejection both of the distinction between mind and matter and the distinction between a method and an object of analysis. [157] In so doing, and in tying the dialectical method to his holistic view of history, Marx's conception of 'ideology' as alienated or false consciousness contains a further element of speculativeness, since it places Marx's conception in the mainstream of what is often referred to as the 'historical' mode of explanation.

Karl Popper, in his famous confutation of the historicist conception, describes it as "an approach to the social sciences which assumes that *historical prediction* is . . . [t]he principal aim, and which assumes that this aim is attainable by discovering the 'rhythms' or the 'patterns,' the 'laws' or the 'trends' that underlie the evolution of history." [158] It is not my intention at this point to discuss the wider ramifications of historical explanation and the philosophy of history as a subject matter; nor do I wish to argue for or against the merits of Popper's critique or to evaluate Marx's contribution to the whole question. [159] However, the historicist charge is relevant to our analysis of the concept of ideology, and therefore this particular aspect of Marx's more general historicist conception must be touched upon, however briefly.

The particular Marxian usage of 'ideology' which we are considering here is historicist for the simple reason that not only does

Marx juxtapose 'false consciousness' against 'true consciousness,' but he also makes this juxtaposition in eschatological and therefore historicist terms. That is, he predicts the attainment of true consciousness as a *historical* phenomenon, as the end product of a *teleological* conception of history. Furthermore, he does so on the basis of his Hegelian notion of the dialectic, without which the Marxian view of human destiny would be impossible. History for Marx is a dialectical development and growth; or to put it otherwise, history materialistically defined has within itself a logic which ineluctibly propels it towards an end state: the stateless society or, what is of more significance here, a state of consciousness which will no longer be false in the sense of being alienated from the praxis of authentic man.[160] It is undeniable that dialectical historicism as a method of explanation and prediction is a curious if potent blend of imaginativeness, fatalism, and wishful thinking; and furthermore, that given its own terms, it cannot be refuted or demonstrated (hence its charm to many). However, the dialectical method *qua* logic of inquiry and explanation has been given a thorough refutation. Essentially this refutation is based on the logical argument that if we admit the truth of two contradictory statements, then from these two premises we can deduce the truth of any and all statements and the truth of their contradictions as well.[161] The dialectical process as a principle of knowledge rests upon assumptions which are thoroughly metaphysical and therefore is either accepted on faith or rejected as meaningless, depending on what we take to be reality and what we take to be illusion. The fact that reality in its manifold particularities demonstrably exhibits many conflicting forces (which sometime lead to good, often to misery) is quite irrelevant to either of these issues, since that is an apperception with regard to empirical phenomena and therefore is a subject matter for empirical investigation not logical construction or deduction.

As to historicism, Popper has given us an ingenious confutation of it, which can be amended to refute Marx's conception of the teleological nature of true consciousness and which as a consequence makes his assertions regarding false consciousness extremely dubious at best. Popper has argued that (1) the course of human history is strongly influenced by the growth of human knowledge;

(2) we cannot predict, by rational or scientific methods, the future growth of our scientific knowledge; (3) we cannot, therefore, predict the future course of human history.[162] I have argued that Marx must hold to proposition (1) if he does not insist upon 'social existence' as an 'idealess' and therefore simply instinctive existence. Therefore if proposition (2) is valid—and Popper gives a logical argument supporting such validity—and if instead of "scientific knowledge" we substitute "true ideas" or "true consciousness," then statement (3), reinterpreted in terms of the future state of "human consciousness" rather than "human history," leads us to submit that we cannot predict the future state of human ideas or consciousness.[163] And yet this is precisely what Marx did. Furthermore, if we leave Popper's argument as it stands and accept Marx's proposition that 'social existence' determines 'consciousness,' and if we also assume that to Marx 'social existence' is a historical datum or condition, then the same conclusion follows: if we cannot predict the history of social existence, then we cannot a fortiori predict a future consciousness determined by it.

Marx's justification for this prediction is, however, not difficult to unearth: he defines 'ideology' as alienated consciousness in terms of his conceptual system in such a way that any statement of it as a societal phenomenon is true by definition and therefore becomes unfalsifiable as a statement regarding the empirical nature of ideology. Consequently, for him to make any empirical generalizations about ideology is to commit the fallacy of conceptual circularity—the failure to distinguish between definitional and empirical statements. This is what he does when he, on the one hand, insists that the "premises from which we begin . . . can . . . be verified in a purely empirical way," and then goes on to state, on the other hand, that 'social existence' determines 'consciousness' but is not determined by it—on the assumption that this is an empirical proposition rather than being a definitional predication: an axiomatic given of his conceptual framework.[164] As a result, his conceptualization of "ideology" is such that it by definition cannot tell us anything about 'ideology' as an empirical characteristic of individuals and society. Another form of circularity is what can be called definition by future retrodiction: a definition of something in the present (say 'ideology' as 'false consciousness') in terms of the converse of a predicted future state of affairs ('true consciousness'). Such definitions always remain vacuous: they say nothing and can be used to say anything and everything.

So much for Marx's conception of ideology in terms of his epistemological anthropology. In summary it can be said that since both his epistemology and his view of the nature of man are thoroughly speculative in the metaphysical sense, this conception of ideology is obviously unacceptable for contemporary explanatory purposes in the social sciences. It in fact involves a begging of the question on a rather magnificent scale. Were it not for his claims to being scientific rather than metaphysical and the fact that his contributions to the subject matter of 'ideology' *qua* 'alienation' have been increasingly emphasized during the past decades, there would perhaps have been little purpose in treating it in as detailed a manner as has been done here.

We can now therefore turn to Marx's second main usage of "ideology": that which I have characterized as being definable in terms of his materialist sociology. It is undoubtedly the conception which Marxism as an intellectual tradition in Western social commentary and social science has popularized and which consequently is most often associated with his name. It is sometimes forgotten, however, that this usage has its philosophical and sociological anchorage in the above conception, of which it in a certain sense is little more than a 'sociological' reflection, to use a Marxian locution.

CRITIQUE OF MARX'S SOCIOLOGICAL CONCEPTION OF IDEOLOGY

It is sometimes submitted that Marx did not discount the social efficacy or importance of ideas, that his frequent and pugnacious outbursts against the 'ideological' nature of the ideational realm was directed not against ideas as such but only against certain *types* of ideas exhibited by his learned contemporaries and against certain misconceptions about the social function of ideas held by intellectuals in Germany and elsewhere. "In his treatment of the problem of ideology," one commentator has written,

Marx did not imply that ideas were unimportant. It was a blockage in the realm of ideas which prevented men from taking the action necessary to bring the social order into line with changed economic conditions. Ideas were being used, consciously or unconsciously, to maintain an outdated *status quo*, and these ideas, which constitute the 'false consciousness' of the epoch, had to be combatted and exposed, and replaced by others more in tune with reality. But he insisted that so long as this 'battle of ideas' was carried on a purely theoretical level, among the intellectuals themselves, it would fail to resolve the confusion and in fact would only add to it. The mass of the people would remain unaffected by the wrangling of the intellectuals themselves, who by isolating themselves from the masses and from the political struggle, would lack the touch-stone of reality against which to test the meaningfulness or otherwise of their verbal disputations. [165]

It is asserted that Marx was not attacking ideas as a system of thought but certain intellectualist delusions about the relationship between ideas, knowledge, and society—the role, in other words, of ideas in politics and how it had been misconstrued by the intelligentsia.

There seems to be some validity to this claim. Indeed, Marx proclaimed this to be his purpose in his preface to *The German Ideology* where (as we have already noted above) he writes:

The first volume of the present publication has the aim of uncloaking these sheep, who take themselves and are taken for wolves; of showing how their bleating merely imitates in a philosophic form the conceptions of the German middle class; how the boasting of these philosophic commentators only mirrors the wretchedness of the real conditions in Germany. [166]

This augers an attack against the naiveté of "the new German revolutionary philosophers," but what actually follows is, however, a series of much broader claims and propositions regarding the genesis and function of ideas in society—premises from which Marx not only is able to deduce the particular delusions of quasi-revolutionary thinkers, but the general misconceptions about the relationship between ideas and the social system which are shared by the public as a whole in any given historical epoch. "The ideas of the ruling class," Marx continues magisterially, are in every epoch the ruling ideas: i.e., the class which is the ruling *material* force of society, is at the same time its ruling *intellectual* force. The class which has the means of material production at its disposal, has control at the same time over the means of mental production, so that thereby, generally speaking, the ideas of those who lack the means of mental production are subject to it. The ruling ideas are nothing more than the ideal expression of the dominant material relationships, the dominant material relationships grasped as ideas; hence of the relationships which make the one class the ruling one, therefore, the ideas of its dominance. The individuals composing the ruling class possess among other things consciousness, and therefore think. Insofar, therefore, as they rule as a class and determine the extent and compass of an epoch, it is self-evident that they do this in its whole range, hence among other things rule as thinkers, as producers of ideas, and regulate the production and distribution of the ideas of their age: thus their ideas are the ruling ideas of the epoch. For instance, in an age and in a country where royal power, aristocracy and bourgeoisie are contending for mastery and where, therefore, mastery is shared the doctrine of the separation of powers proves to be the dominant idea and is expressed as an 'eternal law.'[167]

Marx then continues by linking this description of the relationship between classes and their supporting ideologies to his conception of the division of labor and the resulting division between active and passive groups within the same ruling class:

the division of labour . . . manifests itself also in the ruling class as the division of mental and material labor, so that inside this class one part appears as the thinkers of the class (its active, conceptive ideologists, who make the perfecting of the illusion of the class about itself their chief source of livelihood), while the others' attitudes to these ideas and illusions is more passive and receptive, because they are in reality the active members of ths class and have less time to make up illusions and ideas about themselves.[168]

This passage introduces not only the active 'theoreticians of society,' but juxtaposes these—within the same class—against the 'active,' nonthinking members, who in Marx's view are the real moving forces of the ruling class and who thus provide it with its real power. He then adds, in the same paragraph, that the "existence of revolutionary ideas in a particular period presupposes the existence of a revolutionary class; about the premises for the latter sufficient has already been said above."[169] But then Marx says the following on the same topic:

> For each new class which puts itself in the place of one ruling before it, is compelled, merely in order to carry through its aim, to represent its interest as the common interest of all the members of society, that is, expressed in ideal form: it has to give its ideas the form of universality and represent them as the only rational, universally valid ones. The class making a revolution appears from the very start, if only because it is opposed to a *class*, not as a class but as the representative of the whole of society; it appears as the whole mass of society confronting the ruling class.[170]

Here he obviously had gone one step further in that he no longer delimits the role of ideas to existing societies but, instead, points to their role in societal change, that is, to their role in a revolutionary situation.

These extensive passages, all taken from *The German Ideology* in order to stay within the same referential context, are interesting to us for a particular reason. They highlight the kinds of ostensibly *sociological* statements made by Marx on the relations between ideas and society. He of course has much more to say on the subject, but these statements will suffice for our purposes. Their sociological nature is apparent in the fact that what we have here are propositions focusing on society or segments of society rather than on the individual or on the nature of knowledge. In short, they direct us to the *functional* role of ideas; and as such they purport to say much more than what was claimed in the passage quoted on page 72. Marx's purpose is to show the far-reaching implications of 'consciousness' as being a *societal* function; that is to say, he here indicates the role of ideology in the social system. His *materialism* is equally apparent, both in the text itself and from the fact that the framework presented here is that of 'ideology' defined as the ideational efflux of class-systems, that is, a definition in terms of the material substructure-superstructure model. It is for these reasons that we can speak of these propositions regarding the function of ideology as being definable in relation to his materialist sociology rather than with reference to his epistemological anthropology.

These statements are also of interest for a different reason. They exemplify four types of propositions, commonly distinguished with reference to the following forms of predication: (a) the evaluative, (b) the descriptive, (c) the explanatory, and (d) the prescriptive. Thus, first of all, when Marx writes that the ideas of his contemporary, putatively 'revolutionary' intellectuals are of no social or political consequence but are mere illusions, that his purpose is the "uncloaking [of] these sheep," and so forth, he is engaged in *evaluating* their ideas in terms of their 'revolutionary' goals. He considers their ideas worthless in bringing about social change, since they, as mere intellectuals, are simply the 'idealistic' dupes of the German bourgeoisie. Secondly, when he claims that the "ideas of the ruling class are in each epoch the ruling ideas," and so on, he is *describing* the nature and function of ideas in society, and particularly those of the ruling class. Furthermore, when he writes that the "division of labour . . . manifests itself-. . . so that . . . " he gives an *explanation* for what he had previously described, and this in terms of the division of labor within the ruling class. And finally, when he avers that "each new class . . . is compelled . . . to represent its interest as the common interest . . ." he is quite explicitly *prescribing* the role of ideas in revolutionary social change.

The question facing us here is the following: are these propositions regarding the role of 'ideology' in society sociologically viable and therefore, ipso facto, are they statements regarding the realm of the 'ideological' as a socioideational category which may prove to be of conceptual interest in the definition of the term for our purposes? For if so, then there are prima facie reasons for taking seriously Marx's sociological (and extremely influential) use of 'ideology.' If not, then there is reason to question the thrust of his whole argument. Let us look at each type of proposition in turn.

'Ideology' as an Evaluative Concept

The query we have to pose here is, in a fundamental sense, the following: does Marx, in his use of 'ideology' in conjunction with evaluating the role of ideas in society, make his judgment in terms of a concept which has the evaluative component built *into* it as a conceptual characteristic, or in terms of a purportedly neutral concept, which nevertheless leads him to a negative evaluation of the *denotata* subsumed by it? In other words, is his renouncement of the ideas of his intellectual adversaries—the "German ideologists" to whom the book is directed—an evaluation of things subsumed *under* the concept of ideology, or is it a component part *of* the concept itself? The methodological difference between these two types of concepts is obviously of no small importance for the use of concepts in making statements or evaluations.[171] For example, if the first type of concept is used and if a negative (rather than a positive) evaluation is built into it as an inherent part, then it follows that such statements as "I don't like the Republican ideology," or "The ideology of the Labour party is reprehensible," are tautological. When, on the other hand, a neutral conceptualization is used in conjunction with the two examples cited, they obviously say something significant as *evaluations:* for the phenomena in question are then negatively judged not because they are 'ideologies' but because they are, respectively, 'Republican' or 'Labour' ideologies. Another way of putting this distinction is that whereas the use of the first type of concept can only lead to *one* type of evaluation (in the above case, negative), the use of the second can lead to either a positive or a negative evaluation, to a mixed evaluation, or to no judgment whatsoever, depending on what *denotata* are subsumed by the concept in each case and our evaluations of the *latter*. In short, the use of the first type of concept is evaluatively *predeterminative,* while the use of the second is not.

Now it seems to me to be a basic tenet of the social sciences—indeed of the methodology of science in general—that a concept which has an evaluation built into it as a predeterminative conceptual characteristic is not a bona fide acceptable scholarly concept, despite its many other uses. This does not mean, of course, that the social sciences are or should be value free in a simpleminded, positivistic or other sense. Rather, as a fundamental tenet this requirement guarantees the legitimate role of values in analysis while exorcising from it value judgments which are nothing but terminological trivialities of the tautological kind.[172]

With respect to Marx, it appears difficult to me to justify his use of 'ideology' as *not* being a usage of the concept that is evaluatively predeterminative in the above sense. It is a fact, first of all, that Marx never approved of anything or anybody associated in his mind or writings with "ideology," "ideologists," or "ideological-ness," and that he never once characterized himself or his ideas in these terms (a practice which, as we shall see in the next chapter, was not followed by some of his most illustrious heirs).[173] Further-more, in distinction from the derogatory use of the term as popu-larized by the Bonapartist regime, it is quite justifiable, I believe, to claim that in Marx's pejorative use of the term the dyslogistic component is conceptual rather than being simply terminological. If we were to argue against Marx's 'ideological' judgments, we would have to do so not on the basis of what Charles Stevenson has called 'persuasive definitions'—definitions based on the emotive use of language—but with reference to his conceptual and, it would seem to me, his philosophical framework as a whole.[174] Insofar as Marx's thought is a self-contained system, his concep-tualization of "ideology" is clearly a *systemic* component of it in the strict sense and so too is the evaluative meaning inherent in the concept.

Secondly, 'ideology' as used by Marx is *necessarily* a concept which is evaluatively predeterminative, for the reason that the yardstick which he uses in characterizing ideas as 'ideological' or not is the Marxian philosophical system, which does not allow an evaluation of ideas in other terms than their conformity or noncon-formity to the demands of this system of thought as a whole.[175] Since any judgment of ideas in terms of a particular philosophy or set of doctrines is necessarily a normative judgment ('doctrinaire' in the strict sense of the word) the use of a concept integral to it is ipso facto the use of a predeterminative criterion. This indictment is compounded by the metaphysical nature of the Marxian philos-ophy and especially of its epistemological claims, which incorpo-rate an explicit denial of the legitimacy of values as distinguished from positive knowledge.

This denial is, indeed, the crucial issue. As Max Weber was later to emphasize time and again, one of the fundamental problems with Marx is his failure to recognize or admit that basic viewpoints or value premises are essentially arbitrary; that values as such have their own, independent existence; and that by not allowing for this, Marx was unable—or refused—to accept the crucial distinction between the nature of scientific analysis, on the one hand, and the normative standpoint of the analyst, on the other. Thus while, in Weber's view, the norm for the former is what he called *Wertfreiheit,* which seeks to guarantee the scientific validity, that is, the testability, of our propositions, the norm for the latter is an individual *Stellungsnahme,* or choice, in terms of what is worthwhile knowing, a determination which cannot be scientifically proven but which ought to adhere to the dicates of 'intellectual honesty'—to what Aristotle called the 'intellectual virtues.'[176] By denying this—basically Kantian—standpoint, by claiming that our ideas or basic *Stellungsnahmen* are determined by society in the form of ideology, Marx effectively cuts himself off from the possibility of making either bona fide evaluations with regard to a given subject matter, or empirical generalizations that are testable according to the accepted canons of scientific methodology.[177] Weber quite rightly points to the Procrustean bed of the Hegelian metaphysic as being responsible for this state of affairs in Marxian thought.[178]

Insofar a we seek a conceptualization of 'ideology' that, at least in principle, does not affect the *Wertfreiheit* of its subsequent utilization in analysis and that consequently does not deny the legitimacy of value judgments as a necesary adjunct of the analytic process, Marx's usage gives us nothing at all to build on, despite its great influence on intellectual history. The problem of values in social science is both fundamental and complex; and although it may with some justification be said that Weber erred in being somewhat too optimistic about its solution, Marx erred in a much greater and debilitating way by refusing to recognize it as a seminal issue at all.[179]

'Ideology' as a Descriptive Concept

In our second passage from *The German Ideology* Marx gives a description of ideology in terms of what he calls "the ruling ideas" —that is, he is describing in general what these 'dominant ideas' are. However, a close reading of the text reveals that we are, in fact, served with two descriptive definitions rather than one. We are told, first of all, that the "ideas of the ruling class are in every epoch the ruling ideas"; in other words, the 'ruling ideas' are posited in terms of the ideas of the 'ruling *class*.' Secondly, we are informed that the "ruling ideas are nothing more than the ideal expression of the dominant material relationships," that is, the 'ruling ideas' are described as being the ideational expression of the dominant *material* conditions.

These two statements are different in descriptive and methodological import, and should therefore be scrutinized with particular care. The difference between them is perhaps best illustrated by making two common distinctions in methodology: between abstract and nonabstract terms, and between two kinds of the former. Nonabstract or nontheoretical terms refer to direct or indirect observables, such as a "marked ballot" or an "X-ray plate," and are consequently easily and confidently verifiable. The meaning of abstract terms cannot, however, be specified simply in terms of observations, since they refer either to abstract observables, such as 'government,' or to concepts whose meaning is contained within theories from which they are semantically inseparable (thus, for example, 'Oedipus complex' would be meaningless if disassociated from psychoanalytic theory).[180] These last two types of terms are also sometimes called, respectively, "constructs" and "theoretical terms."

With these two distinctions in mind, I think that we can admit, first of all, that the two statements above belong to the 'abstract' rather than to the 'nonabstract' category. This follows from the fact that the "ruling ideas" of which Marx speaks are obviously neither directly nor indirectly observable—in fact, no cognitive phenomena in and of themselves are. Furthermore, it seems more or less clear to me that while Marx uses "ruling ideas" as a construct in his first proposition above, the second use of it can only be properly understood with reference to the larger Marxian framework, in the same sense that the "Oedipus complex" is a theoretical term explicable only in terms of Freud's whole propositional system.[181]

Making these distinctions is methodologically of great importance, since these different types of terms serve different functions in inquiry—functions which are often confused with one another, to the detriment of both meaning and analysis. Thus if, in a given context of inquiry, the same term is used both as a construct and as a theoretical term, the result can only lead to a muddle. This is precisely the consequence of Marx's two descriptions of what he calls the "ruling ideas." For the last sentence in the relevant passage above is a curious one, given the definitions which have just preceded it. "For instance," he writes, "in an age and in a country where royal power, aristocracy and bourgeoisie are contending for mastery and *where, therefore, mastery is shared*, the doctrine of the separation of powers proves to be *the dominant idea* and is expressed as an 'eternal law'." (Emphasis added.) The curious thing about this assertion is the fact that given three classes and not one, we would expect from Marx's first definition that *three* different 'ruling ideas' would vie among one another for dominance; and yet we are given only *one* such 'ruling idea,' namely, the principle of the division of power itself. It is not difficult to understand how Marx arrives at this conclusion, since his description of the ideas of a particular form of society follows from his second, theoretical conception of the 'ruling ideas' rather than from the first. However, and this is the important thing to notice here, he is using this definition as if it were a construct rather than a theoretical term as defined above. That is to say, the statement is such that it can only be predicated on the analytical level of his construct, since it describes the particular ruling idea of a group of classes of a *specific* kind rather than being an expression of the material conditions underlying *any* kind of society. Another way of saying this is that while Marx ostensibly is describing the *actual* 'ruling idea' of a given society, he is doing this in terms of a construction which logically is a description which he has abstracted *from* the actual ideational configurations of this society consisting of three different, clashing classes. By speaking in terms of this higher level of abstraction as if it were on the same analytical level as that of his description of the 'ruling ideas' as a construct, he is making the same mistake as when one describes the feelings of inhibition of a person as in *actuality* being an expression of the 'superego' of that person. The notion of the superego is only a way—one among others—of speaking *about* inhibitions and cannot therefore at the same time be equated *with* such inhibitions. Once this is done, we are allowing a 'theoretical term'—in this case, the "superego"—a causal efficacy in human affairs. But doing this is in fact committing the fallacy of reification; and as Kaplan has noted, this fallacy "is more than a metaphorical sin, it is also a logical one. It is the mistake of treating a notational device as though it were a substantive term, what I have called a construct as though it were observational, a theoretical term as though it were a construct or an indirect observable."[182]

What Marx has reified here is the 'doctrine of the separation of powers.' When he writes that it "proves to be the dominant idea and is expressed as an 'eternal law'," we immediately have to ask ourselves the following two questions: (i) to whom does this doctrine "prove to be the dominant idea"?; and (ii) who pronounces it to be "an 'eternal law' "? It seems clear to me that the answer to (i) is that it shows itself to the *observer* in question, that is, to Marx himself, whose interpretation of the phenomena at hand is this doctrine. Thus he is obviously abstracting from what he is observing: this doctrine is something which he, almost in a Kantian sense, brings to his description rather than finding it there. But when we look at (ii), the answer that we find is that what Marx has brought to his analysis—his doctrinal interpretation—is at the same time imputed by him to be an inherent characteristic of a particular society. That is to say, it is the members of this society who are said to declare this doctrine to be an eternal law, not Marx—and by so doing the characteristic at the same time acquires some form of societal efficacy *qua* doctrine, if only in the form of a rationalization. In short, an analytic, interpretative category is at the same time declared to be an empirical factor inherent in the phenomenon being described. To do this is clearly to reify the doctrine of the division of power.

Underlying this fallacious form of categorization there is a deeper and more fundamental problem involved in Marx's descriptive use of 'ideology,' namely, his utilization of an undifferentiated class concept in speaking about ideology as the superstructural efflux of societies. Weber pinpointed this problem long ago in his insistence on the nonempirical nature of social wholes or collectivities, and thus on the ideal typical character and function of such constructions as 'class' in sociohistorical analysis. His main target was Marx and his conception of 'society,' 'class,' and similar notations as being *living entities* rather than abstractions. It is apparent that in Marx's use of 'class' we have, once more, a typical and methodologically debilitating case of his *holistic* and *essentialist* interpretation of analytic constructs. What Marx refused to acknowledge is that in a crucial sense a concept such as 'class' is the result of a double degree of abstraction: in defining it we first abstract the components of what we subsume under 'class' in the sociological sense, and then we posit, on the basis of these selected aspects of reality, the further abstraction of 'class' itself. It is thus clear that 'social class' can never be an aggregation of discrete individuals in time and space (such as a crowd at a corrida or at Lords), nor is it definable in terms of such natural classificatory criteria as *genus* and *species*.[183] Accordingly, although it is true, as Kaplan has pointed out, that individuals and their complex properties and relations are the empirical indications and references for collective terms, these terms remain artifacts and therefore cannot be reduced to individuals in the sense that the 'whole' constitutes the sum of its parts.[184]

And yet this is what Marx does in his use of the concept of class. A Gordon Leff makes clear, he "regards class as an actual entity, at once the source of economic, social, legal, institutional and ideological life and the agent in their development. Marx . . . endows class both with ontological and empirical meaning; it is the underlying reality of which all societal forms are an expression, and, as we read earlier in Marx's analysis, class provides the dynamic for all change."[185] The effect of this hypostatization of the abstract category of class is very unfortunate and bedevils Marx's analysis of ideology in at least four different ways.

First of all, it endows a mental construct with causal instrumentality, an attribution which methodologically is wholly unacceptable. Insofar as Marx allows an analytic category to have power with regard to concrete aspects of reality, he is simply being cognitively incomprehensible. And when this leads to the proposition that productive relations—on the basis of which class is defined—determine the nature of man's intellectual, artistic, and moral production, we have nothing but nonsense technically defined.[186] Secondly, Marx's definition of class leads to reductionism of a clear-cut variety—the reduction of all human behavior, including the 'ideological,' to 'class' in one of its forms. This subsumption of the whole of society under one of its aspects also has the paradoxical result of subsuming Marx's materialism under an idealist umbrella. Leff has noted that "we are here nearer to a form of Platonism or medieval realism than to materialism; for although the material conditions are made the determining factors they are conceived not in terms of actual individuals but as self-subsistent natures or essences or wholes, which are autonomous of the individuals which comprise them."[187] Mannheim, as we shall see in a subsequent chapter, avoided this fallacy by speaking simply of 'historical settings' and the 'collective historical experiences of groups' as *existentially* related to various interpretations or *Weltanschauungen*. Marx, however, spoke a very different language; and his basic philosophical premises made such a view quite impossible.

Thirdly, and more specifically with regard to 'ideology,' we are asked to believe not only that the 'ideational efflux' of any given society is unitary, but that any change in this efflux is moved and monitored by a force outside any empirically identifiable human agency, to wit, the abstract concept of class and the productive relations (also an abstraction) defining and underlying it.[188] To so believe is certainly to misconceive, in the footsteps of Hegel, both the nature and interplay of men and ideas in history, and the function of the descriptive categories we employ in order to comprehend what is, after all, a very complex and variable set of empirical phenomena. Such a belief assumes not only that social science concepts have the same methodological status as those of natural sciences, but that history can be explained in the same way that we explain the falling of an apple, that is, without reference to that human instrumentality called purposiveness. This assumption rests on a view of historical and societal change which is ultimately static and predeterministic. Given man as a conscious agent, its import is fatalistic and indeed reactionary in a quietistic manner.[189] No wonder that Lenin could not accept this doctrine but resolutely averred the importance of the human will in the political and revolutionary process.

Finally, by anchoring ideology to class, Marx is asking us to accept the logical absurdity that an abstraction is capable of having a 'consciousness.' Indeed, it is very questionable if 'class' even when defined in terms of an empirically identifiable group rather than in terms of productive relations can have a 'consciousness' in any meaningful sense of that word. Either way it is difficult to see how such a 'consciousness' can be anything but an emanation of an abstruse, transcendental kind. It was on this basis, for example, that Weber castigated the romantic notion of the 'national soul' so popular in German historiography of the late nineteenth century, and compared it (and rightly so) with the Marxian historicist conceptions. [190] In both cases we have the attempt to link an ideational abstraction *causally* to a societal construct, rather than interpretatively ex post facto. It is one thing to speak of the 'spirit' of an epoch or age, of its *Weltanschauung*, in terms of an *interpretation* of that age and something quite different to assume that this belief system in actual fact stood in some causal relationship to that age. While the former is an evaluative interpretation on the part of the observer or interpreter, the latter is an assumption resting upon patently metaphysical supports. It is the failure to recognize this that has led 'vulgar' Marxists to assert that Kant's epistemology is the result of the rise of the industrial age, or to allege that a society of hierarchical estates produced the fugue. [191] The blame here, I am afraid, lies not wholly with vulgar Marxism. [192]

'Ideology' as an Explanatory Concept

If the scientific usefulness of a concept is preeminently determined by its explanatory power, then it is obviously of interest to inquire how Marx's conceptualization of "ideology" fares in this respect. The question here is mainly one of conceptual significance, as discussed in the first chapter; our query addresses itself to the nature of the propositions generated by Marx's sociological formulation of 'ideology' as the 'ruling ideas' of the ruling class of society.

The first question we have to ask is: has Marx defined 'ideology' as the 'ruling ideas' in such a way that it can be used to propound propositions which are not true by definition, that is, not contained within the meaning of the concept itself? Let us look once again at the preceeding statement by Marx that the "ideas of the ruling class are in every epoch the ruling ideas." If we ask ourselves *why* ideology (as the ruling ideas) is the ideas of the ruling class rather than that of another class, then the answer seems plain: it follows from the definition of what constitutes the ruling class. The argument which Marx gives appears to be of the following syllogistic kind: (i) the ruling class determines the "extent and compass of an epoch . . . [and it does] this in its whole range"; (ii) its members "possess among other things consciousness, and therefore think"; and thus (iii) these members of the ruling class determine the ruling ideas—"thus their ideas are the ruling ideas of the epoch." In short, we have a circular explanation: or, to put it otherwise, we have no explanation at all. Marx also purports to give a slightly different explanation. He maintains that the ruling class not only regulates the material production but also the "production and distribution of the ideas of their age." But this, too, is a tautological explanation. The attribution of distributory power to the ruling class follows from the fact that it *is* the ruling class.

However, in the passage following the one referred to above, we do find a different use of 'ideology' as the 'ruling ideas.' In it Marx introduces the concept of the 'division of labor' and tries to explain why the ruling class's ideas are ideological. He writes: "The division of labour . . . manifests itself also in the ruling class as the division of mental and material labour, so that inside this class one part appears as the thinkers of the class (its active, conceptive ideologists, who make the perfecting of the illusion of the class about itself their chief source of livelihood). . . . " Of the significance of the genesis of the division of material and mental labor Marx had earlier written, as we have already noted, that from "this moment onwards consciousness *can* really flatter itself that it is something other than consciousness of existing practice, that it *really* represents something without representing something real. . . . " In other words, the 'division of labor' inevitably makes 'mental labor' an activity in illusion-making and illusion-believing; and inasmuch as the 'ruling ideas' of the ruling class are a product of its 'mental laborers' these ideas are, a fortiori, illusory and therefore ideological.

Two things have to be said about this explanation: (i) it depends on Marx's metaphysical conception of 'consciousness' in society, which forms the main premise in his explanation and which therefore permeates the whole explanation; (ii) 'ideology' is not used to *explain* anything, since the only independent variable which we have here is Marx's concept of the 'division of labor.' Indeed, "ideology" does not seem to be a substantive term at all in this context since it is used as the notational equivalent of not only "illusory ideas" but "ideas" in general.

On the other hand, in this passage we do have an attempt to explain the *role* of the 'ideologist' within the ruling class. He appears as the 'theoretician' of the class, who takes it upon himself to produce "the illusion of the class about itself." This is, however, a circular explanation of the functional role of the 'ideologist,' and in no way explains in what respect such a person is different from a 'thinker,' an intellectual, or what Marx would later call himself, 'a laborer of the head.' Marx attributes 'ideologicalness' to all members of the 'thinking' category of the social dichotomy resulting from the division of labor, with the consequence that the use of 'ideology' here in no way qualifies the nature of a 'thinker' or distinguishes him from another member of the same occupational category. In brief, the term is superfluous as a characterization of the role of a certain group of people; consequently it has no explanatory power. Even Marx's inclusion in this passage of the 'revolutionary class' as a causal variable if and when a new ideology gains dominance is an escape route of the circular kind: it contains no explanatory and thus predictive utility but is simply true by definition ex post facto. [193]

'Ideology' as a Prescriptive Concept

When we come to the last of the four passages excerpted from *The German Ideology* we also come to a significant and revealing paradox in what Marx had to say about the relationship between society and ideas in terms of the substructure-superstructure model. This paradox is contained in the following two propositions: that the "existence of revolutionary ideas in a particular period presupposes the existence of a revolutionary class"; but that "each new class . . . is compelled . . . in order to carry through its aims . . . to give its ideas the form of universality. . . . " Marx here appears to admit to the *function* and *necessity* of ideas in changing social conditions and structures, despite his statement that social consciousness is determined by society but does not determine it. He does this by *prescribing* what form a "class making a revolution" should give "its ideas . . . to carry through its aims," namely, "to represent them as the only rational, universally valid ones." The advice is undoubtedly sound, but is Marx in a position to give it?

I do not think so; nor do I believe that Marx ever solved this contradiction in his social theory—nor, given his premises, that this is possible. Certainly the following symbiosis of philosophy and the proletariat in social revolution is unsatisfactory:

Just as philosophy finds its *material* weapons in the proletariat, so the proletariat finds its *intellectual* weapons in philosophy. . . . Philosophy is the head of this emancipation and the proletariat is its heart. Philosophy can only be realized by the abolition (*Aufhebung*) of the proletariat, and the proletariat can only be abolished by the realization of philosophy.[194]

However metaphorically suggestive this predication may seem, we here have a dichotomy which is unabridgeable except in a metaphysical realm devoid of ordinary logic and common sense. Quite clearly, the 'realization of philosophy' is either the realization of the 'logic of history,' which is ineluctible, or it involves 'philosophy' in an instrumental and volitional sense—as the active and purposive use of ideas in social action and change. If the former, then Marx or any other philosopher is merely a vehicle for a transcendental force which 'uses' him just as much as Hegel's Spirit used ordinary men. If the latter, then Marx has not given 'ideas' their proper due in his philosophical premises. "Material force," Marx wrote in the same year as the passage above, "can be overthrown only by material force; but theory itself becomes a material force when it has seized the masses."[195] This, however, is not an acceptable solution to Marx's dilemma either and merely highlights even further his intense efforts to account for the role of ideas in social change while at the same time retaining his inverted, materialized Hegelian framework. How ideas can become 'material force' is only explicable if we first divest ourselves of the strict substructure-superstructure metaphor and admit that ideas, just as institutional, legal, moral, religious, and other non-'materialistic' forms of social life, are dynamic aspects of man's activity *qua* social being.[196] As variable phenomena they may, on the one hand, delimit the scope of this activity; but they may also lead man on toward new kinds of social life. Unfortunately Marx's premises give us no means for accounting for such efficacious forms of ideational-*cum*-practical activites in social systems.

This leaves us with one more aspect to be considered: the role of the intellectual in social change. Marx, as we know, never came to the point of working out an extensive theory of social stratification; and as Avineri has suggested, this is surmisably a result of his own ambivalence "over the place to be allotted to the intellectuals . . . within his own theory of social classes."[197] However, Avineri's solution to the problem is not, as I have already attempted to show, adequate or convincing—it simply does not square with Marx's social epistemology.[198] The question is, after all, how ideas can seize the masses in order to become a 'material force,' if we at the same time accept the Marxian propositions about ideas and society as expressed in his conception of ideology. Does not such a "seizing of the masses" by an idea or ideas presuppose a process of 'ideologicalization,' and as a result also presuppose a category of individuals whose function it is to instill the right *activating* ideas in the proletariat? As we shall see in the next chapter, this is precisely what Marx's most eminent follower believed to be a sine qua non for revolutionary action. That Lenin also called these individuals 'ideologues' or 'ideologists,' and his own doctrines the 'socialist ideology,' is but a further instance of irony in the fleckered history of our term.

NOTES

1. See Arne Naess, *Democracy, Ideology and Objectivity—Studies in the Semantics and Cognitive Analysis of Ideological Controversy* (Oslo, 1956), pp. 148ff. (hereafter referred to as *Democracy, Ideology and Objectivity*) and George Lichtheim, *The Concept of Ideology and Other Essays* (New York, 1967), pp. 4ff. (hereafter referred to as *Concept of Ideology*).
2. See Lichtheim, op. cit., p. 7. See also Hans Barth, *Wahrheit und Ideologie* (Zurich, 1945), pp. 16ff., and Richard H. Cox ed., *Ideology, Politics, and Political Theory* (Belmont, 1969), pp. 10ff.
3. Quoted in Cox, op. cit., p. 11.
4. Ibid., p. 10.
5. Quoted in Lichtheim, op. cit., p. 7. Author's translation.
6. Naess, op. cit., p. 152.

7. *See* Irving Louis Horowitz, *Philosophy, Science and the Sociology of Knowledge* (Springfield, 1961), pp. 14ff., and David Minar, "Ideology and Political Behavior," *Midwest Journal of Political Science* 5 (November 1961): 318.

8. *See* Horowitz, op. cit., pp. 14ff.

9. Quoted by Horowitz, op. cit., p. 18 (from Bacon's *Novum Organum,* published in 1620).

10. *See* Lichtheim, op. cit., pp. 9f., and Horowitz, op. cit., pp. 25ff.

11. Barth, op. cit., p. 17. Author's translation.

12. Lichtheim, op. cit., p. 8.

13. *See ibid.,* p. 5.

14. *See* Naess, op. cit., p. 150f.

15. Lichtheim, op. cit., p. 5.

16. Robert Nisbet, "The Nemesis of Authority," *Encounter* 39, no. 2 (August 1972): 19.

17. Naess, op. cit., p. 151.

18. Ibid.

19. Ibid., p. 153.

20. Lichtheim, op. cit., p. 46.

21. It seems probable, however, that the early Marx, long ignored by orthodox Marxists and critics of Marx alike, was more of an explicit humanist than the later, more 'scientific' Marx, or the Promethean Marx, about whose character Lewis S. Feuer has some acerbic things to say in his "Karl Marx and the Promethean Complex," *Encounter* 35, no. 6 (December 1968): 15ff.

22. *See* George Lichtheim, *Marxism: An Historical and Critical Study* (New York, 1961), pp. 39f. (hereafter referred to as *Marxism*).

23. Karl Marx and Friedrich Engels, *The German Ideology* (Moscow, 1968) p. 37. This work will hereafter be referred to as *G.I.*

24. Lichtheim, *Marxism*, p. 39.

25. John Plamenatz, *Ideology* (London, 1970), p. 32.

26. Hume's chief philosophical work is *Treatise on Human Nature*, written in France between 1734 and 1737 and published in complete form three years later. A recent edition is L. A. Selby-Bigge, ed., *A Treatise of Human Nature* (Oxford, 1978), 2d. ed.

27. *See* Bertrand Russell, *History of Western Philosophy* (London, 1961), pp. 634f.

28. Ibid., p. 640.

29. Ibid., p. 676.

30. Ibid., pp. 684ff.

31. Ibid., p. 680.

32. Plamenatz, op. cit., p. 35.

33. Ibid., p. 33. *See* Russell, op. cit., pp. 680f.

34. *See* Karl Popper, "What Is Dialectic?" *Mind*, n.s. 49 (1940): 403ff. and Peter Winch, *The Idea of a Social Science and Its Relations to Philosophy* (London, 1958), pp. 10ff.

35. Kant posited knowledge as a function of understanding: "This act we shall call by the general name of *synthesis*, in order to show that we cannot represent to

ourselves anything as connected in the object, without having previously connected it ourselves, and that of all representations *connection* is the only one which cannot be given through the objects but must be carried out by the subject itself, because it is an act of spontaneity." Quoted in Norman D. Livergood, *Activity in Marx's Philosophy* (The Hague, 1967), p. 14. Italicized in the original.

36. *See* Plamenatz, op. cit., p. 35.

37. Ibid.

38. Ibid., pp. 38ff.

39. Lichtheim, *Concept of Ideology*, p. 13.

40. Ibid.

41. G. R. G. Mure, as quoted in ibid.

42. For an analysis of Hegel's philosophy of identity and especially of how it influenced the thought of Feuerbach and Marx, *see* Gerd Dicke, *Der Identitätsgedanke bei Feuerbach und Marx* (Cologne, 1960), pp. 15ff. Karl Popper's treatment of it is, of course, most extensive in his *The Open Society and Its Enemies*, 2 vols. (London, 1962), 2: 40f, 306f., 393ff. For a more succinct discussion, see his "What Is Dialectic?" pp. 403ff.

43. *See* Julius I. Löwenstein, *Vision und Wirklichkeit* (Basel, 1970), p. 30 and Popper, "What Is Dialectic?" pp. 414ff.

44. For a brief consideration of Hegel's activist epistemology with reference to Marxian thought, see Livergood, op. cit., pp. 1ff.

45. For an analysis of Hegel's conception of history, *see*, e.g., Popper, *The Open Society*, 2: 27ff.; Herbert Marcuse, *Vernunft und Revolution* (Neuwied am Rhein, 1962), pp. 200ff.; and John Plamenatz, *Man and Society* (London, 1963), 2: 146ff.

46. Popper, "What Is Dialectic?" p. 416.

47. The short quotation comes from Robert Heiss, *Die grossen Dialektiker des 19. Jahrhunderts* (Cologne, 1963), p. 95. *See also* Löwenstein, op. cit., pp. 30ff.

48. Lichtheim, *Concept of Ideology*, p. 15.

49. *See* Robert Tucker, *Philosophy and Myth in Marx* (Cambridge, 1969), pp. 31ff.

50. *See* Livergood, op. cit., pp. 14ff. For the relationship between Hegel and Marx there exist more than a few works of quality and eminence. Amongst the best are the following: Isaiah Berlin, *Karl Marx* (London, 1948), pp. 35ff.; Sidney Hook, *From Hegel to Marx: Studies in the Intellectual Development of Karl Marx* (New York, 1950); Plamenatz, *Man and Society*, 2; Tucker, op. cit.; Shlomo Avineri, *Karl Marx: Social and Political Thought* (Cambridge, 1971); Popper, *Open Society*, 2. *See also* Günther Hillman, *Marx und Hegel* (Frankfurt am Main, 1966). For a discussion of the roots of the dialectic as a philosophical method, *see*, e.g., Hans Köhler, *Gründe des dialektischen Materialismus im europäischen Denken* (Munich, 1961). *See also* Gordon Leff, *The Tyranny of Concepts* (London, 1969), pp. 92ff., and *History and Social Theory* (London, 1969), pp. 155ff.

51. Marx's ties to German idealism are complex but incontrovertible. The purpose of the preceding pages has been to highlight, without too much detail, the most fundamental of these. However, if one were to say in a few sentences what the quintessential nature of this connection is, one could probably do no better

than Lichtheim when he writes that the certainty that reality can be apprehended through philosophical reflexion and not through empirical perception "constitutes the inmost essence of German idealism, and the source of its unbridgeable opposition to every form of empiricism. Insofar as Marxism embodies a similar conviction, with particular respect to history, it is still within the tradition of classical German philosophy." Lichtheim, *Marxism*, p. 8.

52. Lichtheim, *Concept of Ideology*, p. 15.

53. Karl Marx and Frederick Engels, *Collected Works* (London, 1975), vol. 4, *The Holy Family*, p. 85.

54. Ibid., p. 79.

55. *See* Lichtheim, *Marxism*, p. 6.

56. *See* ibid., pp. 33ff., and *Concept of Ideology*, p. 14.

57. Marx and Engels, *GI*, p. 662.

58. Tucker, op. cit., p. 81. Chapters six and seven provide a richly annotated exposition of Marx's debt to Feuerbach, as well as of Feuerbach's own thought and debt to Hegel.

59. Quoted in ibid., p. 87.

60. It should be noted that Feuerbach used the word *man* in a generic sense alone. Thus Tucker writes: "His human subject is the human race, the species (*Gattung*). The species is the real thing, and individual man is simply a particular instance of the life of the species. God, or absolute self, is an idealized image of the positive attributes of the species. . . . " Ibid., p. 88. Marx, who was very well aware of this aspect of Feuerbach's thought, made much of it in his later polemics against the latter, despite his own frequent use of the concept of *Gattungswesen*. As we shall see below, Marx's own conception tends to suffer from the same affliction as that of Feuerbach.

61. Quoted in ibid., p. 81.

62. Marx/Engels, *GI*, p. 37.

63. Avineri, op. cit., p. 68.

64. *See* A. James Gregor, *A Survey of Marxism* (New York, 1965), pp. 21f.

65. Marx/Engels, *GI*, p. 659.

66. Quoted in Livergood, op. cit., pp. 21f. *See also* Avineri, op. cit., pp. 65ff.

67. Tucker, op. cit., p. 97.

68. *See* ibid., p. 40. In the history of Marxist movements, and in the literature in general there is, however, a lack of consensus regarding the nature and extent of the influence on Marx of Hegel's thought. As to Marxism itself, Engels, Plekhanov, Lenin (during his later years), and Lukács are the most prominent examples of Hegelian Marxists, especially with reference to the importance allotted the Hegelian notion of the dialectic in their thinking. As to non-Marxist historians and scholars, Tucker, Avineri, Lichtheim, Plamenatz, and Gustav A. Wetter, among others, support the preeminence accorded Hegel in the development of Marx's thought. However, there are those, like Karl Löwith and Herbert Marcuse, who insist on an almost complete lack of continuity between the two. Thus Löwith, e.g., has maintained that between themselves, Marx and Kierkegaard destroyed the Hegelian outlook and philosophy. There is also, as Z. A. Jordan has pointed out, a middle group of interpreters, whose members admit

both a continuity and a fundamental break between Hegel and Marx. Jordan regards Sidney Hook's *From Hegel to Marx* as the preeminent example of this exegetic approach. He himself also appears to belong to this school of thought, the contours of which are admittedly vague and ambiguous. *See* Z. A. Jordan, *The Evolution of Dialectical Materialism* (New York, 1967), pp. 65ff. As to the question of Marx's beholdenness to Hegel in his later years as distinguished from those of his youth, Morris Watnick has made the pertinent observation that "The best proof that the later Marx was as much under Hegel's influence when he wrote *Capital* as he was in his younger days was supplied by the draft notes of his economic analysis." Morris Watnick, "Relativism and Class Consciousness: Georg Lukács," in L. Labedz, ed., *Revisionism* (New York, 1962), p. 154fn. The draft notes were published as *Grundrisse der Kritik der politischen Ökonomie* (Moscow, 1939).

69. E. H. Carr, *What Is History?* (London, 1963), p. 18.

70. *See* Tucker, op. cit., p. 101.

71. Quoted in ibid.

72. *See* ibid., pp. 97, 99ff. *See also* Manfred Friedrich, *Philosophie und Ökonomie beim jungen Marx* (Berlin, 1960) and Kurt Lenk, *Marx in der Wissenssoziologie* (Neuwied, 1972), pp. 114ff.

73. *See* Barth, op. cit., p. 124.

74. For an excellent analysis of Marx's conception of human nature, see Part 2 in Bertell Ollman's *Alienation: Marx's Conception of Man in Capitalist Society* (Cambridge, 1971), pp. 75ff. *See also* Joseph J. O'Malley, "History and Man's 'Nature' in Marx," *Review of Politics* 28, no. 4 (October 1966): 508ff.

75. Tucker, op. cit., p. 185.

76. Ibid. As has been pointed out more than once, what Marx called *Entfremdung* would reappear, in this century, in Max Weber's conception of *Rationalisierung*. In fiction it is, of course, above all Kafka who most searingly has portrayed the workings of this phenomenon—though not in Marxist terms, despite Lukács' attempts to turn Kafka into a Marxist, albeit not a full-fledged one. With regard to Tucker's interpretation, see Istvan Meszaros's fierce critique in *Marx's Theory of Alienation* (London, 1972), pp. 331ff.

77. Lichtheim, *Concept of Ideology*, p. 20.

78. Marx as quoted by Tucker, op. cit., p. 102.

79. *See* Barth, op. cit., p. 123, and Lichtheim, *Marxism*, pp. 48ff., for a summary of Marx's original statements regarding man's alienation through his productive activity (as worked out in the so-called *Paris Manuscripts*). *See also* Friedrich, op. cit., pp. 123ff.

80. Quoted in Lichtheim, *Marxism*, p. 49.

81. Quoted in ibid.

82. Marx/Engels, *GI*, p. 43.

83. Ibid., p. 38.

84. Ibid., p. 43.

85. Ollman points out that Marx presents 'alienation' as signifying four broad relations holding within human life: man's relation to his productive activity, to his product, to other men and to the species. Ollman, op. cit., p. 137. *See also* pp.

137ff., and Meszaros, op. cit., pp. 14ff., for a similar fourfold division. I have on the whole dealt with the first two, since it is mainly in terms of these that Marx uses the concept of ideology. It is interesting to note that in Ollman's stimulating analysis of 'alienation' we hardly find any mention at all of the concept of ideology itself. Similarly, the concept plays a negligible role in Meszaros's polemic study.

86. *See,* e.g., Avineri, op. cit., pp. 96ff., and Leff, *The Tyranny of Concepts,* pp. 115ff., for a discussion of these roots. See also Tucker, op. cit., pp. 73ff.

87. Leff, *Tyranny of Concepts,* p. 119.

88. *See* ibid. and Avineri, op. cit., p. 97. But cf. the early Hegel's thought on the alienation of labor with Marx's own. *See* Georg Lukács, *Der junge Hegel* (Berlin, 1954), pp. 369ff., and Watnick, op. cit., pp. 155f. fn.

89. Peter Berger and Stanley Pullberg, "Reification and the Sociological Critique of Consciousness," *History and Theory* 4, no. 2 (1965): 198.

90. Avineri, op. cit., p. 97. *See also* Löwenstein, op. cit., pp. 73ff., and Leff, *Tyranny of Concepts,* pp. 115ff.

91. *See* Avineri, op. cit., pp. 98.

92. Cf. Watnick's formulation:". . . the 'alienation of labour' as a sociological derivative of the self-alienation of the Absolute Idea." Watnick, op. cit., p. 154.

93. Avineri, op. cit., p. 97.

94. As to the 'fetishism of commodities,' see Berger and Pullberg, op. cit., pp. 198f.

95. Marx/Engels, *GI,* p. 42. *See also* Barth, op. cit., pp. 127ff.

96. Marx/Engels, *GI,* p. 37. *See also* Franz Jakubowski, *Der ideologische Überbau in der materialistische Geschichtsauffasung* (Frankfurt am Main, 1968), pp. 8ff.

97. *See* the Preface to "The Critique of Political Economy" in *Selected Works* (New York, n.d.), 1: 356.

98. Marx/Engels, GI, pp. 37f.

99. Ibid., p. 61.

100. *See* Barth, op. cit., p. 162.

101. Marx/Engels, *GI,* 38.

102. John Plamenatz, writing about the "Marxian Uses of the Word 'Ideology' " in his *Man and Society* (London, 1963), 2: 323ff., distinguishes between three such usages: (i) an all-inclusive sense, according to which "ideology" is used to denote "the entire system of ideas which men use to describe the world and to express their feelings"; (ii) the sense, wider than the third but narrower than the one above, according to which the term stands for "all theories and doctrines which are not scientific, and also all normative concepts"; and (iii), a sense which equates the term not with "all normative concepts, but only those which serve the interest of some class or group, and also all theories and doctrines which are not scientific. This sense is prominent when Marx or Engels is trying to explain the behaviour of social classes." These distinctions are very useful, although they have been made for a purpose somewhat different from mine. They do not, however, stand in opposition to the above distinction between the structure and function of 'ideology'; indeed, the first two usages as described by Plamenatz more or less fit into my first category, while the third clearly belongs to

my second class. The fit is not perfect, of course, but neither need it be for the purposes of the present analysis.

103.   Kurt Lenk, in his *Marx in der Wissenssoziologie*, makes a distinction between two Marxian usages of the term "ideology," the first of which refers to the early Marx and his discussion of thought in isolation from praxis, and the second to ideology as 'false consciousness.' *See* op. cit., pp. 134f. In the sense that the former category is primarily a philosophical one, while the latter is sociological, this categorization follows my classification. I would, however, want to put more stress on the *class*-relatedness of 'ideology' in the sociological usage of the concept, which makes it more than merely a synonym for 'false consciousness.' Plamenatz brings out this aspect very clearly in his tripartite classification. In addition, I have stressed that both the philosophical and the sociological concepts deal with 'false consciousness,' whereas Lenk seems to imply that this notion is applicable only to Marx's later usage.

104.   For detailed discussions on the continuity between the young and the the the mature Marx, *see* in particular: Tucker, op. cit., Eugene Kamenka, *The Ethical Foundations of Marxism* (London, 1962), and Avineri, op. cit. But also cf. I. M. Zeitlin, *Marxism: A Re-Interpretation* (Princeton, 1967). *See also* Ollman, op. cit., and Meszaros, op. cit. For a recent and excellent German bibliography on *Marx-Studien* in general and Marx's *Ideologiekritik* in particular consult Kurt Lenk, ed., *Ideologie: Ideologie und Wissenssoziologie* (Neuwied/Berlin, 1967), pp. 433ff. *See also* Isaiah Berlin's more biographical account in his *Karl Marx* (London, 1948), pp. 1ff.

105.   *See* Helmut Dahm, "Der Ideologiebegriff bei Marx und die heutige Kontroverse über Ideologie und Wissenschaft in den socialistischen Ländern," *Studies in Soviet Thought* 12, no. 1 (April 1972): 40ff., for a discussion of the Soviet view in these matters.

106.   Ollman, op. cit., p. 3.

107.   Quoted in ibid., p. 4.

108.   Ibid., p. 5.

109.   Lichtheim, *Marxism*,, p. xvi.

110.   Herbert Marcuse, *Soviet Marxism: A Critical Analysis* (1958; reprint ed., Harmondsworth, 1971).

111.   On the question of how to achieve such a dialogue and what the obstacles to it are, *see*, e.g., the articles by Charles Taylor and Istvan Meszaros in B. Williams and A. Montefiori, eds., *British Analytic Philosophy* (London, 1966), pp. 227ff. and 311ff. respectively.

112.   Kuhn's position is given in the now classic *The Structure of Scientific Revolutions* 2d ed. (Chicago, 1970). Feyerabend's views on these topics can be found, e.g., in his book *Against Method* (London, 1975). As to critiques of their standpoints, *see*, inter alia, I. Lakatos and A. Musgrave, eds., *Criticism and the Growth of Knowledge* (Cambridge, 1970); I. Scheffler, *Science and Subjectivity* (Indianapolis, 1967); and C. R. Kordig, *The Justification of Scientific Change* (Dordrecht, 1971).

113.   Maurice Cornforth, *The Open Philosophy and the Open Society* (London, 1968), p. 37.

114. Ibid., p. 5
115. Williams and Montefiori, op. cit., p. 230.
116. Marx/Engels, *GI*, p. 665. Emphases added.
117. R. G. Collingwood, *The Idea of History* (Oxford, 1948), p. 123.
118. Plamenatz, *Ideology*, p. 42.
119. Ibid.
120. *See*, e.g., John Mepham, "The Theory of Ideology in Capital," *Radical Philosophy* no. 2 (Summer 1972): 12ff.
121. *See* Shlomo Avineri, "Marx and the Intellectuals," *Journal of the History of Ideas* 28, no.2 (April-June 1967): 276.
122. H. Lefebvre, *The Sociology of Marx* (London, 1968), p. 66.
123. The first quotation found in Cornforth, op. cit., p. 118, the second in Löwenstein, op. cit., p. 68. Author's translation.
124. *See also* Avineri, "Marx and the Intellectuals."
125. Quoted by Leff, *History and Social Theory*, p. 164.
126. *See* Plamenatz, *Ideology*, pp. 42f. *See* also ibid., pp. 46ff. 50, 58ff. for various suggested forms that such a relationship between *Bewusstsein* and *bewusste Sein* can take.
127. For a discussion about the ambiguities and confusions inherent in these Marxian propositions, *see*, e.g., A. James Gregor, *Contemporary Radical Ideologies* (New York, 1968), pp. 64ff.
128. Peter Berger writes of the sub- and superstructure model that "at least in Marx's early writings . . . the relationship between the two is clearly a dialectical one. In later Marxism, the dialectic is lost in a mechanistic understanding of sub- and super-structure in which the latter becomes a mere epiphenomenon (Lenin— a 'reflection') of the former." Peter Berger, "Identity as a Problem in the Sociology of Knowledge," *Archives Européennes de Sociologie* 7, no. 1 (1966): 110fn. *See also* Richard Ashcroft, "Marx and Weber on Liberalism as Bourgeois Ideology," *Comparative Studies in Society and History* 14 (1972): 138ff. Engels, during his old age, argued along a less 'deterministic' line; *see* Note 199 below.
129. *See* Barth, op.cit., pp. 162f.
130. Marx/Engels, *GI*, p. 31.
131. Klaus Hartmann, *Die Marxsche Theorie* (Berlin, 1970).
132. Dahm, op. cit., p. 68.
133. Hartmann, op. cit., p. 555. Author's translation.
134. Dahm, op. cit., p. 68. Author's translation.
135. Hartmann, op. cit., pp. 557f. Author's translation.
136. Ibid., p. 563. Author's translation.
137. Lenk, *Marx in die Wissenssoziologie*, p. 286; Hartmann, op. cit., p. 563. Author's translation.
138. *See* Dahm, op. cit., p. 69.
139. Hartmann, op. cit., p. 565.
140. Mannheim, op. cit., p. 137. *See also* pp. 110ff.
141. Avineri, "Marx and the Intellectuals," pp. 276f.
142. Marx/Engels, *GI*, p. 11.
143. Ibid., p. 43.

144. Ibid., p. 38.

145. *See* Lewis S. Feuer, "Marxism and the Hegemony of the Intellectual Class," *Transactions of the Fifth World Congress of Sociology* (Brussels, 1964): 83.

146. Tucker, op. cit., p. 96.

147. Karl R. Popper, *The Poverty of Historicism* (New York, 1961), p. 76. For an analysis and criticism of holism, *see* pp. 17ff., 76ff. The musical examples in the text come from Popper's arguments.

148. *See* ibid, pp.27f. For an analysis of essentialism and nominalism in European intellectual history, *see* Lewis S. Feuer, *The Scientific Intellectual* (New York, 1963), pp. 83ff.

149. Klaus Knorr and James N. Rosenau, eds., *Contending Approaches to International Politics* (Princeton, 1969), p. 93. For a discussion of reductionism as a valid form of explanation, *see*, e.g., Ernest Nagel, *The Structure of Science* (New York, 1961), pp. 345ff.

150. Quoted in Robert K. Merton, *Social Theory and Social Structures* (New York, 1957), p. 364.

151. Marion Levy in Knorr and Rosenau, op. cit., p. 93.

152. Quoted in Leff, *The Tyranny of Concepts*, p. 184.

153. Popper, *Poverty of Historicism*, p. 78fn. However, *see* Ollman's defense of holism in terms of a philosophy of internal relations, in Ollman, op. cit., pp. 249ff. Emphases added.

154. Levy in Knorr and Rosenau, op. cit., p. 99.

155. Reinhard Bendix, *Max Weber: An Intellectual Portrait* (Garden City, 1962), p. 476. Thus, e.g., Weber in adopting Tönnies's famous distinction between *Gemeinschaft* and *Gesellschaft* preferred to use, respectively, the terms *Vergemeinschaftung* and *Vergesellschaftung*. These are active nouns and are unfortunately not translatable into English.

156. Quoted in Löwenstein, op. cit., p.37. Author's translation.

157. For an orthodox Marxist attack on treating Marxian dialectics in terms of the Hegelian conception, *see* R. O. Gropp, "Die marxistische dialektische Methode und ihr Gegensatz zur idealistischen Dialektik Hegels," I, II, *Deutsche Zeitschrift für Philosophie*, 2 (1954): 69ff., 344ff.

158. Popper, *The Poverty of Historicism*, p. 3. Emphasis added.

159. As to Popper's critique, *see*, e.g., Leff's critical comments in *The Tyranny of Concepts*, pp. 95ff. For Marx's contribution to historiography and the philosophy of history, see inter alia, M. M. Bober, *Karl Marx's Interpretation of History* (Cambridge, Mass., 1927); Karl Federn, *The Materialist Conception of History* (London, 1939); E. J. Hobsbawm, "Karl Marx's Contribution to Historiography," *Marx and Contemporary Scientific Thought* (The Hague, 1969), p. 197; and Gordon Leff's two books, already cited. Also cf. the exhaustive German bibliography on historicism in Lenk's *Ideologie: Ideologiekritik und Wissenssoziologie*, pp. 437ff.

160. *See* Löwenstein's short but incisive discussion in op. cit., pp. 71ff.

161. *See* Popper in "What Is Dialectic?", pp. 403ff., and Sidney Hook, *Dialectical Materialism and Scientific Method* (Manchester, July 1955).

162. Popper adds two more conclusions which can be derived from his premises: "(4) This means that we must reject the possibility of a *theoretical* history; that is to say, of a historical social science that would correspond to *theoretical physics*. There can be no scientific theory of historical development serving as the basis for historical prediction. (5) The fundamental aim of historicist methods . . . is therefore misconceived; and historicism collapses." *Poverty of Historicism*, pp.viff. I shall deal with *Historismus* as contrasted with historicism in the chapter on Mannheim and the sociology of knowledge. Author's emphases.

163. With reference to this proposition Popper writes: "The decisive step in this argument is statement (2). I think that it is convincing in itself: if there is such a thing as growing human knowledge, then we cannot anticipate today what we shall know tomorrow. [Emphases deleted.] This, I think, is sound reasoning, but it does not amount to a *logical proof* of the statement. . . . My proof consists in showing that *no scientific predictor*—whether a human scientist or a calculating machine—*can possibly predict, by scientific methods, its own results*. Attempts to do so can attain their result only after the event, when it is too late for prediction; they can attain their result only after the prediction has turned into a retrodiction." Ibid., pp. viiff. Emphases added.

164. Marx/Engels, *GI*, p. 31.

165. Charles Madge, *Society in the Mind* (New York, 1964), p. 64.

166. Marx/Engels, *GI*, p. 11.

167. Ibid., p. 61. Emphases added.

168. Ibid., pp. 61f.

169. Ibid., p. 62.

170. Ibid. Emphases added.

171. *See* Naess, op. cit., pp. 154ff., where an argument along these lines is presented.

172. The problems associated with the term "value"—"that unfortunate child of misery," as Kaplan quotes Weber—are complex, and it is not my intention to give these any but the most cursory attention. This is not really necessary at this point, since the problem of values only becomes acute when (among other factors) the meanings of terms have acquired normative ambiguity; and my belief is that in Marx's use of 'ideology' we find no such ambiguity. For it is explicitly 'value-loaded,' to use Gunnar Myrdal's terminology, and its use by Marx is clearly one of an 'appraising value judgement' (to use Nagel's phrase) as distinguished from a characterization which does not entail an appraisal. Or as Alasdair MacIntyre has written, "for Marxism the key descriptive expressions in our vocabulary are also evaluative. Nor is this merely a matter of such expressions being composites in which a descriptive component is joined to the expression of an evaluative choice. For in a Marxist view, values are not chosen, they are given; indeed, the view that values are not given but chosen is, in a Marxist view, one of the given evaluations of a liberal, individualistic society. For it itself embodies an evaluative attitude." *Against the Self-Images of the Age* (London, 1971), p. 92. In a word, the term "ideology" is very obviously biased in the technical sense, and it is Marx's open acceptance of its biased nature that makes his use of it evaluatively predeterminative. This bias not only suffuses Marx's selection of problems, but also the meaning

he attributes to events as well as the facts presented for accounting for this meaning. Marx's rejection of 'objectivity' as both a state of mind and a norm in analysis undoubtedly led him to be unconcerned about this whole *Problematik*. See Kaplan, op. cit., pp.370ff. (the quote above is to be found on p. 370), for a concise and balanced presentation of the problem of values in analysis.

173. For the ludicrous proposition that Marxism is both a science and an ideology, *see* Walter Hollitscher, "Der Ideologiebegriff in marxistischer Sicht," *Proceedings of the Fourteenth International Congress of Philosophy* (Vienna, 1968), p. 509.

174. *See* Charles L. Stevenson, *Ethics and Language* (New Haven, 1944), pp. 206ff. "In any 'persuasive definition'," Stevenson writes, "the term defined is a familiar one, whose meaning is both descriptive and strongly emotive. The purport of the definition is to alter the descriptive meaning of the term . . . without . . . any substantial change in the term's emotive meaning. And the definition is used, consciously or not, in an effort to secure, by this interplay between emotive and descriptive meaning, a redirection of people's attitude." Ibid., p. 220. My argument is that (a) "ideology" had acquired an ambiguity and vagueness by the early 1840s which, together with the emotive meaning attached to it, made it a perfect instrument for a 'persuasive' definition (*see* Naess, op. cit., p. 153); that (b) Marx was aware of this fact (*see* ibid., pp. 153f., 271 fn. and Lichtheim, *On the Concept of Ideology*, p. 18fn); that (c) he accepted and utilized this depreciatory connotation of the word; but that (d) Marx did not stop here, simply using it as a *Schimpfwort* or as a means for changing attitudes in the Stevensonian sense, but instead (e) redefined it in terms of his larger conceptual framework, by linking its meaning to the question regarding the relationship between 'ideas' and 'society,' in which operation he was deeply influenced by his Hegelian roots. In short, it acquired a new *technical* meaning, but not a normatively neutral one. It should be added that while an evaluative *concept* necessarily emotively charges the word or term which is used to refer to it, an emotively charged term does not necessarily imply an evaluative concept—or any concept at all. As I have previously argued, the derogatory use of "ideology" by the Bonapartist regime was terminological rather than conceptual; and the point here is that with Marx it is no longer simply a question of terminology but of conceptualization. In line with this interpretation, a contemporary Soviet philosopher, V. A. Jadov, has in his book *Die Ideologie als Form der geistige Tätigkeit der Gesellschaft*, published in Leningrad in 1961, given the following explication of the Marxian usage of 'ideology': "Marx and Engels were the first to introduce the expression 'ideology,' viewed as a sociological term, into scientific discourse. They used this concept in *The German Ideology* wholly in the sense of a false reflection of concrete reality . . . As used by Marx and Engels the expressions 'ideology' and 'ideological' are no less derogatory than was the case with Napoleon. However, in distinction to the latter, this derogatory meaning did not [in the case of Marx and Lenin] pertain so much to the practical helplessness of the ideologues in everyday life *as to the theoretical invalidity of their mental constructions.*" Quoted by Dahm, op. cit., pp. 39f. (my emphasis).

175. *See* Leff, *History and Social Theory*, pp. 165ff.

176. Quoted by Löwenstein, op. cit., p. 154.

177. We shall take up this problem of the nature of choice, the value problem, and the question of objectivity in the discussion of Mannheim's 'historism' in a subsequent chapter.

178. Weber's critique of Marx was not, however, intrinsically antagonistic; rather, he saw in Marx's work much that was seminal to an understanding of society and history. Consequently he tried to give the Marxian propositions a methodologically acceptable anchorage rather than rejecting them outright and in toto. Karl Popper pays a similar tribute to Marx. He states that "Modern Marxists believe that they know a great deal. They are wholly lacking in intellectual modesty. They flaunt a little knowledge in an oversized terminology. My reproach does not apply to Marx or Engels. They were formidable and original thinkers who did have new ideas, many of which were not easy to formulate." Popper, "On Reason and the Open Society," *Encounter* 38, no. 5 (May 1972): 17.

179. For a short but excellent discussion of Weber's methodological critique of Marx, *see* W. G. Runciman, *Social Theory and Political Theory* (London, 1965), 43ff. *See also* Löwenstein's admirable book, op cit., pp. 153ff.

180. *See* Kaplan, op. cit., pp. 54ff., for an elaboration of these distinctions.

181. These distinctions are obviously not cut-and-dried, and thus the four categories will have to be treated as somewhat fluid. But while the meaning of Marx's first description of 'ruling ideas' does not necessarily invoke his larger framework—indeed, to a certain extent the statement can be considered to be true by definition—his second proposition can only be understood in terms of his own particular philosophical system and the relationships which he posits between 'material production' and the dialectics of history.

182. Kaplan, op. cit., p. 61.

183. *See* Leff, *History and Social Theory*, pp. 168ff. *See also* Löwenstein, op. cit., pp. 155ff.

184. Kaplan, op. cit., p. 81; *see also* pp. 80ff., and Nagel, op. cit., pp. 380ff.

185. Leff, *History and Theory*, p. 170.

186. I should add that although the Marxian determinism above—or its vulgar Marxist variant (it is not always easy to know where the one ends and the other begins)—has to be rejected, this by no means indicates that we cannot 'date' art with reference to a historical period and its 'social situation.' Mannheim's thesis to this effect is not only justifiable but is indeed sensible—a point which any decent book on the history of art can testify to. *See* Mannheim, op. cit., pp. 243ff. This procedure does, however, involve Mannheim in the problems of 'imputation'—see his argument in ibid., pp 276f.—to which we shall return in a subsequent chapter.

187. Leff, *History and Social Theory*, p. 170. For an analysis of how Marx's definitions of 'class' and 'ideology' affect explanation, *see* pp. 172ff.

188. *See* ibid., pp. 171ff.

189. Among those who reacted against this aspect of Marxism most deeply was Georgii Plekhanov, whose whole *The Development of the Monist View of History* (published in 1895) is a brave attempt to extricate Marxism from the charge of fatalism and quietism, and of ignoring 'ideals' and 'individuals' in sociohistorical development.

190. *See* Löwenstein, op. cit., p. 153.

191. *See* Ernst Bloch, *On Karl Marx* (New York, 1971), p. 146.

192. Mannheim, despite his many mistakes, did not fall for this kind of silly talk. *See* Mannheim, op. cit., p. 214.

193. It is often decried that Marx never came to finish his third volume of *Das Kapital*, that he broke it off just as he was about to deal with the notion of class. Had he not done so, the evidence suggests that a more sophisticated Marxian treatment of social stratification would have been available. In *The Eighteenth Brumaire of Louis Napoleon* he does in fact suggest a meaning of the concept which is not simply that of property differentiation but also involves a more activist, communal group conception. *See* Avineri, "Marx and the Intellectuals," pp. 269ff, and Leff, *History and Social Theory*, pp. 174ff.

194. Avineri, "Marx and the Intellectuals," p. 270.

195. Ibid., p. 278.

196. Engels, during the final years of his life, appears to have realized the need for a more subtle and differentiated approach to this question (especially when confronted with the simplicities of *Vulgärmarxismus*). *See* Leff's discussion in *The Tyranny of Concepts*, pp. 184f.; and for a discussion of Weber's rejoinder to this Marxian *Problematik, see* Löwenstein, op. cit., pp. 157ff.

197. Avineri, "Marx and the Intellectuals," p. 269. *See also* Feuer's "Marxism and the Hegemony of the Intellectual Class," pp. 83ff.

198. It is with regard to this point that Feuer makes the cogent statement that "a profound dilemma . . . would have confronted Marx and Engels if they had tried to develop a theory of the intellectual class. They would not have been able to do so without abandoning either their materialist conception of history or their idea of the self-emancipation of the working class." Ibid., p. 83. Lenin, as we shall see in the immediately following chapter, drew the consequences of this ineluctable choice by rejecting the ability of the working class to 'spontaneously' move toward a socialist revolution.

3

LENIN AND THE CONCEPT OF IDEOLOGY

THE LENINIST CONCEPTION OF IDEOLOGY

INTRODUCTION

"There can be no revolutionary movement without a revolutionary theory," Lenin enjoins in a famous passage in *What Is to Be Done?*, first published in exile more than seventy years ago.[1] On the face of it, this dictum (which he owes to Plekhanov) does not appear to deserve the significance and acclaim which has come its way since then. For it seems to express nothing more than the rather truistic notion that revolutions are not nurtured in a 'theoretical' vacuum—that revolutionary movements, being a function of purposive human actions, are inconceivable without ideas or doctrines purporting (in some sense at least) to define, explain, and proclaim the nature of the goals being sought and the reasons for the means being used in the pursuit of these. But what may appear to be a truism to us today was certainly not meant to be simply a commonsense reminder by Lenin on the subject matter of revolution. On the contrary, what we have here is a heated and explicit injunction, a programmatic and polemical answer to the query raised in the title of his pamphlet. As such it is nothing less than a rejoinder—in substance if not directly—to Marx's claim that the existence of revolutionary ideas in a given epoch presupposes the existence of a revolutionary class, or to Engels's depiction of revolutionary socialism as a 'reflex' in the minds of the proletariat of the conflict between the forces and the mode of production.[2] Although all three of these propositions tie revolutionary ideas, doctrines, or theories to a revolutionary structure and situation, the thrust of Lenin's position is almost diametrical in substance to that of the other two: for while Marx appears to have been arguing for the thesis of the deterministic, epiphenomenal subordination of theory to sociohistoric structure, of the ideational to the material, of ideas to praxis, and while Engels posits an almost automatic and symbiotic genesis of socialist ideas once an obvious revolutionary reality obtains, Lenin's declared emphasis is clearly placed on the direct and causal significance of ideas in human activity and thus on the prior necessity of revolutionary theory if revolutionary class-action is to be made possible and achieve its goals. His reasons for enjoining this dictum are twofold: (i) "there can be no talk of an independent ideology formulated by the working classes themselves in the process of their movement"; and (ii) the "*spontaneous* development of the working-class movement leads to its subordination to bourgeois ideology."[3] This being the case, Lenin continues with his characteristic and insistent decisiveness, then "the only choice is—either bourgeois or socialist ideology. There is no middle course. . . ."[4]

In the history of the term "ideology" the importance of these passages in *What Is to Be Done?* cannot be overemphasized. As a landmark in this history Lenin's tract occupies a natural and central place next to *The German Ideology*, with which it is also kindred in spirit and temperament in more than one respect, although the latter was not published as a whole until almost ten years after Lenin's death. Both are highly polemical and acrimonious in tone, with ad hominem diatribes and clearly defined animosities flowing through their pages with notable if not always elegant ease. Both are also relatively youthful works, and neither is in itself regarded as a major theoretical or philosophical contribution within the oeuvre of their respective authors (nor were they meant to be). In addition, both are centrally concerned with utilizing the term "bourgeois ideology" for one purpose or another, a primary one being that of wielding it as an eristic weapon to discredit the ideas of those who are so forcefully put to task in these two books. Finally, in terms of the larger spectrum of intellectual and political discourse, both of these pamphlets can be said to constitute an essentially factional contribution to debate among 'socialists' and 'radicals' of one hue or another rather than being disputations with opponents who clearly belong to a fundamentally different or opposite camp in either German or Russian politics and intellectual life (hence the effective pejorativeness of "bourgeois ideology" as a disputational battle-ax). Both are representative examples of the intense polemical—or, as some would say, 'ideological'—cut and thrust that has been such a noteworthy factor within the various radical, socialist, and generally oppositional movements in Europe ever since their earliest days.

But it is not due to these similarities that Lenin's short work deserves its place next to *The German Ideology*. Rather, this claim rests primarily on the significant differences between his and Marx's doctrines on, and usage of, 'ideas' and 'ideology' as highlighted in this pamphlet—differences which would later profoundly affect not only Marxist doctrine in particular but also modern political and intellectual history in general. Of these, the most important to us as a baseline is the adumbrated doctrine of the duality of ideology, that is, Lenin's thesis of the two ideologies, either of which excludes the other and which together exhaust the universe of ideas, doctrines, and beliefs. As we have already noted, these two are the bourgeois and the socialist ideologies, beyond which there is none other; for as Lenin notes rather inconcinnously, "mankind has not created a 'third' ideology, and moreover, in a society torn by class antagonisms there can never be a non-class or above-class ideology."[5] The fundamental difference between this dualistic, zero-sum conception of 'ideology' and the Marxian notion of it as a single, 'idealistic' and 'alienative' epiphenomenon contained solely within the boundaries of bourgeois consciousness is immediately apparent, and need therefore not concern us extensively here (we need simply to remember Marx's celebrated if somewhat belated comment that he was not a Marxist). What needs some explication, however, is Lenin's own and very singular contribution to the history and usage of this concept, together with the far-reaching implications of this usage to the theory and practice of what is officially known today as Marxist-Leninism. For what Lenin established here, and Stalin brought to full bloom, is a meaning of the term which has become one of its pervasive interpretations in the contemporary literature.

LENIN'S REFORMULATION OF THE MARXIAN CONCEPT

In distinction to Marx, who derives his doctrine of ideology as false or mystifying consciousness from a basically ontological conception of the nature of man as species-being, Lenin's conception is a direct derivative of the sociological concepts of 'class' and especially 'class conflict.' Hence it is not only a broader, simpler, and far more palpable doctrine than that of Marx, but also (probably because of this) an eminently practical one, well suited to a frame of mind which, as Trotsky writes, was above all dominated by the ambition of being "the great engineer of history" rather than—as in the case with Marx—"the midwife of revolution."[6] The basis for the dualistic nature of ideology which Lenin posits is thus not difficult to ascertain; it is a direct function of the bifurcated structure of class societies and of the need of the working class to do battle with the bourgeoisie on all fronts of the struggle if the aims of revolution and socialism are to be achieved.[7] Lenin's point is that of these fronts the theoretical is at least as important as any other, contrary to the accepted, putatively Marx- and Engels-inspired tenets of his revolutionary comrades. Consequently, Lenin maintains, the inherent conflicts of a class-divided society are necessarily paralleled in theory, that is, in ideology; as a result partisanship has to extend beyond the political and economic struggle to the theoretical and indeed philosophical spheres, into the struggle of and over mind and consciousness, in which impartiality is as impossible as within the other and more tangible forms of the revolutionary movement. To think otherwise was, as Lenin put it, both silly and naive.[8] If there can be any doubt about this, he feels free to claim the immense authority of Engels (and through him, that of Marx) in order to buttress his argument. He notes with emphasis that Engels recognized "*not two* forms of the great struggle of Social-Democracy (political and economic), as is the fashion among us, *but three, placing the theoretical struggle on a par with the first two.*"[9]

But Lenin does not stop here, since he is by no means prepared to subscribe to a 'reflected,' deterministic or, in the terminology of his day, a 'spontaneous' notion of the origin and nature of revolutionary ideology in class societies. On the contrary, as we have already noted, Lenin was not only pessimistic about the ability of the working masses in creating an ideology of its own, but also submitted that the 'spontaneous development' of the labor movement is such that it inevitably leads to its subordination to bourgeois ideology.[10] Given the Marxist roots of his intellectual development (though these were undoubtedly intertwined with, and sometimes dominated by, some peculiarly Russian ones), the reasons he proffers for this negative appraisal of the 'ideological' viability of the proletariat are no less surprising than they are significant.[11] "But why," he thus speaks for the reader,"... does the spontaneous movement, the movement along the line of least resistance, lead to the domination of bourgeois ideology? For the simple reason," he answers, "that the bourgeois ideology is far older in origin than socialist ideology, that it is more fully developed, and that it has at its disposal *immeasurably* more means of dissemination."[12] The significance of this passage lies in the fact that by giving these empirical rather than historicophilosophical reasons for the dominance of the bourgeois ideology, Lenin at the same time signals the possibility of an ideological counterattack on the part of socialism which, if launched with the proper insight, the appropriate means, and a strong and pronounced will, can exert itself successfully viz-à-viz bourgeois ideology in terms of the very factors which have sustained the dominance of the latter.[13] What we have here is nothing less than an *empirical* interpretation of the *ideologicalization* of the bourgeois class, and flowing from it, a theory of, and thus a blueprint for, the ideologicalization of the working masses. Contained within this explanation of the appeal of bourgeois ideology we also have, in a nutshell, three of the most significant elements which define Lenin's conception of the ideological phenomenon: the historical, the doctrinal, and the instrumental factors, corresponding to the three reasons which he submits in his explanation. Taken together, and given Lenin's particular explication of each in terms of his revolutionary goals, they obviously provide a potent blend for revolutionary action. Thus it is necessary that we look at each in turn if we are going to do sufficient justice to the Leninist conception and usage of 'ideology.'

Ideology and History: Lenin's Voluntarism

Lenin's submission of the historical factor as important for the dominance of bourgeois ideology is significant above all for the fact that—despite his avowed Marxism—it is based on a voluntaristic rather than on a primarily deterministic interpretation of the historical process.[14] Thus, in his view, history consists above all of men dominating other men rather than being the matrix of more transcendental and ineluctible forces. Or, to put it differently, his conception of the historical process is that of a series of power plays for which history provides the arena for political action and willful human dominance, giving victory to the contender or contenders whose arsenal of insight and strength in all its various forms proves to be the most efficacious and appropriate as dictated by the givens of the particular historical situation and framework at hand (hence, we can perhaps add, his decisiveness in October 1917). This is not to say, however, that Lenin thought that a recognition of the centrality of human action precludes a belief in historical necessity, or that history does not contain inherent laws which are clearly recognizable and inescapable. Rather, emphasizing the great similarities between Marx and Darwin, he cast the idea of historical determinism into an evolutionary mold, while at the same time pointing out that the belief in definite laws of historical evolution does not necessarily contradict the notion of the historical efficacy of human determination.[15] Thus Lenin writes—and this recognition came to him early in his career, as evidenced here—that "the idea of historical necessity does not in the least undermine the role of the individual in history; all history is made up of actions of individuals, who are undoubtedly active figures."[16]

But Lenin's emphasis on the importance of human action in history does not stop here. Rather, in viewing history voluntaristically in his way, he was obviously searching not only for explanations of the past, but also for historical guides of how to act in the present and the future. "The real question," he continues in the passage just quoted, "that arises in appraising the social activity of an individual is: what conditions ensure the success of his actions, what guarantee is there that these actions will not remain an isolated act lost in a welter of contrary acts."[17] The activist bent of Lenin's mind is clearly discernable in this query; and it was above all this urge to learn from history in order to do something about it which "eroded the Marxian historical determinism which was ultimately replaced by a revolutionary activism based on the principle of voluntarism."[18] Given this interpretation of historical actions, in addition to his activist conception of the role of ideas in the revolutionary struggle, the lesson to be learned from the historically determined dominance and viability of bourgeois ideology is thus plain to Lenin: namely, the need for the activating will of the revolutionary on the battlefront of the ideational arena in which a purposive, militant, and well-conceived countervailing attack is of the utmost importance if the back of the 'spontaneous' or 'instinctive' appeal of bourgeois ideology is to be effectively broken.

In this connection two further, essentially Darwinian aspects of Lenin's historical outlook should be noted: his deep respect for, and preoccupation with, the power bestowed by history and the 'laws of its motion' upon those who have gained a dominant position in society; and his elitist conception of how such power is gained in the historical development of mankind. It is in part due to the former that he felt compelled to castigate his comrades-in-arms for their naive trust in 'spontaneity' and the lack of respectful insight into the strength of the historically dominant bourgeois class which this betrays—an insight which the proper study of history ought to have imprinted upon their minds.[19] It is because of his pronounced elitism that he gave such a fervent appraisal of the positive need for 'conscious' control of the masses as a "motive power of revolution" (to use the words of Marx).[20] In his view, the failure to recognize in history the strength of its immanent laws was the signal weakness of his revolutionary compatriots; for it is precisely and only in the discovery of these that a firm foundation for action could be laid, while ignoring or misinterpreting them could only lead to the continued 'spontaneous' dominance of the ruling class over the labor movement which Lenin was so keen on emphasizing. It is only by making use of these laws rather than submitting to them, he insists, that the revolutionary movement in Russia—and with it the masses of individuals—can be led consciously and purposively toward the predetermined goals which define the raison d'être of this undertaking.[21] This is obviously a "manipulative theory of history" and as such it stands in marked contrast to the orthodox Marxism of the turn of the century.[22]

The call is thus for two factors, both equally important in Lenin's view to the success of revolution, and both defining the role of 'ideology' in his usage of the term. The first is the doctrinal, which consists in the establishment of the incontrovertible truths about history and society as guiding lights for action; and the second is the instrumental, which lies in the application of these doctrines in mobilizing and purposive action. In more practical terms, the call is for the *ideologist* and the *party*, both of which Lenin regarded as absolutely essential for a socialist upheaval on Russian soil. Together they form the *avantgarde* of the revolution, and separately the one cannot function without the other if the dominance of the working masses is to be achieved outside the realm of utopian thought.

Ideology and Doctrine: The Ideologist qua Avantgarde

The doctrine of the necessity and efficacy of an active 'theoretical' battle vis-à-vis bourgeois ideology has, to Lenin's mind, two different if interrelated corollaries: the doctrine of the induced or aroused proletariat consciousness and the doctrine of the absolute partisanship of philosophy. The former refers to an emotive, affective, and conative dimension of the revolutionary movement, while the latter is essentially an injunction directed toward the cognitive characteristics of the philosophical countercheck to bourgeois ideology, which he has found to be so necessary. While the former doctrine is predicated in terms of the nature and function of 'consciousness' in revolutionary change—with specific reference to the consciousness of the masses—the latter directs itself not to 'consciousness' as such but to the nature and structure and the ideational contents of the philosophical underpinnings of socialist ideology. In Lenin's view, this philosophical aspect, which involves a direct confrontation in the sphere of ideas with bourgeois ideology, is functionally different—with regard to the revolutionary process—from the need to arouse the revolutionary will of the workers in a society dominated by the 'spontaneous' appeal of bourgeois ideology. Although both doctrines refer to the use of ideas in social change, the former involves a social and utilitarian feature while the latter embraces the intellectual, essentially 'theoretical' aspects of the revolutionary's role in radical change. This conforms not only with his elitist conception of the revolutionary movement, but also with his seemingly fundamental rejection of the Marxian notion of the 'reflexive' character of ideas in history and society. These differences between the two corollaries to Lenin's activist doctrine of revolutionary theory make it necessary for us to treat each separately and in more depth, since both emphasize equally important aspects of the meaning of 'ideology' as bequeathed to us by the Leninist legacy. But as we shall see later, these differences are more apparent than real, just as in Lenin's thought the symbiotic relationship between theory and practice, between ideas and action, is much more pronounced than the distinction above may suggest. Indeed, as Leonard Schapiro writes, in "no man before Lenin have action and thought been so closely interrelated that it is usually impossible to say whether the action was dictated by the thought, or the thought inspired by its utility for a particular course of action."[23]

(i) *The Doctrine of the Induced or Aroused Proletariat Consciousness*

Marx's lifelong fulminations against all forms of idealism—and historical idealism was not the least important of these—in essence constituted an attack on voluntarism in the name of material determinism in general and the doctrine of historical materialism in particular. Lenin, as we have noted, reintroduced voluntarism into post-Marxian socialist theory in the form of his activist principle, at the same time as he continually insisted that he was in no fundamental way diverging from the materialist conception of history as explicated by Marx and Engels. He could do this by maintaining that while, on the one hand, he believed in the possibility of a purposive human determination of the historical process, such action could only be efficacious, on the other hand, if and only if human actions are guided by a proper understanding of the laws of social development and their application as outlined and explained by the materialist conception of history. This certainly gives the appearance of being skillful sophistry on the part of Lenin, at the same time that it illustrates two fundamentally different functions of any given theoretical construction—in this case the 'materialist conception of history.' For while "Lenin and Stalin were anxious to make use of the materialist conception of history as a guide to action, . . . Marx and Engels . . . considered it only as a guide to study, that is, as we would say today, as a point of view which enables us to organize, analyze, and explain social and historical development."[24]

However, if it were merely a case of two different but equally legitimate uses of the same abstraction, there would be little need for Lenin's subtle sophistry or for the immense doctrinal battle which took place in Russia before his substantial modifications of the Marxian dicta were accepted as official dogma. While in general it is quite acceptable to speak of different purposes or functional levels being involved in inquiry, the Marxian theory of historical materialism is usually considered to have a contrary peculiarity: in principle the theory is such that it would be logically contradictory to accept and adhere to it while at the same time propagating its utility as a 'guide to action.' Indeed, as we have seen in the previous chapter, it is to a large extent precisely on the basis of this fact that Marx could and did insist that his doctrines were not 'ideological,' since they could not, by definition, serve as 'ideal,' purposive 'rationalizations' in the sphere of human history. For had Marx admitted that 'ideas'—even his own—could determine actions, either directly or indirectly, then the very essence of his materialist, reflected conception of 'ideology,' and with it his more embracing ideohistoricist theses, would immediately have fallen to pieces. Therefore, the very function of Marxian theory which Lenin made into the cornerstone of his philosophical indebtedness to Marx is precisely the function which Marx himself appears emphatically to have repudiated as being neither philosophically legitimate nor empirically feasible. It is thus not without reason—though he undoubtedly had his own specific, not altogether orthodox reasons—that Plekhanov could accuse Lenin of revisionism by submitting that his voluntarism struck "at the roots of the philosophical, sociological, and economic doctrines of Marx and Engels."[25]

Yet it is also a fact, and certainly an ironic one, that in a certain crucial sense Lenin's utilitarian and instrumental approach to knowledge adheres closer to the spirit of one of Marx's most reverberating injunctions than does the practice of Marx himself. Thus, if the assessment is correct that Lenin viewed the task of social science to consist primarily if not solely in the acquisition of knowledge on the basis of which revolutionary social action toward predetermined socialistic goals could be effectualized, then Lukács is wholly justified when, shortly after Lenin's death, he gave the following appreciation of Lenin's legacy: "Marx's concluding thesis on Feuerbach, that the philosophers hitherto only have interpreted the world, but that their preeminent task is to change it, has, it can be said without any exaggeration, found its most adequate personification in Lenin and his work."[26] This certainly seems to be a fair appraisal of Lenin's general philosophical credo and of his belief and trust in the use of ideas to propel the revolution toward the desired socialist end state.

But if the philosophically revisionist character of Lenin's voluntarism lies in his activist interpretation of the functional worth of ideas as ideology, its more tangible and concrete Marxian unorthodoxy is to be found in his assertion that while, on the one hand, the socialist consciousness of the working class is "the only basis that can guarantee our victory," this 'consciousness' is, on the other hand (to quote George Lichtheim), "an extraneous element, not rooted in the 'spontaneous' life process of the working class, but injected into it by the radical intellectuals who are the carriers of the socialist world-view."[27] In arguing for this latter notion, that the 'spontaneity' of the masses has to be molded by the 'conscious' intervention of a small vanguard of revolutionaries, Lenin quotes extensively and appreciatively from Karl Kautsky's writings, in which the latter had insisted that the "socialist consciousness is something introduced into the proletariat class struggle from without and not something that arose within it spontaneously."[28] The reason which Kautsky gave for this was that "modern socialist consciousness can arise only on the basis of profound scientific knowledge"; and the "vehicle of science is not the proletariat, but the *bourgeois intelligentsia.*"[29] To which Lenin adds, rather happily, that by their "social status, the founders of modern scientific socialism, Marx and Engels, themselves belonged to the bourgeois intelligentsia."[30] What Kautsky was reacting against was the 'revisionist' argument that while "Marx had asserted that economic development and the class struggle create, not only the conditions for socialist production, but also, and directly, the *consciousness* of its necessity," the case of England—"the country most highly developed capitalistically"—proved the opposite, since it had the least developed socialist consciousness in Europe.[31] He rejected the "allegedly orthodox-Marxist view" from which this apparent contradiction is deduced, and instead reaffirmed the proposition (which the Austrian Social-Democratic party had expressed in its program) that the task of the party "is to imbue the proletariat with the *consciousness* of its position and the consciousness of its task."[32] Lenin, on his part, not only fully agreed with all of this while at the same time castigating his fellow revolutionaries for their lack of proper consciousness and initiative: he also made this view into one of the indisputable tenets of his political philosophy and revolutionary leadership. It is also from this perceived need to inject 'conscious' control *into* the working-class movement—of creating, from without, the proper 'consciousness,' both as a positive force and as a bulwark against the 'spontaneous' tendency toward the trade-unionism and bourgeois ideology which Lenin decried so emphatically in *What Is to Be Done?*—that he developed his doctrine of an avantgarde control *over* this movement by a select, highly disciplined, and 'theoretical' cadre of professional revolutionaries. As we shall see below, this in effect amounted to the "political expropriation of the proletariat" by a small group of the bourgeois, revolutionary intelligentsia of Russia; and it is as such that Lenin's position in this matter was attacked from both the left and right wings of the European and especially the Russian Social-Democratic movement.[33]

(ii) *The Doctrine of the Absolute Partisanship of Philosophy*

Building on the Leninist thesis of the unconditional antagonism or contradiction between, and thus the incompatibility of, bourgeois and socialist ideology, the doctrine of the absolute partisanship of philosophy is, in turn, derived from the unbridgeable division between the bourgeois and proletariat classes. That philosophy cannot stand above this concrete antagonism, that it is, on the contrary, immanently and necessarily involved in it, follows from Lenin's tripartite division of the socialist struggle, and especially from his injunction that in this struggle "the role of vanguard fighter can be fulfilled only by a party that is guided by the most advanced theory."[34] Furthermore, in Lenin's view (and here he wishes, as always, to speak as a true follower of Marx and Engels) the alternatives which philosophy offers are clear-cut, just as the choice which socialism has to make is unarguable: there are two and only two kinds of philosophical systems, namely, idealism and materialism, both of which are readily recognizable as the historicoideational emanations of the historical process and the class antagonisms contained in it. In sum, partisanship is an inherent attribute aof philosophy itself, a function of its principles and premises and therefore coeval with it, synchronous with its history, and a coefficient of its development. "Recent philosophy," Lenin posits, "is as partisan as was philosophy two thousand years ago."[35] Since the proletariat class is the only 'revolutionary' class, that is, the only historically 'progressive' social structure of the modern era, it is only from that philosophy which is in tune with this 'progressiveness' of history and of its 'motion' as reposited in the dynamics of the working-class movement, that 'scientific knowledge' about historical development and evolution can be drawn, and upon which the 'most advanced theory' can be built.[36] This is what has been referred to as Lenin's postulate of a meta-theoretical identity between socialist ideology and science, a doctrine which remained more or less intact in the Soviet Union until Stalin's death and which has come under critical scrutiny there only during the past decade or so.[37]

Lenin, following in Engels's footsteps, identified philosophy with dialectics and subscribed to Engels's definition of philosophy as the "science of the general laws of motion and development of Nature, human society and thought."[38] This subsumption of science under philosophy is justified not only on the grounds that it is philosophy alone which can provide science with the requisite epistemological and methodological foundation, but also because of the belief, consonant with Lenin's antipositivistic stance in general, that only philosophy, and thus no particular science by itself, can formulate laws of the highest 'theoretical' generality— laws to which all phenomena throughout time and space can be said to be subject.[39] It is in these absolute laws, which ultimately are those of the dialectic, that Lenin found (to use Herzen's famous words) "the algebra of revolution."[40] Dialectics, however, was regarded as a dark and empty Hegelian box if not linked to an epistemological anchorage which held it solidly to reality and the experienced world of mankind, while at the same time being valid in a supraempirical or philosophical sense. Materialism provided this 'naturalistic' coupling, and although Lenin gave the impression that he had taken this concept unadulterated from the pen of Engels, it is clear that Lenin's view of it differs in some important respects from Engels's. Engels had defined 'materialism' in an absolute and genetic sense: matter is all that exists and is real, and mind is simply the highest product of matter.[41] Our perceptions are thus simply the reflections *caused* by the external, material world, which in its essence is all that exists and is as such the only reality.[42] Consequently, the concept of mind, designating the phenomena of sense perception, thought, and consciousness, refers merely to the "emergent qualities of matter organized in a particular way."[43] This conception—'to be is to be material'—is obviously ontological, and the rudimentary theory of knowledge flowing from it, that the world is more or less the way that it appears to us, is usually called naive realism. Engels, who reputedly had little interest in epistemological questions in themselves, regarding them as unproblematic, felt assured that a commonsense view of the natural sciences supported it.[44]

Lenin, however, having been made aware of the epistemological weaknesses in Engels's view by the increasing phenomenalist attacks upon it (based in part on the revolution in the natural sciences at the turn of the century, particularly in physics), saw the need for a revised and less ontological and metaphysical definition of matter.[45] The result was a definition which had epistemology itself as its mainstay, and which for that reason is known today as epistemological materialism (to distinguish it from absolute or ontological materialism). As he himself acknowledges quite explicitly, Lenin found it in Berkeley's *Treatise Concerning the Principles of Human Knowledge*, in which the latter had presented this ancient doctrine in its Lockean version in order, as we all know, to refute both it and Locke.[46] Lenin was not, of course, impressed by Berkeley's reasoning and instead wholeheartedly accepted the very view which the bishop had worked at so brilliantly to confute. The view which Berkeley had rejected and which Lenin made into his fundamental philosophical premise in *Materialism and Empirio-Criticism*, his major theoretical work, published almost exactly two centuries after Berkeley's magnum opus, is that of "the absolute existence of sensible objects in themselves, or without the mind," as Berkeley writes, or in Lenin's own words, that "[T]hings exist independently of our consciousness, independently of our sensations, outside of us. . . ."[47]

This definition differs from that of Engels because it does not define the nature of materialism ontologically but merely claims the existence of matter as being independent of the human mind. It is an epistemological definition since the assertion that "materialism is the recognition of the external world, that is, of the existence of things outside and independent of our mind" is a variant of epistemological realism, which rests on the claim that 'objective reality' exists 'outside our mind.'[48] Matter, Lenin argues, "is known to us only as that which produces, or is capable of producing, certain impressions on our senses. All that is known about matter for certain is its power to produce these effects."[49]

The problem with the causal theory of perception had been that while it can serve as an argument supporting naive realism, it equally well serves the purposes of phenomenalism; and it was the phenomenalists whom Lenin regarded as his main philosophical opponents, and who therefore are the main nonpolitical protagonists in *Materialism and Empirio-Criticism*. While the causal theory can be called upon to give credence to the belief that material objects exist independently of our perception, and while it can be pointed to as accounting inferentially for the source of our mental images, it cannot by itself guarantee that the external world *corresponds* to the forms and qualities which perception ascribes to it. In other words, this theory cannot give an adequate argument to support the view that phenomena as perceived by us are not different in essence from 'things-in-themselves'—that is, the external world. And yet, in Lenin's view, there "is definitely no difference in principle between phenomenon and the thing in itself, and there cannot be any such difference."[50] In support of this he argued that while "for idealism there is no object without a subject . . . for materialism the object exists independently of the subject and is reflected more or less adequately in the subject's mind."[51] "Matter," he continues elsewhere in *Materialism and Empirio-Criticism*, "is a philosophical category denoting the objective reality which is given to man by his sensations, and which is copied, photographed and reflected by our sensations, while existing independently of them."[52] This doctrine is usually referred to as the copy theory of perception, and Lenin made it into an integral part of epistemological materialism in order to buttress the weaknesses of the causal theory of perception.[53] Matter not only *causes* our sensations but also gives us more or less true *copies* of things "as they would be if they remained unknown, that is, as they are in themselves" (as one commentator writes).[54]

The conclusion which Lenin draws from these epistemological premises is clear-cut and precise in its partisanship. "To regard sensations as images of the external world, to recognize objective truth, to hold the materialist theory of knowledge—these are all one and the same thing."[55] To think otherwise in any manner whatsoever is both to reject a view "which is shared by natural science to this day," and to succumb either to full-fledged idealism or to agnosticism (of which he accuses Hume and Kant, following Engels's example).[56] Both these designations carried with them a judgment of the deepest philosophical disapprobation, connoting subjectivism, solipsism, and muddleheadedness—all favorite Leninist profanities. Furthermore, materialism (and Lenin often used this term as synonymous with epistemological materialism) is not only the sole 'true' philosophical and therefore scientific 'line' but also the only doctrine which recognizes the essence of nature itself and the immutable laws of the dialectic which govern all of life. As he writes, "the recognition of theory as a copy, as an approximate copy of objective reality, is materialism."[57] Given Lenin's strict copy theory, we are strongly tempted to interpret this in no other way than as the assertion that nature itself speaks to us through epistemological materialism—that Lenin's doctrine is nothing less than a "more or less adequate" reflection of the objective world itself.

Indeed, Lenin's characterization of ideology in terms of partisan philosophy can be viewed as a happy instance of the smooth dovetailing of form and content; it is an idea which, almost in the Hegelian sense, is contained within, while at the same time determining the truth of, its own predication. Or as Z. A. Jordan writes, the "materialist theory of truth comprises the claim of being itself an incontrovertible truth."[58] This trait of Lenin's philosophical mind is perhaps nowhere more starkly exhibited than when he repudiates the pejorative connotations of the term "dogmatism," instead claiming for it a veridical denotation defined in terms of the concept of verisimilitude. For "dogmatism," Lenin writes, expresses nothing else but truth as "the *correspondence* between the consciousness which reflects nature and the nature which is reflected by consciousness."[59] The argument for the 'dogmatic' nature of materialism as ideology-cum-philosophy—that it represents the absolute truth precisely because of its correspondence to objective reality—is seen to encase, at the same time, the requirement that this truth be adhered to dogmatically. In other words, to Lenin the truth-value of the materialist philosophy of socialist ideology was seen as residing in the inherent 'dogmatism' of materialism as the only valid philosophical conception of reality. There is therefore no longer a necessary contradiction between 'science' and 'ideology' since 'correct' or 'true' ideology, that is, the proletariat ideology, is the only force which can guarantee and foster scientific truth, which in turn informs the correctness of socialist ideology.[60] This is a proposition which Marx probably would have found extremely dispiriting both to the exercise of creative praxis in general and to scientific creativity in particular.

But Lenin's insistence on the absolute partisanship of philosophy is not only a characteristic of *Materialism and Empirio-Criticism* but is already clearly spelled out in the revolutionary strategy in *What Is to Be Done?* and in its call for the exercise of theoretical warfare. Lenin's emphasis in it is placed not only on the need for theory as such, but on the need for a very specific kind of theory, one which not only draws "firm and definite lines of demarcation" during "a period of theoretical disorder," but which also renounces any kind of "eclecticism in the formulation of principles."[61] What Lenin reacted against so strongly was the slogan of "Freedom of Criticism" and the charges, raised under its banner by some Marxist intellectuals, of " 'Dogmatism, doctrinairism,' 'ossification of the party—the inevitable retribution that follows the violent straitlacing of thought'," and so forth.[62] In Lenin's view, these charges and the various calls for an open, critical debate "conceal unconcern and helplessness with regard to the development of theoretical thought"; they manifestly illustrate "that the much vaunted freedom of criticism does not imply substitution of one theory for another, but freedom from all integral and pondered theory; it implies eclecticism and lack of principle."[63] And in answer to his opponents' reference to Marx's letter on the Gotha Program, in which the latter writes that "Every step of real movement is more important than a dozen programs," Lenin mixes indignation with sarcasm and exclaims that to "repeat these words in a period of theoretical disorder is like wishing mourners at a funeral many happy returns of the day."[64] Significantly, it is only a few lines after this that Lenin makes his famous statement, that there can be no revolutionary movement without a revolutionary theory.

The import of these passages is clear. Although in *Materialism and Empirio-Criticism* the major villain is Ernst Mach (or, more directly, Alexander Bogdanov) and epistemological phenomenalism, in one form or another, while here it is Eduard Bernstein and political reformism, the injunction is the same: the absolute necessity of an unvacillating and thorough commitment to the doctrinal principles of the socialist, materialist ideology.[65] Furthermore, given Lenin's unconditional assertion, that if " 'freedom of criticism' means freedom for an opportunist trend in Social-Democracy, freedom to convert Social-Democracy into a democratic party of reform, freedom to introduce bourgeois ideas and bourgeois elements into socialism"; and given, in addition, his injunction that the "task now devolved upon the Social-Democrats . . . is . . . the task of combatting the new trend" of 'freedom from criticism'—then it becomes clear that Lenin is saying more than one thing when he so strongly emphasizes the need for 'revolutionary theory' if the revolutionary movement in Russia is to succeed in its aims.[66] For as we have already noted, he is not simply enjoining the need for a *theoretical* struggle, which should be placed on a par with the political and the economic struggle; instead, he is also insisting in the strongest terms possible that this theory be *revolutionary*. From what we have just read, Lenin seems to say that by 'revolutionary' he here means, among other things, a cognitive and ideational quality which is nothing less than the converse of the qualities which he has castigated. A closer reading of the text certainly justifies this interpretation. The significance of all this to us is not difficult to ascertain, since it is precisely the creation of such revolutionary theory—one which brooks no criticism, deviation, or concession—that Lenin identified with the establishment of socialist ideology.

The step from advocating revolutionary *ideology* to prescribing the creation of a strong cadre of revolutionary *ideologists* is short, and Lenin certainly did not hesitate to take it. Indeed, it can be argued with much justice that the upshot of the first part of *What Is to Be Done?* lies precisely in the establishment of the need for socialist ideologists as distinguished from ivory-tower socialists, "professors," "critics," and other quasi-revolutionary, "flabby," and sentimental beaux esprits, whose contributions to the revolution Lenin disowned with even more fervor than that with which Marx deflated and abased the revolutionary pretensions of the Young Hegelians of the early 1840s.[67] But while Marx's diatribes were in essence those of the exasperated but dedicated philosopher and theoretician, Lenin quite clearly was here not nearly as interested in philosophic discourse and inquiry itself (in distinction to the dark days of his Swiss exile during the war years) as in the more concrete concerns of revolutionary action. Given his activist bent, together with his voluntaristic and elitist interpretation of the historical process and of the function of ideas in it, it is tempting to argue that in the final analysis the step which Lenin took was not so much from ideology to the avantgarde ideologist, from theory to practice, as the other way round.

Thus Lenin, in his pamphlet, did not ask what is to be 'thought' or 'theorized,' but rather what is to be *done*. When he maintains that "the role of the vanguard fighter can be fulfilled only by a party that is guided by the most advanced theory," he is not merely arguing for the need for 'theory' but for the kind of theory which is required *in order to fulfill* the role of the vanguard fighter. It seems that it is the role or function of the avantgarde ideologist which is foremost in Lenin's mind, not revolutionary theory or ideology; and since it is precisely this function to which 'ideology' is to contribute in order to fulfill its purpose, the needs of the vanguard fighter *qua* Leninist ideologist—as the imbuer of a socialist consciousness—can be viewed as the real subject matter of Lenin's theorizations. Seen from this perspective, it is not difficult to understand why Lenin was so adamant about the absolute partisanship of materialist doctrines and philosophy. For this quality, and the dogmatic, doctrinaire traits which cluster around it, is contained within and indeed defines the Leninist conception of the 'party' itself as the exclusive organizing, arousing, and mobilizing vanguard of revolution. [68]

Ideology and Organization: The Party as Instrument

"We should dream!" Lenin suddenly exclaims toward the end of *What Is to Be Done?*, amid a hortative account of the prosaic detail of revolutionary organization and of the need for an all-Russian revolutionary newspaper. "I wrote these words," he immediately adds introspectively, "and became alarmed."[69] The dream that frightened the otherwise so unperturbed Lenin was that of a "mobilized army" which would "rouse the whole people to settle accounts with the shame and the curse of Russia"; and the principal cause for his alarm—a question which sent a "cold shiver" down his spine and made him wish for "but a place to hide in"— was whether "a Marxist has any right at all to dream, knowing that according to Marx mankind always sets itself the tasks it can solve. . . . "[70] As if for once lost for words to justify his emphatic but disquieting answer to a question which continued to disturb him throughout his life—the question of the relationship between man's concrete social reality and his human aspirations and visions —he refers the reader to a rather obscure article by the critic I. D. Pisarev on the "Blunders of Immature Thinking." " 'There are rifts and rifts,' wrote Pisarev of the rift between dreams and reality," Lenin notes and continues:

My dream may run ahead of the natural march of events or may fly off at a tangent in a direction in which no natural march of events will ever proceed. In the first case my dream will not cause any harm; it may even support and augment the energy of the working man. . . . The rift between dreams and reality causes no harm if only the person dreaming believes seriously in his dream, if he attentively observes life, compares his observations with his castles in the air, and if, generally speaking, he works conscientiously for the achievement of his fantasies. If there is some connection between dreams and life, then all is well.[71]

To which Lenin adds, himself once more, that "of this kind of dreaming there is unfortunately too little in our movement."[72] The significant quality of Lenin's dreams is their practical rather than visionary aspects; he could find legitimacy only for those dreams which could be realized concretely in the here and now. Hence, although *What Is to Be Done?* is above all a "theory and a panegyric of the Party" as the bearer and vanguard of socialist consciousness and revolution, we find in his dreams little or nothing of the 'spiritual' dimension and mission which, for example, Lukács so forcefully identified with the party as the "historical form and . . . active bearer of class-consciousness."[73] Thus if we make the distinction which Lukács makes between social and political revolution, of which only the former entails a 'reform of consciousness'—and this is the only true Marxian revolution in Lukács's eyes—while the latter simply means an overthrow of government, it is evident that although Lenin obviously did not reject the long-range goals which a radical transformation of society and humanity entails, his whole being and all his efforts were directed toward realizing a more immediate and concrete dream: the acquisition of political power and its tools.[74]

This ambition explains, first of all, the fundamental difference between 'true consciousness' as defined in Marxian nonalienative terms, on the one hand, and Lenin's elitist, partisan and activist conception of 'consciousness' as a mobilizing force within the revolutionary vanguard, on the other. It also illuminates the crucial relationship which Lenin posits between the 'ideological' task of the vanguard vis-à-vis the 'spontaneity' of the working-class movement. For 'ideology' as 'consciousness' is fundamentally *political* in nature, despite Lenin's strenuous attempts to identify it with scientific, objective truth; and it is political in the simple sense that the concern is with the acquisition and exercise of power, for which the cooperation of the masses is, as Lenin iterated time and again, a prime necessity. It is in view of this function that 'ideology' *qua* revolutionizing 'consciousness' not only provides such an effective raison d'être for the organizational and partisan structure of the Leninist party, but also with equal plausibility is able to define and above all justify the politico-revolutionary function of the party within the social and historical universe of mass politicization. That is, as a political instrument ideology is made to serve the dual role of, on the one hand, legitimizing the 'party' as both the incarnation (Lukács would later speak of *Gestalt*) and the institutionalized organization of revolutionary consciousness and, on the other, of explaining and justifying the role of this organization in imprinting such a consciousness upon the slow-moving, instinctively 'spontaneous,' and essentially nonrevolutionary mentality of the masses of workers as the recalcitrant arrière-garde. In both cases it is a question of buttressing the claim of the Leninist party to political hegemony in the mass revolutionary movement —of establishing, at a time of great factional flux within the Russian socialist movement, the need for a highly centralized, organized, and powerful revolutionary apparat in battle against the prevalent 'bourgeois' forces. "Give us an *organization* of revolutionaries," Lenin exclaims, "and we will overturn Russia."[75]

This is, of course, an enormous claim for the political sagacity and historical potency of a small group of individuals, lacking little of the characteristics of Hegel's Men of History whose "particular purposes contain the substantial will of the World Spirit. . . . They see the very truth of their age and their world, the next genus, so to speak, which is already formed in the womb of time."[76] This is elitist voluntarism in its most uncovered form, but it is not, as history has shown us, a goal beyond the realm of the possible. And while Lenin, during the first years of this century, deviated from the classical Marxian conception of the socialist revolution only to the extent that he insisted that a revolutionary party possessing the proper ideology was a necessary condition for success, by 1917 (in *Imperialism*) he appears to have taken the next and final logical step and "began to suggest that a revolutionary party was not only a necessity, but also the necessary and sufficient condition for revolution," as A. James Gregor has written.[77]

Lenin's conception of 'ideology' is, therefore, a notion which in a very fundamental sense is inextricably tied to his organizational conception of how to dominate men both in the revolutionary process itself and in the exercise of the political power to be gained through it. To us, who have the benefit of a late-twentieth-century historical hindsight, this organizational concept might not appear to be as visionary a dream as Lenin made it seem (we would perhaps even think the reverse). But at the time that Lenin wrote these words—a period that was a veritable pinnacle of disorganization, factionalism, and failure among radical Russians—he stood alone in his insight into the immense organizational effort called for if history (and, in particular, the vast masses of czarist Russia) was to be manipulated toward the goals of Marxist theory. Consequently, the 'Party' as wellhead, determinant, and regulator of radical sociopolitical change is a conception which, in the history of political ideas, is almost synonymous with the towering figure of Lenin. And so is 'ideology' as the active ideational and doctrinal force which is used to guide, justify, and structure the political 'will' of the people through a 'party' speaking both for and to it.

That ideology was conceived of as an active force with immense practical consequences for the organizational efforts of the party is abundantly clear, finally, from the emphasis which Lenin gives, in the final parts of *What Is to Be Done?*, to the establishment of an all-Russian socialist newspaper.[78] Its purpose, as Lenin states quite explicitly, is to spread 'propaganda' within the proletariat populace—that is, to educate and guide it, to coordinate and give a blueprint for the bricklaying (to use Lenin's own analogy) which is the sine qua non of revolutionary organization. "This newspaper," Lenin writes graphically,

would become part of an enormous pair of smith's bellows that would fan every spark of the class struggle and of popular indignation into a general conflagration. Around what is in itself a very innocuous and very small, but regular and *common*, effort, in the full sense of the word, a regular army of tried fighters would systematically gather and receive their training. On the ladders and scaffolding of this general organizational structure there would soon develop and come to the fore Social-Democratic Zhelyabovs from among our revolutionaries and Russian Bebels from among our workers, who would take their place at the head of the mobilized army and rouse the whole people to settle accounts with the shame and the curse of Russia.[79]

Here Lenin spoke as a true prophet.

'Ideology' as "an enormous pair of smith's bellows": this is, in a nutshell, Lenin's answer to the question whether his dreams are 'soluble' in the Marxian sense, that is, whether the revolutionary task which he has posited for mankind—or at least for the masses of Russia—is commensurate with the world of the possible as defined both by the Marxian cosmology and the givens (as perceived by him) of the social and political structure of Russian society. Revolution *is* a realistic dream, Lenin affirms, because even if only a small group believes seriously enough in it, and organizes itself and works conscientiously for its achievement, then the dream will become real because the dream exists within the group as the kind of belief system which, in the final analysis, determines all collective, concerted and purposive human endeavors in history. As Nicolas Berdyaev has written of the Leninist party, if "this insignificant minority is entirely possessed by the gigantic idea of the proletariat, if its revolutionary will is stimulated, if it is well organized and disciplined, then it can work miracles; it can overpower the determinism which normally controls social life."[80] 'Ideology' as the unifier of theory and practice, of means and ends, in the form of the self-fulfilling, teleological prophecy as entrusted to revolutionary organization:this is, perhaps, the greatest contribution to the history of both political philosophy and social transformation which we should associate with the name of Lenin. As a doctrine it is, also, deeply ironic, given Lenin's constant appeals to Marx's authority; for it entails nothing less than the belief that the superstructure brings its own basis into existence.[81]

It is evident that any critical analysis of the Leninist concept of ideology will have to take cognizance of the fact that Lenin used it in at least two different senses and for two purposes. The first of these is the philosophical usage, exemplified most clearly by *Materialism and Empirio-Criticism,* and the second is his identification of 'ideology' with mass political action and organization, which is a mode of use formulated most forcefully in *What Is to Be Done?* As the reader no doubt will notice, this broad distinction between a philosophical and sociopolitical frame of reference is not entirely new in the history of our concept. We have already found it in the short introductory discussion of the French idéologues, as well as in the more substantial analysis of the Marxian critique of ideology. For the sake of convenience we may label these two Leninist usages as, respectively, the *dogmatic* and the *mobilizing* conceptions of ideology. The appositeness of these terms is perhaps already apparent and should become even more so in the critical discussion to follow.

A CRITIQUE OF THE LENINIST CONCEPTIONS OF IDEOLOGY

INTRODUCTION

Not unlike most other ideational traditions, Leninism is neither a clear-cut nor uncontroversial intellectual and doctrinal edifice. On the contrary, like Marx's writings, if to a lesser extent, it has been the object of many heated altercations, both within the official orthodoxy of Marxist-Leninism as explicated and administered by the Soviet Communist party, and within the many scholarly debates over the years—both Marxist and non-Marxist —which have had no connection with Soviet doctrine or policy. Whatever the particular aspect of Lenin's ideas discussed, the upwelling question has not unsurprisingly centered around "what did Lenin really say"(to use the title of a recent book in German); and it is of course as an important a query as it is unamenable to a definitive answer.[82] As a legitimate concern it cannot be either slighted or ignored, nor can it be expropriated by any particular group as its exclusive property, on the basis that this group alone is competent and justified in resolving the question. It is therefore necessary that I say a few words on the particular stance taken in this discussion and critical analysis of Lenin's notions on the nature and role of 'ideology.'

First of all, and with regard to the question of the published works by Lenin on which the body of my analysis builds, I can only submit that in concentrating on *What Is to Be Done?* and *Materialism and Empirio-Criticism*, a choice has been made which seems natural in view of the fact that the concern in this study is with the concept of *ideology* and the particular philosophical and concrete doctrines supporting it, and not with any other matter, however seminal it may be to a fuller understanding of Lenin's thought as a whole. In addition, and this is by no means a minor point in an analysis of the *major usages* of 'ideology' in the history of ideas, these two works have always been, and still are, regarded as cornerstones of official Marxist-Leninism; and it is, after all, this doctrine or set of doctrines which has been the primary force which has stamped Lenin's thought—and thus what is to be regarded as the Leninist conception of ideology—on modern sociopolitical history and intellectual life.[83] Marx, fortunately or otherwise, never achieved a similar official and powerful executor of his legacy, and it is perhaps because of this that Leninism as an *intellectual system* is rather more cut-and-dried in the history of ideas than is the case with Marxian thought. This also makes it somewhat easier to determine what is to be regarded as the preeminent contours of Lenin's philosophical and doctrinal achievement.

This brings us to our second point, one which was already raised earlier in the discussion on Marx. That is, should Lenin's thought be analyzed and criticized 'immanently,' as a system of ideas not meaningfully comprehensible in terms of non-Leninist —or rather, non-Marxist—terminology and philosophy? I have argued against this position with regard to Marx in terms of two different considerations, one of principle and the other with reference to the practice of Marxism itself. Both arguments appear to me to be equally relevant here. In addition, however, on perusing Lenin's writings it seems evident that he himself neither adhered to this position nor subscribed to or advocated it. On the contrary, his whole approach in *Materialism and Empirio-Criticism*, his major philosophical work, was clearly that of attacking and trying to refute his opponents in terms of philosophical concepts which he claimed were not only in full accord with the latest developments in scientific method—bourgeois or not—but, he insisted, had been part and parcel of philosophy since its earliest days. As Henri Lefebvre (a prominent French Marxist and Leninist philosopher) has noted, Lenin posed what he perceived to be a 'classical' question in his writings on epistemology and philosophy and gave an answer in terms of the 'classical' division between 'idealism' and 'materialism' (or, as Lefebvre also notes, in terms of the division between Berkeley and Diderot).[84] It is therefore not surprising that it is within this nonimmanentalist tradition that a contemporary British Marxist-Leninist philosopher like Maurice Cornforth self-consciously places himself and Marxism in general as a philosophical tradition of the first order.[85]

This leads us to a different query, since if the above is a valid standpoint, and if Bertell Ollman's interpretation (as discussed in the previous chapter) of the philosophical and terminological immanentalism of Marx's thinking has any validity, then we obviously have to ask ourselves how much of a 'true' or 'genuine' Marxian thinker Lenin in fact was.[86] This is, of course, a major question in the interpretation of Lenin's writings and doctrines—a controversy fully equivalent to the 'early-late' problem in studies in Marxian thought. Most non-Marxist scholars have taken the position that there is indeed a natural discontinuity between Marx and Lenin, both easily recognizable and readily explicable, while official Soviet orthodoxy maintains that the hyphenation of 'Marxism' and 'Leninism' is truly philosophical rather than simply being a traditionally and historically convenient notation without any substantive justification. It is clear that Marx left posterity an "ambiguous legacy" (to quote part of the title of a book on Marxism by Sidney Hook), and that Alisdaire MacIntyre, in an article provocatively titled "How Not to Write About Lenin," makes a sound judgment when he notes that "classical Marxism is a doctrine in which insight into the bourgeois societies of the mid- and late-nineteenth century was bought at the price of all too close a reflection of the categories of that society in theories," and that in consequence "when Marxism came to be applied to new situations . . . would-be Marxists were left with a good deal of freedom, both theoretical and practical."[87] However, it also seems quite appropriate to at least in part accept Leopold Labedz's harsh injunction on the question of the official view regarding Lenin's putative 'orthodoxy' and the old bête noire of 'revisionism,' that "Marx can no more be treated seriously by Marxists, including revisionists, than Aristotle was by medieval theologians, alternatively invoking him and the Bible as the ultimate authority. It is only when Marx the thinker is disassociated from Marx the prophet, and from the movement of which he is the patron saint, that it is at all possible to do him justice."[88] Where does this, however, leave us? It appears to me, at least on the question regarding 'ideology' and the doctrines supporting it, that great hagiographical and hermeneutical skills are called for if Lenin is to be made into a true Marxian follower as distinguished from a Marxist believer. George Lichtheim is thus essentially correct, in my view, when he writes that "if anyone introduced a profound 'revision' of Marxist doctrine, it was none other than Lenin himself. This was immediately perceived by his opponents, who at the time included almost every Marxist of note, from Plekhanov and Kautsky to Luxemburg and Trotsky."[89] This seems to me to be at least as plausible a view as any, especially with regard to Lenin's emphasis on the role of 'ideas' and 'ideology' in the revolutionary movement.

This standpoint does not, of course, denigrate Lenin's contributions, as it is sometimes felt; on the contrary, it upholds the claim that Lenin was an original thinker in his own right, albeit one whose thought was much more suffused with the practical considerations attending revolutionary zeal than was the case with the scholarly Marx (despite the latter's occasional lapses into activistic urges during short periods of political upheaval). Nor is this view in any sense an anti-Marxist standpoint, as it is sometimes asserted —except, of course, if Marx's teachings are regarded as canonical and therefore any bona fide or apparent deviation from these as heretical. Such an attitude cannot in principle be either defended or accepted in any serious scholarly discussion of the subject matter.

With regard to a different aspect of the interpretation of Lenin's thought, it is sometimes said, although not always loudly, that to engage in a critique of Leninism as a philosophical doctrine is to kick a decidedly dead if perhaps once alacritous horse. Lichtheim, for example, whose scholarly sympathy for Marx (if not always for Marxism) was clear though complex and at times ambivalent, notes laconically about Lenin that whatever "the significance of his philosophical writings for the mental climate of the USSR, their purely intellectual standing—whether in terms of traditional Marxist thinking or simply of philosophy in general—is not such as to invite prolonged consideration; perhaps the only thing which needs to be said is that Lenin's naively realistic theory of knowledge is incompatible with the dialectic."[90] Similarly Jean-Paul Sartre, as Louis Althusser reports, regarded Lenin's (and Engels's) materialistic philosophy as both "unthinkable" and—echoing Fichte's ironic criticism of Kant—a 'non-thing' (*Unding*); it cannot, Sartre has insisted, sustain even elementary philosophical scrutiny simply because it is based on a naturalistic, pre-Kantian, precritical, and pre-Hegelian metaphysics (he here probably had in mind Lenin's naive anti-Berkeleianism).[91] And to Maurice Merleau-Ponty, another French philosopher of the Marxist persuasion, Lenin's philosophy was nothing but an "emergency undertaking" in a particular historical situation calling for it.[92] Non-Marxist scholars have, of course, been even less inclined to pay serious consideration to the contributions of Leninist philosophy; on the whole they have regarded him primarily as a revolutionary, not a philosopher.[93] However, such bestowals of philosophical quietus are notoriously a case of the beholder's eyes; philosophical horses, like Peter Pan's fairies, seemingly live and die according to the proclivities of the particular mind at work. The position taken here is that Lenin's concept of ideology is very important to our present concerns, and that insofar as this concept has philosophical underpinnings in his writings, his philosophical tenets—whatever their merit in the final analysis—cannot be ignored or left either unscrutinized or (as we shall see) ungainsaid. Furthermore, it is a palpable fact that even today Leninism as a philosophical credo is accepted by many as the final word, and this not only within the Soviet Union.

One additional, uncontroversial, and essentially semantic factor should be noted before proceeding with a critique of 'ideology' as found in Lenin's writings. This is that in distinction to Marx, Lenin's usage of the term "ideology" by itself was not evaluative but was meant to be descriptive in a more or less normatively neutral fashion. E. H. Carr is at least partially right when he notes that "in Marx, 'ideology' is a negative term," while "in Lenin, 'ideology' becomes neutral or positive—a belief implanted by an elite of class-conscious leaders in a mass of potentially class-conscious workers."[94] He is right in the sense that generically the word "ideology"—and its derivatives—is evaluatively neutral, designating (in Ernest Nagel's sense of being a "characterizing value judgment") a broad class of ideational phenomena, namely, the universe of ideas and philosophical doctrines to be found in any given society.[95] However, the word acquires positive meaning only when qualified in terms of the Marxist dichotomization of society into bourgeois and working classes. Or more properly, it acquires positive meaning (in terms of Nagel's conception of an "appraising value judgment") when qualified as *socialist* ideology. We can perhaps say that conceptually the term "ideology" in Lenin's writings only becomes significant when such an identification is made. In principle, therefore, when speaking of Lenin's conceptions of ideology, we should always clearly indicate which of the two kinds of specific ideologies—the bourgeois and the socialist—we are identifying, utilizing, or analyzing when referring to his usage of the concept. This is not commonly done, however, nor have I found any weighty reasons for changing this practice. Thus I do believe, after all, that Carr is substantially correct in his identification of 'ideology' with Lenin's positive usage: the identification of 'ideology' with 'socialist ideology.' The major reason for this is that Lenin himself was not much interested in 'bourgeois ideology,' and almost exclusively, when writing on the phenomenon of the ideological, thought of it 'partisanly,' namely, in terms of the positive function of ideology in the revolutionary socialist movement and context. Furthermore, I believe it is a correct assessment that the concept which Lenin has bequeathed to posterity is his dogmatic and mobilizing conception of ideology as defined in terms of his revolutionary aims and political practice.

CRITIQUE OF THE DOGMATIC CONCEPTION OF IDEOLOGY

In an article on "Three Views Concerning Human Knowledge," first published in the middle 1950s, Karl Popper makes a fundamental philosophical distinction between what he calls the "Galilean" and the "instrumental" conception of the nature of knowledge. The former view, he writes, rests on the assumption that science as knowledge aspires to attain "a true description of the world," that in the face of the mysteries of the universe its aim is in essence that of uncovering the "reality hidden behind its appearance."[96] This was the standpoint of Galilei on the nature of the Copernican 'System of the World,' and as such constituted the reason for the conflict with the Church which led to his subsequent recantation of this view in the face of the threats of the Inquisition. The instrumental view was stated quintessentially by Berkeley, whose analysis of Newton's concepts (derived from those of the Copernican system) convinced him "that this theory could not possibly be anything but a 'mathematical hypothesis,' that is, a convenient *instrument* for the calculation and prediction of phenomena or appearances; that it could not possibly be taken as a true description of anything real."[97] It was on the basis of this criticism that Hume's epistemological skepticism was submitted and from which Kant drew his conclusion that reality itself was unknowable—that although Newtonian science was true, it was true only of nature, that is, of the *phenomenal* world confronting man's perceptive and conceptive mind.[98] Today, Popper notes, this instrumental view "has won the battle without another shot being fired"; it "has become an accepted dogma" and "may well now be called the 'official view' of physical theory" and has "become part of the current teaching of physics."[99] He adds, parenthetically, that only Einstein and Schrödinger among leading twentieth-century theorists have not submitted to this view of the epistemological nature and ultimate aim of science.

Z. A. Jordan, in his otherwise excellent analysis of the nature and development of Marxist theory and philosophy, makes the rather curious claim that "Lenin's conception of philosophy is an instance of the instrumentalist view in Popper's sense."[100] That is to say, he ascribes to Lenin a standpoint which "renounces the hope of ever understanding anything and sees in science nothing but an instrument devoid of theoretical or cognitive significance and true only in the sense of being operationally and technologically useful."[101] He does add the qualification, however, that Lenin's instrumentalism is neither pragmatic nor technological but, instead, sociopolitical in the sense of being a view which regards knowledge as useful primarily "in guiding and influencing human attitudes and conduct."[102] Despite this qualification Jordan's claim is strange and can perhaps be explained only by the fact that he appears to have obfuscated the distinction—particularly important in the case of Lenin—between the *nature* and *function* of knowledge: the difference between (broadly speaking) the 'philosophical' and 'sociological' aspects of knowledge. The fact is that the Popperian distinction to which Jordan refers is preeminently philosophical in that it refers to the nature of knowledge. Thus to regard Lenin's view as 'instrumental' in terms of Popper's terminology is to fly in the face of the fact that *Materialism and Empirio-Criticism* probably constitutes one of the most intense and concerted *anti-instrumentalist* statements of this century.

Lenin's fundamental hostility to the instrumentalist view is clearly discernible, first of all, in the list of those individuals in the history of philosophy who appear as the most outstanding personae non grata of his own philosophical domicile. Even a cursory glance at this list in *Materialism and Empirio-Criticism* reveals the names of Berkeley, Hume, and Kant as especially noteworthy in this particularly telling respect. This prominence is attributable to the fact that all three of these philosophers were regarded as 'idealists' in one sense or another, that is, as 'instrumentalists' in Popper's terminology. Secondly, Lenin's attacks against phenomenalism and the 'new science' of the physicists were clearly waged as a rather desperate countervailing action vis-à-vis the instrumentalism emerging from the redefinition of 'matter' in physics. The Michelson-Morley experiment, the discovery of the electron, the Lorentz transformation, the Fitzgerald contraction, and other similar scientific developments were clearly undermining the 'naive realism' of classical physics; and it is to Lenin's credit that he perceived how rapidly these contributions to the history and philosophy of science were undermining his Marxist premises while at the same time contributing to the emergence of the 'official view' which Popper has found in contemporary physical theory.[103] It is in this light that we should understand his fulminations against Mach and his followers; for Mach was, as Popper points out, one of the earliest physicists who was both philosophically aware of, and actively engaged in working for, the instrumentalist break with the Galilean view that the 'new physics' entailed.[104]

However, it is not these negative aspects of Lenin's battle against instrumentalism which are of primary interest to us here, but rather his own particular view with regard to the nature of, and interconnection between, reality and knowledge and how this is related to what I have called his 'dogmatic' conception of ideology. This view is quite explicitly Galilean in spirit and gives his philosophical definition of the nature of Marxist ideology the unmistakable cognitive contours which we associate with Leninism. In what follows I shall criticize, as briefly as possible, the main propositions supporting his dogmatic conception of ideology, and touch upon his anti-instrumentalism only when necessary.

I have characterized Lenin's first usage of the concept 'ideology' as 'dogmatic' because it rests on the proposition, submitted by him, that theory should aim at offering 'ultimate explanations'—to use one of Popper's hallmarks of the Galilean view concerning knowledge—and that *only* epistemological materialism can fulfill this purpose. "Such theories," Popper writes of this view of knowledge, "are neither in need nor susceptible of further explanation"; for they purport to "describe the 'essences' or the 'essential natures' of things—the realities which lie behind appearances."[105] It "is sheer ignorance," Lenin answers one critic, " . . . not to know that all materialists assert the knowability of things-in-themseves"; and therefore it is "infinite slovenliness . . . not to realize that the 'objective truth' of thinking means *nothing else* than the *existence* of objects ('things-in-themselves') *truly* reflected by thinking."[106] As he writes elsewhere in *Materialism and Empirio-Criticism:* "From the standpoint of modern materialism, i.e., Marxism, the *limits* of approximation of our knowledge to objective, absolute truth are historically conditioned, but the existence of such truth is *unconditional*, and the fact that we are approaching nearer to it is also unconditional. . . . In a word, every ideology is historically conditioned, but it is unconditionally true that to every scientific ideology . . . there corresponds an objective truth, absolute nature."[107] Furthermore, as we have already quoted Lenin, "To regard our sensations as images of the external world, to recognize objective truth, to hold the materialist theory of knowledge—these are all one and the same thing." These unequivocal statements can be said to be 'dogmatic' for two reasons: they propound a dogmatic, absolute conception of the nature of truthful knowledge; and they comprise the assertion that materialist theory is itself such an incontrovertible truth, or at least the closest approximation to it. But how 'true' is Lenin's epistemological materialism? Let us turn to this question first before considering his concept of the nature of truth itself and the larger issue of the relationship between these doctrines and the partisanship of philosophy *qua* ideology.

Epistemological Materialism

Lenin's definition of materialism is, as we have already noted, epistemological inasmuch as it is a definition of matter not in terms of its immanent nature or properties but in terms of epistemological realism, that is, the proposition that "Things exist independently of our consciousness, independently of our sensations, outside of us. . . ."[108] The major reason why Lenin felt compelled to adopt this definition rather than that of Engels was that he perceived that the instrumentalism growing out of the new developments in physics cast doubts on materialism as classically conceived —mechanistically—while at the same time favoring Berkeleian idealism, the archenemy of any materialist (or realist). It was on this basis that he could accuse Mach of idealism, despite the fact that Mach's phenomenalist position was simply that in the absence of mind nobody could experience anything, while Berkeley had asserted something quite different, namely, that without mind there would be nothing to be experienced.[109]

However, the proposition that 'matter' designates 'objective reality,' that the sole property of 'matter' is that of being the 'objective reality' existing 'outside our mind,' is philosophically deeply problematic, as indeed Berkeley himself had pointed out with great acumen (and many others since him). It rests on the implication that the predicates 'exist' and 'be real' are identical in meaning, and that 'be material' and 'be real' are coextensive. However, given this implication, it is clear that any statement of the kind "Nothing exists but matter" or "Matter is all that exists" is, by itself, without distinctive meaning. First of all, if either of these statements is regarded as true, then it would be contradictory to postulate anything as 'being' immaterial, since anything which is not material does not, by definition, exist. Secondly, any all-embracing proposition of this kind, in which 'existing' is coterminous with 'being,' denotes the 'being' of everything and thus connotes nothing. Or, as one commentator argues against Lenin in this respect, "statements of all-embracing significance are without significance."[110] This was precisely Berkeley's argument against the very position adopted by Lenin; and the two hundred years separating them has in no way whatsoever diminished the relevance of this criticism. The result is that "Lenin's definition of matter effaces the difference between materialism, on the one hand, and objective idealism, immanentalism, or phenomenalism, on the other"; it makes "materialism indistinguishable from mentalism, idealism, or spiritualism."[111] This was certainly not Lenin's intention, but it is nonetheless a result of his epistemological definition of matter.

Furthermore, in defining matter in terms only of the relation of sensations to sensed objects, of the cognizing subject to the cognized object, Lenin lays himself open to an additional and equally fundamental criticism, which is also a criticism of the causal theory of perception. This critique is based on the fact that the perceptual conditions which are both necessary and sufficient to establish the existence of sense-data (and Lenin's theory of knowledge does not question but in fact embraces the existence of sense-data as a fundamental premise) are necessary but not sufficient conditions for establishing the existence of the material objects of which sense-data are said to be an effect.[112] That is to say, our evidence for the existence of the former cannot by itself be taken as evidence for the existence of the latter.[113] Or as Bertrand Russell has written, "in accepting the causal theory of perception we have committed ourselves to the view that perception gives no immediate knowledge of a physical object, but at best a datum for inference."[114] Indeed, in positing a duality between 'consciousness' and 'objective reality,' between a cognizing subject and a cognized object, between an immediately experienced and an unexperienced entity, Lenin is at the same time bound by the logical fact that no direct or valid inference can be drawn from the existence and nature of the former to the existence of nature of the latter. Yet Lenin insisted that matter was the objective reality directly given to us in experience. It is precisely the impossibility of establishing this proposition which phenomenalism had stressed; and Lenin's mistake lay in the fact that while he accepted the phenomenalist thesis that the objective world can only be experienced through the sensations which it causes in us, that is, through sense-data, he at the same time imputed intrinsic properties to matter—properties which are primary in the sense that they do not depend on the interaction between object and subject. It is with regard to these conflicting aspects of Lenin's theory of knowledge that Jordan can maintain that he "seems to have run with the hare and hunted with the hounds, for he endorsed some parts of the phenomenalist argument and at the same time claimed to be in possession of knowledge concerning the existence of material substances which the phenomenalist repudiates. He did not succeed in refuting phenomenalism but simply confronted it with the blank statement that matter is the immediate and indisputably given reality."[115] In so doing, Lenin's materialism becomes an especially glaring example of begging a very fundamental philosophical question.

Lenin did, however, augment his causal theory of epistemological materialism with a proposition which was to provide us with knowledge of the objective world *qua* matter beyond our 'realist' cognizance of its existence as an independent entity confronting our perception. "Matter," we have thus already quoted him, "is a philosophical category denoting the objective reality which is given to man by his sensations, and which is copied, photographed and reflected by our sensations, while existing independently of them."[116] Unfortunately, Lenin's copy theory of knowledge suffers from all the problems associated with his epistemological materialism in general, in addition to some which are peculiarly its own.

As more than one critic has pointed out, the most fundamental of these is perhaps the iconic imagery which this statement suggests, i.e., a proposition in terms of *similarity* rather than a causal representationalism of the Hobbesian kind or the 'sensory signs' of

Helmholtz's theory of the relationship between our sense perceptions and objective reality.[117] This seems to have been Lenin's
expressed intention, despite various attempts to attribute only
causal representationalism to this theory.[118] "Engels," he writes
with approval,

> speaks neither of symbols nor of hieroglyphs, but of copies, photographs,
> images, mirror-reflections of things. . . . If sensations are not images of
> things, but only signs or symbols which have 'no resemblance' to them,
> then . . . the . . . initial materialist premise is undermined; the existence of
> external objects becomes subject to doubt. . . . It is beyond doubt that an
> image can never wholly compare with the model, but an image is one
> thing, a symbol, a *conventional sign*, another. The image inevitably and of
> necessity implies the objective reality of that which it 'images' . . . while
> . . . symbol, hieroglyph are concepts which introduce an entirely unnec-
> essary element of agnosticism.[119]

From this it appears to be clear that Lenin was not speaking of
representationalist realism in his copy theory of perception, but of
a much more pictorially comparable and close relationship between the 'thing-in-itself' and its perceptive 'appearance' in our
minds.

However, the theory that sensations are true copies of external
objects is a form of 'naive realism' which is untenable and indeed
meaningless. If our perceptions provide us with some kind of
'image' of something which is not a content of our perception, then
either this 'image' itself must be a physical object (which nobody
since Democritus or Epicurus seems to have been willing to
accept) or the relationship cannot be that of a portraitlike comparison. This follows from the fact that something which is part of our
perceptive content cannot be a copy of something which is not, by
its very nature, a content of perception.[120] Thus Lenin's copy
theory is either only a metaphor, which he himself appears to have
denied and which in any case would not be of interest to the
philosophical analysis of the relationship between perception and
that which is perceived; or it assumes what it intends to, or at least
should, prove—an assumption which is, furthermore, unverifiable by any imaginable means.[121] Comparability is meaningful
only in the context of two perceived objects, such as when we

compare a photograph with the thing photographed, or a portrait with the person portrayed in it. Such a process of comparison cannot, however, apply to our perceptions, for the statement that we perceive our own perceptions is not simply a semantic oddity but a logical impossibility. Furthermore, if the copy theory is valid, then we can perceive only copies or reflections of things but never the things themselves; therefore, it is impossible to compare our images of things with the things themselves, in which case we can never know if our copies are 'true' or 'false' or even if they are copies at all of objects existing independently of perception. As Jordan has put it, "what the copy theory says might be right, but if it is right we could not know it."[122] The comparability posited by Lenin could only exist if it were possible to transcend experience; but to transcend experience is by definition empirically impossible.[123] Alternatively, Lenin must have had in mind an identity of objects and our perceptions of them which, as one of his Menschevik opponents pointed out in arguing against his epistemological materialism, is fundamentally the Machist position. "But materialism," Axelrod adds, "takes the point of view that sensations, which are aroused by the action of various forms of the motion of matter, are not like the objective processes that give rise to them."[124] In the face of these grave shortcomings raised by Lenin's copy theory of perception, we can only marvel at his insouciance when he claims that not a "single fact was or could be cited" to refute this view, "which is shared by science to this day."[125]

Lenin does not seem to have realized, in addition, that if his copy theory was an attempt to undermine the 'agnosticism' of phenomenalism, of countering instrumentalist claims which, he felt, made "the existence of external objects . . . subject to doubt," then this attempt was doomed to failure from the very start. For the fact is that if we wish to accept the theory that perceptions are 'copies' or 'images' of external objects, then we are forced, by the very nature of the premises involved in this view, into resigning ourselves to never coming in direct contact with either objects existing outside of us or with the individuals surrounding our own private world. We can never pierce the solipsistic veil of the mirror-reflections which are our only direct contact with reality and must as a consequence remain but "monads with no windows" to let in that which lies beyond our perceptions.[126] This, it is clear from Lenin's stated intentions, is exactly the reverse of what he wished to achieve through his copy theory of perception. In short, Lenin was unable to prove either that if the copy theory of perception was right, then phenomenalism was wrong, or that his theory as such is true or valid.[127]

Lenin's Conception of Truth

The proposition that there exists an objective reality, independent of but 'copied' or 'photographed' by the mind is intimately linked to Lenin's conception of the nature of truth. In his view this linkage is quite simple, since (to quote him again on this) the "knowability of things-in-themselves," that is, "objective truth . . . means nothing else than the existence of objects . . . truly reflected by thinking." 'Objective, absolute truth' is, in short, a function of the reflection of 'absolute nature' in our minds; and thus the more 'truly' our minds reflect objective reality, the closer we come to apprehending objective, absolute truth. This is an engagingly simple and elegant doctrine, but it is also philosophically a wholly untenable point of view. It rests on the assumption that (i) the truth of our theories or explanations of reality can be established beyond any doubt, and that (ii) this is possible because what our theories essentially aim at apprehending are the objective realities which lie behind the appearances of perception; that is, it is possible to attain absolute truth because we can achieve *ultimate* explanations.[128] Neither of these views can stand up to closer scrutiny, however much Lenin believed this to be the case.

The first proposition of this Galilean view of knowledge is untenable for the simple reason that it cannot be *proved* but can only be accepted on faith. Why this is so follows from the fact that if this view is to have any relevance to 'real nature' (Marx's standpoint, which Lenin subscribed to wholeheartedly, is precisely that of having established an *empirically* grounded orientation to philosophy contra idealism) then it must restrict the validity of truth-statements to science and experience; and in science and empirical reality no proposition can lay claim to finality, since it is always subject to future empirical confutation. The absolute truths which Lenin claims are possible to apprehend cannot, by their very nature, ever be identified. If, however, the Leninist claim refers to truths of logic and definition, then it cannot be said to be valid for propositions which refer to a reality which is independent of the thought and experience of man, that is, to a world beyond the human conceptual or perceptual apparatus.[129] Either way, truth remains relative to man in time and space and thus to his experience, while Lenin insists that "to every scientific ideology . . . there corresponds an objective truth, absolute nature." The point is: how can we know this to be true?

The second proposition, commonly identified with an 'essentialist' point of view on the nature of knowledge, is equally unacceptable. First of all, as Popper has pointed out, even if we cannot prove that 'essences' of objects do not exist, to assume their existence inevitably leads to obscurantism; and if only for this methodological rather than logical reason—namely, the fact, richly illustrated by the history of science, that the 'essentialist' view hinders the pursuit of fruitful questions by foreclosing inquiry—it should be rejected even as a heuristic assumption.[130] Furthermore, the standpoint that our ordinary world is a mere appearance behind which we have to go to discover the 'real' and 'objective' world is a doctrine which, to quote Popper once again, "has to be discarded once we become conscious of the fact that the world of each of our theories may be explained, in its turn, by further worlds which are described by further theories—theories of a higher level of abstraction of universality, and of testability. The doctrine of an *essential or ultimate* reality collapses together with that of ultimate explanations."[131] For as long as we cannot be 'ultimately' certain about where or how ultimate reality is to be found or apprehended, we cannot be certain about the truths which purport to be ultimate explanations of these.

The thesis that a belief is true if it agrees or accords with objective reality is in principle unverifiable, for the same reason that we cannot know if the copy theory of perception is true or not. It is perhaps due to this that Lenin felt compelled to insist that "To regard our sensations as images of the external world, to recognize objective truth, to hold the materialist theory of knowledge—

these are all one and the same thing." If each entails the other, each also requires a common faith. But at the same time, if any one of these doctrines can be shown to be untrue or unverifiable, it follows that the other cannot be incontrovertibly true. Since his doctrine of truth holds the central position among these, it is not surprising that Lenin considered it to be of prime importance, to the point that at times he regarded the major distinction between materialism and contemporary philosophy to arise from the question regarding the absoluteness or relativity of truth.[132] He failed, however, to show in what manner his dogmatic treatment of truth could be philosophically validated and how an "objective measure or model existing independently of mankind" could be determined and verified.[133] It was in regard to this question, interestingly enough, that he felt compelled to repudiate the 'dogmatic' connotations applied to his conception of truth by his philosophical opponents—not because he rejected this designation and characterization, but because of its pejorative use by those for whom his absolute conception of truth held no appeal. This use of the word, he insisted, was just so much "ancient trash."[134]

Ideology and the Partisanship of Philosophy

Lenin's conception of the inherent partisanship of philosophy is definable in terms of two different but interconnected factors. The first is the strictly philosophical proposition that "behind the mass of new terminological artifices, behind the clutter of erudite scholasticism, we invariably discern(-) *two* principal alignments, two fundamental trends in the solution of philosophical problems." "Throughout the preceding exposition," Lenin continues on the theme of "Parties in Philosophy and Philosophical Blockheads" toward the end of *Materialism and Empirio-Criticism,*

in connection with every problem of epistemology touched upon and in connection with every philosophical question raised by the new physics, we traced the struggle between *materialism* and *idealism.* . . . Whether nature, matter, the physical, the external world should be taken as primary, and consciousness, mind, sensations (experience—as the *widespread* terminology of our time has it), the psychical, etc., should be regarded as secondary—that is the root question, which *in fact* continues to divide the philosophers into *two great camps.*[135]

The second factor is less philosophical than it is historical in the sense that it pertains to the genesis and sociopolitical nature of ideas. Lenin writes in the concluding paragraph of his main philosophical work, that "behind the epistemological scholasticism of empirio-criticism one must not fail to see the struggle of parties in philosophy, a struggle which in the last analysis reflects the tendencies and ideology of the antagonistic classes in modern society. Recent philosophy is as partisan as was philosophy two thousand years ago. The contending parties are essentially . . . materialism and idealism."[136] Lenin refers to Engels (and by implication, when not directly, to Marx) in support of these two doctrines, the first of which can be said to hinge on Engels's genetic materialism, while the latter is a variant of historical materialism.

The reason why Lenin treated these two doctrines as interdependent is to be found in his belief, fostered by Marx and Engels (in, for example, *The German Ideology*), that philosophy and the contending schools of thought which its long history has produced is not simply a function of man's independent powers of ratiocination but reflects, *qua* ideology, the essential nature of the development of societies in history. That is to say, Lenin maintained that all philosophical contentions are in the final analysis *ideologically* determined, and since in modern societies ideology and social class are indivisible, it is the historically natural antagonism between classes—the moving force of history—which produces the partisanship of philosophy. Idealism in philosophy "is merely a subtle refined form of fideism, which stands fully armed, commands vast organizations and steadily continues to exercise influence on the masses, turning the slightest vacillation in philosophical thought to its own advantage."[137] An idealist, to Lenin's mind, is anybody and everybody who is not an unquestioning adherent of materialism as defined by him. However, both of Lenin's doctrines concerning the fundamental partisanship of philosophy are unacceptable, if for different reasons and as a result of different methodological fallacies.

Lenin's thesis of the philosophical division between 'materialism' and 'idealism' suffers, first of all, from what we may call the fallacy of residual dichotomization: the division of a broad range of phenomena into two mutually exclusive categories, the first of which is strictly and narrowly defined (usually eulogistically) while phenomena not belonging to this narrow category are relegated to a broad, polar, and essentially residual class, defined by *ex adverso* or negation with respect to the first. The distinction between 'white' and 'black' sheep is the classical Biblical metaphor of this classificatory practice, while in contemporary politics and intellectual debate (and at a time of less metaphoric sophistication if greater directness of speech) we often tend to think and speak of the 'good' and the 'bad' fellows, or simply of 'us' and 'them.' This is, of course, to do great violence both to fruitful thinking on philosophical issues and to the inherent complexity of the reality underlying these categories, even if such distinctions are ostensibly offered in the name of simplicity and classificatory clarity or parsimony. This form of dichotomization appears to be a congenital affliction of almost all dialectic thought. It is fallacious in science not because it adheres to the principle (so dear to Spinoza and often repeated by Hegel) of *omnis determinatio est negatio*— that any determination involves negation—but because it identifies all phenomena belonging to the residual category of such a dichotomization with a homogenous structure and generification which is simply the converse of the first class of phenomena posited. To say that there is a fundamental distinction between 'fish' and 'non-fish' is prima facie valid if not enormously significant: it at least allows us to identify a 'fish' (if properly defined) and thus to distinguish it from the rest of living organisms. However, to maintain that all 'non-fish' are, say, 'carnivorous mammals' is obviously synonymous to being befuddled or a blockhead, to use two of Lenin's more telling epithets. Yet this is precisely what he does when he divides all philosophers—living, dead, or unborn— into two and only two "great camps": those of 'materialism' and those of 'idealism.' Even Plekhanov, allegedly the "father of Russian Marxism," was closer to a more acceptable classification when he conceded that, apart from materialist and idealist monism, a third, dualistic standpoint is possible, which recognizes both matter and mind as independent entities in the constitution of the universe.[138] But to the mind of Lenin, everybody and anybody who is not a materialist as defined by him is, unwittingly or not, an 'idealist'—which is of course correct, given his premises.

But in what respect was, for example, Mach an idealist in the sense defined by Lenin, that is, in Berkeleian terms? It is indeed very difficult to justify such an assertion regarding the subsumption of phenomenalism under the umbrella of idealism. For what Mach said, in effect, was that the concept of matter is *redundant* in science; and contemporary physical theory has proven him right without in any way transgressing into 'idealist' domains. [139]

Furthermore, had Lenin applied the logic of dialectics to the history of philosophy, he would in fact have had to admit—which he apparently did in his *Philosophical Notebooks*—that a dichotomization of this kind is never as clear-cut as he would wish it to be. This is perhaps why Althusser would not want the history of philosophy to be treated 'historically'—that is, dialectically. By positing philosophy as essentially *ahistorical* Althusser obviously attempts to preserve Lenin's untenable dichotomization; and yet it is clear that the very partisanship which is Lenin's mainstay runs counter to the notion of dialectical change, which he presumed dictated the nature of philosophical understanding itself. The simple fact is that the logic of dialectics cannot allow for static and mutually irreconcilable dichotomizations of this kind, as Mannheim (as we shall see in the next chapter) was to maintain with such force and tenacity. [140]

A third and perhaps even more debilitating fallacy is involved in Lenin's zero-sum dichotomization of philosophy, namely, the assumption that there exists a formal logical relationship of inverse entailment between idealist and materialist epistemology, in the sense that if the former is true then the latter is false, and vice versa. Lenin believed that if he could refute phenomenalism *qua* idealism, this by itself would be proof of the truth of epistemological materialism. However, as Jordan has written, if "it is conceded that Lenin's objections against Machian phenomenalism are valid, this does not imply that Lenin's own views are valid. The refutation of phenomenalism has logically nothing to do with the justification of epistemological realism and its defense against possible objections." [141] Nor, as we have already noted, does Lenin's definition of matter make it unacceptable to "a Hegelian, a Platonist, or an epistemological realist, all of whom are hostile to materialism." [142] In short, the two epistemological standpoints posited by Lenin as wholly contrary are not mutually exclusive. It has also been pointed out that nothing that Lenin objected to in Mach's doctrines refutes methodological phenomenalism—the standpoint that our propositions about physics are formally reducible to statements about sense-data.[143] Indeed, such a view does no harm at all to Leninist epistemology since, as we have already seen, the copy theory of knowledge is precisely such a translation of the 'thing-in-itself' into our perception of it (as a 'thing-for-us' or 'copy') through the mediation of sense-data. Furthermore, Lenin seems to have been unaware of the fact that a defense of the truth of realism is not a support for the truth of materialism; and it is precisely in failing to see this that he missed the whole point of the phenomenalist criticism of the former.[144]

In summary, therefore, Lenin's explication of his belief in the inherent partisanship of philosophy gives us no relevant philosophical or methodological information. It does, however, as we shall see below, contribute to our understanding of the Leninist conception of *ideology* and of his conviction that ideological partisanship necessarily requires the belief that *philosophy* itself is partisan.[145] Such a conviction is, in the final analysis, neither dialectical nor philosophical but biographical, as Nagel has put it, and can easily be recognized as such when its philosophical tenets are related to Lenin's paramount interest in political (or revolutionary) action.[146] Thus, if it is "unconditionally true" that to every "scientific ideology"—and Lenin certainly believed his doctrine to be 'scientific'—there "corresponds an objective truth, absolute nature," then all that we can say for sure about Lenin's 'ideological' conception of the partisanship of philosophy is that it corresponds to an "objective truth" other than that which can be apprehended by the philosophical tools (especially epistemological) which he himself so self-consciously utilized and referred to as authoritative.

The fallacy involved in Lenin's historiographical conception of the partisanship of philosophy, that the partisan struggle within philosophy "in the final analysis reflects the tendencies and ideology of the antagonistic classes of modern society," is that of spurious reductionism, which in this case involves the reduction of philosophical differences to empirical or extraphilosophical sources. This is a form of argumentation *ad hominem* in socio-political and historical terms and is as invalid as the more common and vulgar form of this practice. Philosophical differences can by definition never be reduced to empirical variables, just as we cannot find valid solutions to philosophical problems by nonphilosophical means. (How we *acquire* our points of view is an entirely different question, as is the question of how and why we sometimes change these in the face of empirical factors.) I have already touched upon this fallacy in my critique of Marx's superstructural explication of ideology and need therefore not pursue it further here.

However, we can use some of Lenin's own premises to argue against him on this point. Lenin claims that the partisanship of philosophy is a true proposition because philosophy 'truthfully' reflects objective reality, that is, the bifurcated social reality of class structures, which "in the final analysis" determines the division of all schools of thought in philosophy into two partisan groups. Lenin also insisted that the copy theory of perception, the materialist theory of knowledge, and the doctrine of a reflected and absolute, objective truth "are all one and the same thing," that is, that each of these entails the other in the sense that if any one (or more) is true, then the other are also necessarily true (this seems to be the only meaningful interpretation of this dictum). However, as I have tried to show above, we cannot determine if either the copy theory in particular or epistemological materialism in general is true or not; nor can we know if Lenin's conception of the nature of truth is valid or not, since it hinges on the validity of the other. Therefore Lenin cannot positively assert that the putative partisanship of philosophy (in the first, philosophical sense above) is a reflection of the "tendencies and ideology of the antagonistic classes of modern society." This belief is, therefore, in short, as 'fideistic' as the 'idealism' which Lenin abhores and objurgates with such vehemence. It is also a belief which suffers decisively from the genetic fallacy, since its claim rests on the doctrine that the truth of a statement is fundamentally conditioned by its origin. The putative fact that 'materialism' is a reflection of the proletariat class has no relevance whatsoever to its logical validity or material truth—or to its *philosophical* (as distinguished from 'ideological') partisanship. [147]

This concludes the critique of Lenin's *dogmatic* conception of ideology. My argument is that Lenin's identification of 'ideological' differences with philosophical partisanship does not hold water, for the simple reason that it is based on philosophical premises which are quite unacceptable. These are, as I have tried to indicate, not bona fide philosophically or logically or scientifically supportable doctrines and beliefs; consequently Lenin's attempt to link 'ideology' with philosophic concepts and concerns (and by inference, with methodological and epistemological questions of science) must be regarded as a valiant feat but a patent failure. In short, he was just as unable as Marx to give the concept of ideology a philosophically relevant identity or raison d'être, despite his strong and heated insistence to the contrary. This is not to say, however, that his conception of ideology is of no interest to philosophic inquiry or to the methodology of the social sciences. On the contrary, as we shall see as we now turn to his mobilizing conception of ideology, Lenin's contribution to the history and utility of this concept is great. Although this contribution is not philosophical but empirical and especially political, it has had consequences which the philosopher of social science cannot ignore without peril to an understanding of, and an inquiry into, the nature and function of beliefs in social action.

CRITIQUE OF LENIN'S MOBILIZING CONCEPTION OF IDEOLOGY

"Concrete universality as against more abstract universality," a scholar of Slavic thought surmised some years ago, "—this is the essence of the Russian manner." After explaining himself more fully, he adds, significantly, that on this hypothesis "Lenin's *Materialism and Empirio-Criticism*, though terrible philosophy is . . . of enormous general European significance."[148] The significance which is here intimated is that of the concrete function of universalistic doctrines in social action—or, in the case of Lenin, the function of such doctrines in *revolutionary* social action. Trotsky, in his short and appreciative memoir of Lenin, has expressed a similar judgment on the significance of Lenin's 'Russian manner' as against the 'ivory tower' strands of European Marxism and, more particularly, of Marx's own contributions. "The entire

Marx is contained in the *Communist Manifest*, in the foreword to his *Critique*, in *Capital*. Even if he had not been the founder of the First International he would always remain what he is." Lenin, however, "expands at once into revolutionary action. His works as a scholar mean only a preparation for action. If he had never published a single book in the past he would still appear in history what he now is: the leader of the proletarian revolution, the founder of the Third International."[149] Nicolas Berdyaev, another contemporary of Lenin's (thought at this time already a renegade from Marxism), comes to a similar conclusion. "Lenin was not a theoretician of Marxism like Plekhanov, but a theoretician of revolution; everything he wrote was but a treatment of the theory and practice of revolution. He never elaborated a program; he was interested in one thing only—the seizure of power, and the acquisition of strength to achieve this; and for this reason he triumphed."[150]

It is this aspect of Lenin's conception of the role of ideas—as a mobilizing, revolutionary ideology—which will concern us here; not, that is, the putative epistemological nature of ideology but its concrete function as an *activating belief system* in mass political mobilization. Lenin regarded this function to be crucial to the success of the envisioned revolution; for, as one scholar of political ideas has paraphrased Lenin, "on correct ideology depended the entire future of the revolution. In default of the successful propagation of uncorrupted socialist doctrine the working class would fall under the spiritual sway of the bourgeois order and the cause of the revolution would be lost. We have here," he concludes, "the decidedly un-Marxian implication that ideas determine the course of history."[151] This is, as we have seen, the essence of Lenin's injunctions in *What Is to Be Done?* and its analysis of the requisites of revolution. In view of these dicta and their "un-Marxian" implications, the germane question at this juncture is not if history has proved Lenin right on this point—to the extent that history can 'prove' anything, it has, I feel, done so abundantly—but rather if the particular doctrinal grounds which he offers in explanation and justification of his mobilizing conception of ideology are valid.

Marxist philosophy, Lenin claimed, "is cast from a single piece of steel," and therefore one "cannot eliminate one basic premise, one essential part, without departing from the objective truth, without falling prey to bourgeois-reactionary falsehood."[152] Lenin was here thinking about both the philosophy of materialism in general and historical materialism in particular—a unity which he had expressed even more clearly in his younger days, when he insisted that "materialism is not 'primarily a scientific conception of history'... but the only scientific conception of it."[153] For "until we get some other attempt to give a scientific explanation of the functioning and development of some formation of society... until then the materialist conception of history will be a synonym for social science."[154] The point at issue is: is there any necessary and exclusive relationship between Lenin's activist, voluntarist conception of historical materialism—exemplified most clearly by his mobilizing conception of ideology—and the more embracing materialist philosophy from which it is said to spring and gain coherence? Must we accept Lenin's conception of the nature of social science as synonymous with the materialist view of history in order to comprehend and thus explain the structure and function of ideology which Lenin has posited here? If so, then it is clear that this conception of ideology is strictly delimited and of little consequence to a social science not based on the tenets and premises which Lenin associated with the materialist view of history, society, and philosophy. Our interest in it as a concept is in that case necessarily confined—assuming that the exegetical, hermeneutical or hagiographical modes of analysis are not to our taste—to the ideohistoriographical in a broad and descriptive sense, or to the more strictly historical if we wish to regard it as a significant datum or phenomenon limited to the success of the Bolshevik revolution and its aftermath. However, if we do not accept this point of view, that is, if we believe that there is nothing *doctrinally* or *philosophically* exclusive about this conception of ideology—in the sense that, for example, Marx's conceptions of ideology are peculiarly and exclusively Marxian and cannot be understood apart from his larger philosophical framework—then it becomes available to us as a concept in a completely different manner and for wholly different purposes. The following discussion will show that this is indeed the case—that what Lenin claimed to be a distinctively Marxist doctrine, cast from the same "piece of steel" as the rest of the materialist system, is but a particular instance, if historically very illuminating and innovative, of a more inclusive empirical phenomenon of modern social reality, to wit, the phenomenon of ideology as an "action-oriented system of ideas" (to use Carl Friedrich's definition) or, in Daniel Bell's words, as "the conversion of ideas into social levers" in mass politicization. [155] That Lenin was a consummate wielder of action-oriented and mass-directed ideas and ideals nobody can deny; but my thesis is that nothing which he says about the specific *contents* (especially philosophic) of these is relevant to the structure and *function* of the ideas which he so successfully utilized for his own particular revolutionary purposes.

Lewis Feuer, in a psychologically rich if short (and rather acerbic) analysis of Lenin's person and ideas, notes that he "is the only man in history who wrote an epistemological book as part of his tactical plan to defeat another faction within his party." [156] But why was this so important to him? Why did he, as Berdyaev submits, read a whole philosophic literature in order simply to expose, in *Materialism and Empirio-Criticism*, the ideas of Mach and Avenarius, whose interest in revolutionary political action was certainly negligible, if it is true that he at the same time had little time for, nor interest in, philosophical contemplation and analysis but, on the contrary, was possessed of an outlook on life which was singlemindedly "adapted to the technique of revolutionary conflict" and the seizure of power? [157] Why did Lenin the impatient man of action find philosophical and especially epistemological questions so important to the success of revolution? Lenin himself gave us two answers, the one philosophical and the other socio-psychological. While he believed that the latter necessarily entailed the former as a major premise, it is my contention that only the latter is analytically significant and empirically relevant to the social sciences, while the former is part and parcel of the inherent speculativeness of epistemological materialism and thus of no import whatsoever to the social sciences and its study of empirical phenomena.

Lenin's first answer is his assertion that materialism is the only scientific conception of history and provides the only absolute, objective frame of reference for discovering the laws of nature to which all social relations and historical processes conform.[158] "The most important thing," Lenin writes of the significance of the materialist philosophy for understanding historical change and development, "is that the *laws* of these changes have been discovered, that the *objective* logic of these changes and of their historical development has in its chief and basic features been discovered."[159] "The highest task of humanity," he continues, "is to comprehend this objective logic of economic evolution (the evolution of social life) in its general and fundamental features, so that it may be possible to adapt *to it* one's social consciousness and the consciousness of the advanced classes of all capitalist countries in as definite, clear and critical a fashion as possible."[160] On the following page in *Materialism and Empirio-Criticism* his identification of historical with epistemological materialism becomes even more clear-cut. "Materialism in general recognizes objectively real being (matter) as independent of the consciousness, sensation, experience, etc., of humanity. Historical materialism recognizes social being as independent of the social consciousness of humanity. In both cases consciousness is only the reflection of being, at best an approximately true (adequate, perfectly exact) reflection of it."[161] The significance of Lenin's epistemological concerns is thus to be found in his belief that in order to acquire the necessary and correct social consciousness for revolutionary action, a '*true*' understanding of the laws and logic of social change has to be established. For if this is not done, that is, if men do not correctly comprehend the true nature of social evolution (or revolution), they cannot *act* in accordance with the only efficacious patterns which history has set for social change and development. This is the essence of his dictum of the necessity of theory for revolution and as such permeates his whole conception of materialism as a guide to action. It is also this premise which underlies his activist conception of the ideologist as the vanguard of the revolution, whose task it is to bring the *correct* consciousness to a recalcitrant and 'spontaneously' trade-unionistic or quasi-bourgeois working class in order that revolution may be accomplished.

However, this view of an inherent historical logic and of absolute, objective historical laws, conceived of as factors of the external world and therefore independent of man's perceptive and reasoning faculties, is as untenable as the Marxian historicism from which it is derived.[162] Even Marx himself, toward the end of his life, appears to have had second thoughts about a universal *passe-partout* (or key) to historical events and facts; he denounced the employment of "the skeleton key of some general historico-philosophical theory the highest merit of which lies in its supra-historicity," perhaps because he came to feel that such a key, by explaining everything, explains nothing.[163] Furthermore, and this is especially evident in Lenin's historicism and that of his followers, a conception which posits laws of social change in Darwinistic-evolutionist terms, that is, in terms of the 'objective laws of Nature' which Lenin defended so vigorously and exten-sively, is bound to lead to the reification of a conceptual scheme which, as I have tried to show above, can never be proved to be a 'real' reflection of the external world. Marx offered to dedicate *Capital* to Darwin, and (to quote E. J. Hobsbawm) "would hardly have disagreed with Engels's famous phrase at his graveside, which praised him for discovering the law of evolution in human history, as Darwin had done in organic nature."[164] Lenin's con-ception of historical materialism, while premised on an episte-mology which differs in important respects from that of either Marx or Engels, apparently embraced this comparison and identi-fication uncritically and in so doing subscribed to a historiographi-cal view of the relationship between ideas and social action which, though instrumental in a political sense, has been fateful because it has no valid foundation in empirical social and political theory.[165]

Lenin's second answer is most clearly spelled out in *What Is to Be Done?* and in its injunction that "only short-sighted people can consider factional disputes and a strict differentiation between shades of opinion inopportune or superfluous."[166] What the Rus-sian Social-Democratic movement needed, on the contrary, was to combat the "freedom of criticism" which is simply a slogan for "unconcern and helplessness with regard to the development of theoretical thought" and "implies eclecticism and lack of princi-ple."[167] For ultimately " 'freedom of criticism' means freedom for an opportunist trend in Social-Democracy, freedom to convert Social-Democracy into a democratic party of reform, freedom to introduce bourgeois ideas and bourgeois elements into socialism."[168] In short, Lenin insists, if the revolutionary goal is to be achieved in Russia, "we must first of all draw firm and definite lines of demarcation" and, referring to Marx's point of view, "not allow any bargaining over principles . . . or make theoretical 'concessions'."[169] This is, as we have seen above, also an essential meaning of his demand for 'revolutionary theory' in the socialist movement, and of his dogmatic and doctrinaire insistence that in the theoretical or doctrinal field no concessions can be made to ideas which do not further the true revolutionary task of Social Democracy. Why? Because, he cries out heatedly, "to belittle the socialist ideology *in any way, to turn aside from it in the slightest degree* means to strengthen bourgeois ideology" and thus *a fortiori* the status quo.[170]

Lenin, Berdyaev writes, "had no philosophical culture," but instead "fought all his life for that integrated totalitarian view of life, which was necessary for the struggle and for the focusing of revolutionary energy. . . . He fought for wholeness and consistency in the conflict. The latter was impossible without an integrated dogmatic outlook, without a dogmatic confession of faith, without orthodoxy. He demanded deliberate thought and discipline in the struggle against everything elemental; this was his basic theme."[171] The stress in this description of Lenin's thought is placed—and rightly so, it seems to me—on the conative and affective utility or function of theory and doctrine, rather than on its philosophical contents in terms of descriptive or analytic validity. Lenin, another commentator has written, viewed theory as "but a device, bent to the requirements of the goal which tradition bequeathed to him. It was natural, therefore, that Lenin's distinctive ideas about revolution dealt mainly with tactics, the *how* rather than the *why* of revolution."[172] It is in this sense, in the question regarding the function of knowledge rather than its philosophical nature, that Jordan is quite correct in ascribing an *instrumental* view of knowledge to Lenin, even though he perhaps overemphasizes Lenin's lack of interest in philosophical queries per se. "Lenin was not guided by the philosopher's or scientist's interest in truth. His tactics, which he himself stated explicitly, were intended to produce a definition of matter and materialism that would be secure from change and never become outdated." Lenin, Jordan adds in further describing this functional view in doctrinal matters, regarded this security as desirable and necessary, if any political and social objectives were to be achieved. He believed that people would not fight effectively for socialism and communism unless they were materialists. They would not become materialists, however, unless adherence to materialism carried a simple, clear and invariant meaning. Philosophy had only an instrumental value; it was a means for the attainment of some superior aims."[173]

Thus, in the face of the struggle for which Lenin prepared and organized others, the "highest merit of the Marxian doctrine was that it bound the theory and practice of this struggle for emancipation into one inseparable whole from which the revolutionaries could draw their convictions and which provided them with rules for action."[174]

Here we have, it is my judgment, the central root to Lenin's insistence on the need for a partisan revolutionary theory in revolutionary action: a partisanship which has little to do with the philosophical differences between 'idealism' and 'materialism,' or with different shades of the latter, but which, on the contrary, is thoroughly strategic in outlook and tactical in intent in its prescription of "what is to be done" if mass revolutionary mobilization and upheaval is to be achieved. This latter goal was Lenin's prime motive, and hence we can perhaps understand why he spent so much time, energy, and venom in an attempt to guarantee an epistemological defeat of his factional opponents within the socialist movement.[175] "The book," Feuer writes of Lenin's philosophic treatise, "has more invective per page than any other work written in the history of philosophy," and this is perhaps excusable—if true—in as impatient a man of action as Lenin, who (in addition to having Engels's *Anti-Düring* and its tone of voice as model) viewed philosophical differences and doctrinal altercations as essentially a nuisance in the face of the far greater problem of consolidating a political movement in order to proceed to the real order of the revolutionary business.[176] This utilitarian view of ideology as an integrated, dogmatic, holistic, and authoritarian set of ideas or doctrines, serving as an effective sociopsychological means to mass politicization, is the essence of Lenin's answer to the question what power ideas can have over human life. As a guide to action this is a view which, as history has acknowledged,

Lenin put into practice with consummate skill. It is also a position on the *function* of knowledge—as an *instrumental* force in social change—which, significantly, requires or ideally calls for a *dogmatic* interpretation of the structure of knowledge. There is, given this view of ideology, no real contradiction between Lenin's epistemological dogmatism and his instrumentalist or pragmatic conception of the function of ideas. If ideas are to have the conative efficacy in mass mobilization which Lenin's historical voluntarism attributed to them and which he utilized in his revolutionary tactics, they necessarily have to be posited as absolutely true, as the only authoritative system of beliefs and frame of reference, and as the source ne plus ultra for our answers to all queries, both philosophical and sociopolitical.[177]

It is of great significance to note, in addition, that the instrumentality which Lenin attributed to ideas in general and specifically to socialist ideology could be effective despite the fact that neither his epistemological nor his historical materialism can be shown to be valid but possess, instead, fundamental and debilitating shortcomings. As I have already indicated, it is my contention that the importance of Lenin's concept of ideology as a phenomenon of social and political beliefs in action has in principle little or nothing to do with the truth or falsity of the doctrines on which it is so ostensively premised.[178] We are here, in fact, confronted with the *persuasive treatment* of ideas, and in such a treatment the strictures of epistemic logic are as irrelevant as the potentially effective structures of sociopsychological logic are of paramount importance. For as I have intimated earlier, Lenin's conception of ideology can in the final analysis be viewed as being predicated not on scientific grounds but in terms of the dynamics of the self-fulfilling prophecy and its predictive power. Of this phenomenon Robert Merton has written in his classic essay that its logic is such that what "is, in the beginning, a false definition of the situation evokes a new behavior which makes the originally false conception come *true*."[179] W. I. Thomas, once the dean of American sociologists, regarded this phenomenon as a basic element of social life, a factor of great if neglected import in the analysis of human endeavor. "If men define situations as real," he states as a fundamental theorem in social logic, "they are real in their consequences."[180]

Or as Merton writes, "men respond not only to the objective features of a situation, but also, and at times primarily, to the meaning this situation has for them. And once they have assigned some meaning to the situation, their consequent behavior and some of the consequences of that behavior are determined by the ascribed meaning."[181] He also points out that this phenomenon is peculiar to human affairs, that is, to the sphere of purposive, volitional actions; and (as others, especially Heisenberg, have stressed in criticism of dogmatic realism), we find it in nature, that is, in the physical sciences, only as a consequence of the effects of human observational intervention in it.[182] Lenin's voluntarism is a clear recognition of this characteristic of human actions, just as the laws leading to the 'predictions' or 'prophecies' of his historical materialism (based on the 'laws of Nature') can be viewed as reifications—efficacious in defining and directing historical actions and situations—which in their hypostatized forms condition the very processes which are 'objectively' or 'scientifically' predicted. "The scientific analysis of the movement of capitalism," Bukharin once acknowledged openly, "is only a means of foreseeing, and foresight itself is only a means for practical activity."[183] Lenin was perhaps not as candid in his writings, but his practice proved to be an illuminating example of this insight into a basic aspect of social reality.

It is obvious that the ideal conditions for making these kinds of historical 'predictions' or 'prophecies' are those in which a man of action possessing rich theoretical or, more particularly, doctrinal gifts is able to create deep feelings of partisanship and unity among men in order to motivate them to act concertedly for a common aim. Such motivation requires, in addition, the kind of confidence which is best achieved if it is based on the unperturbable belief and trust that history is on one's side and vice versa, and that success is, consequently, inevitable and imminent. Marx had a keen insight into these historical and social mechanisms, but it was Lenin who perfected these tools of ideological motivation and made them into effective revolutionary instruments. William James once emphasized that "faith creates its own verification," and that in such cases—that is, when the achievement of goals is ultimately determined by the willingness to exert oneself and by the confidence that the final outcome is within palpable reach—it is "the part of wisdom to believe what one desires."[184] Lenin proved the revolutionary meaningfulness of this wisdom to the extent that at the time of Stalin's height of power it became part of orthodoxy to believe that the 'superstructure' brings its own 'basis' into existence not only in theory but in applied science and practice as well (Lysenkoism thus becoming—no fault of Lenin's —the apogee of the voluntarist interpretation of Marxist-Leninist thought).[185] In the process Lenin also showed that historical materialism, insofar as it exhibited a 'prophetic' or 'predictive' utility with regard to the process of sociopolitical change, was ipso facto invalid in terms of its own premised 'laws of Nature.' In short, the basic assumptions of Marx's historicism were proved false to the extent that Lenin's utilization of it as 'ideology' proved to be instrumentally effective.

However, and here we come to the key of Lenin's success in utilizing 'ideology' for mass mobilization and to the reason why this conception retains its significance for contemporary social and political science, this dogmatic-*cum*-instrumental view of knowledge and ideas in the social sphere can only be related to, and function within, the empirical reality of a society if it is solidly anchored to it not merely as a set of variable and individual or atomistic belief-systems alone but, more importantly, as an *organized* system of integrated and disciplined thought and action (something which the Russian Orthodox Church no doubt knew well, as evidenced in the excerpt from its Short Catechism quoted in the Epigraph). The history of ideas and doctrines is richly strewn with potential orthodoxies and absolutistic beliefs, but these have, on the whole, remained locked within the covers of thick and musty tomes and are of minimal interest except to those whose self-imposed task or calling is to explore diligently the dustier enclaves of literary repositories. Lenin's contribution to this genre would probably have remained within this category were it not for the fact that his temperament was inherently and incorrigibly activist and his genius organizatorial rather than philosophical. "In its struggle for power," he intoned, "the proletariat can become, and inevitably will become, an invincible force only when its ideological unification by the principles of

Marxism is *consolidated by the material unity of an organization* which will weld millions of toilers into an army of the working class."[186] It is due to this recognition that Lenin's conception of an activist, mobilizing ideology cannot be separated from the notion of the vanguard ideologist and the organizational structure of an omniscient and all-powerful party which gives the ideologist the requisite tools for forming and guiding social and political reality. In a significant sense, therefore, the 'ideological' characteristics of Lenin's 'materialism' can in the final analysis be viewed as primarily being a 'theoretical' extrapolation from the concrete, functional, and strategic-tactical needs of organization as defined by him. One can perhaps even venture to suggest that when he enjoins that there can be no revolutionary movement without revolutionary theory, he is really saying that without revolutionary ideologists organized into a revolutionary party there can be no genuine revolution.

In conclusion, the truth of the matter seems to be that Lenin (as to some extent Marx) appears not to have wholeheartedly trusted in, nor given much for the worth of, an independent realm of ideas. But he certainly did believe in the *use* of ideas as an effective manipulative instrument for collective action in history—as a vehicle, in the hands of the dedicated ideologist, for arousing and channeling the potential revolutionary consciousness of oppressed masses. That such use could be made most effectively of a cognitively 'closed'—that is, dogmatic and authoritarian—system of ideas and beliefs is a notion which, as modern history has proved time and again, betrays an impressive insight into the social logic and psychology of mass movements. But in reducing the role of theory and philosophy to a tool for mass politicization—of justifying the *cognitive* nature and value of ideas in terms of the strategic considerations of *affective* mass mobilization—Lenin reveals that the doctrine of the partisanship of philosophy as ideology, rather than being an inherent trait of the history of philosophy or thought, is really nothing else but an efficacious substantiation of the doctrine of the aroused revolutionary consciousness. While Lenin should be credited with reintroducing the role of the idéologue *qua* ideologist into the history and theory of social change, he at the same time established a specification of the nature and function of this role which is as far removed from its original conception as his philosophical doctrines and sociopolitical goals are from those of the post-Enlightenment idéologues of a century earlier.

NOTES

1. V. I. Lenin, *Collected Works*, 45 vols., vol. 5 (Moscow, 1964), 5: 369 (these works hereafter referred to as *CW*). For a short introduction to this pamphlet, see S. V. and Patricia Utechin's translation of *What Is to Be Done?* (Oxford, 1963), pp. 1ff. The importance of this polemic work within Leninist thought as a whole has been much debated. John Plamenatz, for example, views it simply as a pamphlet "written for the benefit of a small band of Marxists harassed by a powerful and intolerant bureaucracy," while Adam B. Ulam writes that this work "was to guide Lenin through the intra-Party struggle that began in 1903 and lasted through the Revolution of 1917." John Plamenatz, *German Marxism and Russian Communism* (London, 1954), p. 227, and Adam B. Ulam, *Lenin and the Bolsheviks* (London, 1966), p. 176. Alfred G. Meyer, who views Lenin not so much as a practical revolutionary but more as a political philosopher in his own right, stresses that this pamphlet has relevance only to Lenin's conception of the party, which, though not unimportant within Leninism, is a subsidary aspect of Lenin's philosophy, which centers around his treatment of dialectics and the economics of imperialism. *See* Alfred G. Meyer, *Leninism* (Cambridge, Mass., 1957), pp. 1ff. Robert Nisbet, on the other hand, writes that "Lenin's *What Is to Be Done?* . . . is probably his major work from any point of view, certainly from that of the adaptation and reorientation of Marxism to which I have just referred." Robert Nisbet, *The Social Philosophers* (New York, 1973), p. 293. Within the Soviet Union, as S. V. Utechin writes, "the *Short Course* of party history, which was the alpha and omega of the theoretical training of party cadres under Stalin, stated that 'the theoretical theses expounded in *What Is To Be Done?* later became the foundation of the ideology of the Bolshevik party'." As to the post-Stalinist era, the official textbook of party history gives a more or less similar appreciation of the importance of this work. Utechin, op. cit., pp. 1f. *See also* pp. 35f., which gives a short appraisal of the weight given to it in the literature. Cf. also Reidar Larsson, *Theories of Revolution* (Stockholm, 1970), pp. 196ff. and 305ff. The title of Lenin's tract is taken verbatim from a Russian novel by Chernyshevsky, a veritable fountain of revolutionary sentiment and much read during the end of the last century. Reportedly, it was very much admired by Lenin, especially during his younger days.

2. Marx's claim can be found in Karl Marx and Friedrich Engels, *The German Ideology* (Moscow, 1968), p. 62, while the reference to Engels is contained in Larsson, op. cit., p. 111. Engels's own statements on this question can be found (as cited by Larsson) in, e.g., Karl Marx and Friedrich Engels, *Werke* (Berlin, 1954-1968), 20: 250, 265; 22: 250, 254 (this collection is commonly referred to as *MEW*).

3. Lenin, *CW*, 5: 384. Author's emphases.
4. Ibid.
5. Ibid.
6. Quoted in Z. A. Jordan, *The Evolution of Dialectical Materialism* (New York, 1967), p. 273.
7. *See* Helmut Dahm, "Der Ideologiebefriff bei Marx und die heutige Kontroverse über Ideologie und Wissenschaft in den sozialistischen Ländern," *Studies in Soviet Thought* 12, no. 1 (1972): 45.
8. *See* Jordan, op. cit., p. 273.
9. Lenin, *CW*, 5, p. 370. For descriptions and interpretations of the intense struggle which occurred within Russian Marxism around the turn of the century—leading to the Bolshevik-Menschevik rift of 1903-1905—see, inter alia, Plamenatz, op. cit., pp. 191ff.; L. H. Haimson, *The Russian Marxists and the Origins of Bolshevism* (Cambridge, Mass., 1955), pp. 75ff.; E. H. Carr, *The Bolshevik Revolution of the Soviet Union* (London, 1960), pp. 7ff.; Leonard Schapiro, *The Communist Party of the Soviet Union* (London, 1960), pp. 19ff.; Adam B. Ulam, op. cit., pp. 160ff.; George Lichtheim, *Marxism* (New York, 1965), pp. 325ff.; Larsson, op. cit., pp. 108ff.; Dietrich Geyer, *Lenin in der russischen Sozialdemokratie* (Cologne, 1962), pp. 187ff.; Theodor Dan, *The Origins of Bolshevism* (London, 1964), pp. 236ff.; and Donald W. Treadgold, *Lenin and His Rivals* (New York, 1955).
10. In a footnote Lenin adds, however, that "it is perfectly true" that "the working class *spontaneously* gravitates towards socialism." But, he adds, this is so only "in the sense that socialist theory reveals the causes of the misery of the working class more profoundly and more correctly than any other theory, and for that reason, the workers are able to assimilate it so easily, *provided*, however, this theory does not itself yield to spontaneity, *provided* it subordinates spontaneity to itself." Lenin, *CW*, 5: 386. *See also* Meyer, op. cit., pp. 29ff. On p. 31 Meyer writes that "whereas Marx believed in the spontaneous growth of working-class consciousness under the impact of capitalist realities, Lenin tended to assume that the workingman was forever doomed to insufficient consciousness, no matter how miserable his conditions." For a different interpretation, see Plamenatz, op. cit., pp. 222ff. Author's emphases.
11. For a discussion of the peculiarly Russian roots of Leninist and Soviet Marxism, *see*, e.g., Gustav A. Wetter, *Der dialektische Materialismus* (Freiburg, 1952), pp. 65ff., and Robert V. Daniels, "Lenin and the Russian Revolutionary Tradition," *Harvard Slavic Studies* 4 (1957): 339ff.
12. Lenin, *CW*, 5: 386. Author's emphases.
13. John Mepham, in an article on the Marxian theory of ideology, argues that these reasons which Lenin gives for the origin and dominance of bourgeois ideology are in the form of a "passing remark," that "this statement is, not surprisingly given its context, incomplete, and is open to misinterpretation. It may suggest a view that is very common but which is, in my opinion, fundamentally mistaken. This view, which is an ideology of ideology, is that the dominance of bourgeois ideology has its basis in the dominance of the bourgeoisie as a class only in the sense that this dominance as a class allows the bourgeoisie to have

monopoly on the production and dissemination of ideas." John Mepham, "The Theory of Ideology in Capital," *Radical Philosophy* no. 2 (Summer 1972): 12. It is clear, however, that Mepham is judging Lenin in terms of a concept of ideology— as the Marxian 'mystification' of the bourgeois consciousness—which is not only inappropriate with regard to Lenin's usage of the concept, but which he also had little use for. Lichtheim appears to make something of a similar mistake—of assigning to the Marxian concept of ideology sole definitional validity—when he writes that "Lenin's employment of the term 'ideology' to denote the content of working-class consciousness represents a misuse of a terminology which as a Marxist he might have expected to treat more carefully." George Lichtheim, "Comments," *Slavic Review* 24, no. 4 (1965): 605. *See* Daniel Bell's reply to this in ibid., pp. 617ff. Istvan Meszaros, in his *Marx's Theory of Alienation* (London, 1970), apparently does not accept either my point of view or that of Lichtheim. He thus argues that "in Lenin's development as a Marxist his grasp of the concept of alienation in its true significance played a vital role." Ibid., p. 93.

14. Regarding Lenin's 'voluntarism,' *see*, e.g., Haimson, op. cit., pp. 46, 100, 111ff., 162, 208; Wetter, op. cit., p. 142; A. J. Gregor, *A Survey of Marxism* (New York, 1965), pp. 210ff.; R. V. Daniels, "Soviet Power and Marxist Determinism," *Problems of Communism* 9, no. 3 (1960): pp. 12ff.; and D. P. Costello, "Voluntarism and Determinism in Bolshevist Doctrine," *Soviet Studies* 12 (1960-1961): 394ff.

15. *See* Lenin, *CW*, 1: 141ff. Undoubtedly Plekhanov's *The Development of the Monist View of History* (1895) influenced Lenin considerably in his Darwinian interpretation of Marx. But Plekhanov was not alone in dwelling explicitly on the similarities between Marx and Darwin; these were, in fact, clearly recognized by Marx and Engels themselves. *See* W. G. Runciman, *Social Science and Political Theory* (Cambridge, 1965), pp. 45f., and Larsson, op. cit., pp. 110f. Plekhanov, however, must be given more exclusive credit for the Leninist modification of Marxian thought into a philosophy of revolutionary action. *See* Larsson, op. cit., pp. 110ff. and Jordan, op. cit., pp. 334ff.

16. Lenin, *CW*: 159.

17. Lenin, *CW*: 159.

18. Jordan, op. cit., p. 355.

19. It is in regard to Lenin's "almost obsessive preoccupation with problems of power" (to use Meyer's words) that he was frequently attacked as a Jacobin and Blanquist—epithets which he apparently did not wholly dislike, although he believed, contrary to Blanqui, that 'power to rule' (as distinguished from 'acquiring power') would have to be based on the masses. For an analysis of Blanquism vs. Marxist theory, *see* Larsson, op. cit., pp. 17ff., 61ff., 87ff., and 115ff. The quote above is to be found in Meyer, op. cit., p. 37.

20. For an analysis of the elitist tendency in Leninism, *see*, e.g., Larsson, op. cit., pp. 196ff. and 322ff.; *see also* pp. 77ff. and 132ff.

21. *See* Wetter, op. cit., p. 141.

22. Meyer, op. cit., p. 41. The view of 'orthodox Marxism' in regard to this question is quintessentially formulated in the *Communist Manifest*, in which we read that "revolutions are not intentionally and capriciously made, but rather

have universally been the necessary consequence of conditions completely independent of the will and leadership of the individual parties and entire classes." Quoted in A. James Gregor, *Contemporary Radical Ideologies* (New York, 1968), p. 68. The *Manifest* as a whole can be found in either Karl Marx and Friedrich Engels, *Selected Works in Two Volumes* (Moscow, 1955), 1: 62, or in *MEW*, 4: 372. Regarding Lenin's putative 'orthodoxy' or 'deviationism' (or 'revisionism'), see my comments later in the chapter and the references included there.

23. Leonard Schapiro, "Lenin's Contribution to Politics," *The Political Quarterly* 35 (1964): 13f.

24. Jordan, op. cit., p. 353. For an opposing view on the question regarding Marx's interest primarily in theory, *see* C. J. Hammen, "Alienation, Communism, and Revolution in the Marx-Engels *Briefwechsel*," *Journal of the History of Ideas* 33, no. 1 (1972): 77ff.

25. Quoted by Jordan, op. cit., p. 210. For an analysis of Plekhanov's own deviations from orthodoxy, *see* Larsson, op. cit., pp 108ff.

26. Georg Lukács, *Lenin* (Neuwied/Berlin, 1967), pp. 90f. For a discussion of Lenin's socialist goals, *see* Daniel Tarschys's study, *Beyond the State* (Stockholm, 1971), pp. 87ff. Author's translation.

27. Lenin, *CW*, 5: 354, Lichtheim, *Marxism*, p. 336. Lenin's ambivalence with regard to the role of the masses in revolution has often been pointed out and debated; *see* e.g., Meyer, op. cit., pp. 37ff.

28. Lenin, *CW*, 5: 384.

29. Ibid., p. 383. *See also* Meyer, op. cit., pp. 31ff. Emphases added.

30. Lenin, *CW*, 5: 375. *See also* Lewis S. Feuer, "Marxism and the Hegemony of the Intellectual Class," *Transactions of the Fifth World Congress of Sociology* 4 (Brussels, 1964): pp. 83ff.

31. Lenin, *CW*, 5: 383. Emphases added.

32. Ibid., p. 384. Within parentheses, the translation at hand explicitly adds that to "imbue the proletariat' *literally* means to "saturate the proletariat." Emphases added.

33. Lichtheim, *Marxism*, p. 337. Lenin does state, rather disingenuously and only in a footnote, that this position does not entail that workers have no part in creating a socialist ideology. However, he adds, they "take part . . . not as workers, but as socialist theoreticians, as Proudhons and Weitlings; in other words, they take part only when they are able, and to the extent that they are able, more or less, to acquire the knowledge of their age and develop that knowledge." Lenin, *CW*, 5: 384. For an analysis of the various attacks on Lenin's intellectual and revolutionary elitism, *see*, e.g., Larsson, op. cit., pp. 234ff. and Meyer, op. cit., pp. 37ff. *See also* Gregor, op. cit., pp. 92ff.

34. Lenin, *CW*, 5: 370. Lenin emphasizes this whole passage.

35. Lenin, *CW*, 14: 358.

36. *See* Wetter, *Sovjetideologie heute*, p. 19.

37. *See* Dahm, op. cit., pp. 37ff.

38. Quoted in Z. A. Jordan, *Philosophy and Ideology* (Dordrecht, 1963), p. 323.

39. *See* ibid., and Jordan, *Evolution of Dialectical Materialism*, pp. 217ff.

40. Quoted in Julius I. Löwenstein, *Vision und Wirklichkeit* (Basel, 1970), pp. 117.

41. *See* Jordan, *Evolution of Dialectical Materialism*, pp. 153, 152.

42. *See* ibid., p. 153.

43. Ibid., p. 152.

44. *See* Jordan, *Philosophy and Ideology*, pp. 324ff.

45. *See* Gregor, *A Survey of Marxism*, pp. 73ff.

46. *See* Lenin, *CW*, 14: 83. For an incisive and detailed discussion of Lenin's epistemological modifications of Engels's view, *see* Jordan, *Philosophy and Ideology*, pp. 325ff. and *Evolution of Dialectical Materialism*, pp. 226ff. *See also* Irving Fetscher's *Von Marx zur Sowjetideologie* (Frankfurt, 1956), especially the first two parts.

47. The quote from Berkeley is found in *CW*, 14: 26, and Lenin's statement, ibid., p. 103. *See also* pp. 22ff. For a highly informative description of the complex of events which led to the publication of *Materialism and Empirio-Criticism*, *see* David Joravsky, *Soviet Marxism and Natural Science, 1917-1932* (New York, 1961), pp. 24ff.

48. Quote found in Jordan, *Evolution of Dialectical Materialism*, p. 211. *See also* pp. 210ff.

49. Ibid., p. 216.

50. Lenin, *CW*, 14: 103. *See also* ibid., pp. 88ff. Lenin's main phenomenalist protagonist was Ernst Mach, who regarded the complexes of sensations which we experience as the 'real' world, as the 'things' of reality. Lenin quite explicitly calls Mach an 'idealist,' and his doctrine "a simple rehash of Berkeleianism." Ibid., p. 42. *See also* pp. 40ff. for Lenin's arguments against Machism, and Jordan, *Philosophy and Ideology*, p. 326.

51. Lenin, *CW*, 14: 63f.

52. Ibid., p. 130. *See also* p. 261.

53. *See* Jordan, *Philosophy and Ideology*, pp. 317ff. for a thorough discussion of the Leninist modifications of the causal theory.

54. Jordan, *Evolution of Dialectical Materialism*, p. 214. That sensations are only "more or less" true copies of reality and not *identical* copies was emphasized by Lenin time and again. Had he regarded them as identical, he feared (with much justice) that he would be accused of idealism. See Lenin, *CW*, 14: 261.

55. Lenin, *CW*, 14: 130.

56. Ibid., p. 59.

57. Ibid., p. 265.

58. Jordan, *Philosophy and Ideology*, p. 351.

59. Lenin, *CW*, 14: 137.

60. *See* Dahm, op. cit., p. 46.

61. Lenin, *CW*, 14: 367, 369, respectively.

62. Ibid., p. 368.

63. Ibid., pp. 368, 369, respectively.

64. Ibid., p. 369.

65. For a discussion of Bernstein's central role in the division of Social Democracy on the Continent, *see*, e.g., Lichtheim, *Marxism*, pp. 272ff., 284ff. In

terms of philosophical epithets, the main villains in Lenin's view were neo-Kantianism, empirio-criticism, and empirio-monism; *see* Wetter, *Der dialektische Materialismus*, pp. 102ff. and 129ff. On Bogdanov's role and position in Russian Social Democracy, *see* S. V. Utechin, "Philosophy and Society: Alexander Bogdanov" in Leo Labedz, ed. *Revisionism* (London, 1962), pp. 117ff.

66. Lenin, *CW*, 5: 355, 369.

67. Lewis S. Feuer, in an article attempting to treat Lenin's dogmatism and factionalism as a function of his psychological makeup, asks himself what Lenin's philosophical method was, and comes to the conclusion that it "was, we might say: usually the method of invective." Lewis Feuer, "Lenin's Fantasy," *Encounter* 35, no. 6 (December 1970): 25. For examples of this method *see*, inter alia, Lenin, *CW*, 14: 50, 116, 145, 182, 195, 239, 264, 296-97, 298-99.

68. *See* Wetter, *Der dialektische Materialismus*, pp. 142ff.

69. Lenin, *CW*, 5: 509.

70. Ibid.

71. Ibid., pp. 509f. For Lenin's continued preoccupation with this problem during his 'philosophic years' while in exile during the war, see his notes to Aritistotle's *Metaphysics*, *CW*, 38: 372ff.

72. Lenin, *CW*, 5: 510.

73. Ulam, op. cit., p. 178. Quote from Lukács in Victor Zitta, *Georg Lukács' Marxism: Alienation, Dialectics, Revolution* (The Hague, 1964), p. 236.

74. For Lukács's distinction, *see* Zitta, op. cit., pp. 234ff. and Georg Lukács, *Geschichte und Klassenbewusstsein* (Berlin, 1923), pp. 218ff. Lenin's only 'utopian' work is the perplexing *State and Revolution* (1917), which contains a futurology which is as simple as it is at odds with the practice which Lenin initiated during this momentous year. For a detailed analysis of Lenin's 'instrumental political utopia,' *see* Tarschys, op. cit., pp. 88ff. *See also* Plamenatz, op. cit., pp. 240ff.

75. Lenin, *CW*, 5: p. 467. Emphasis added. *See also* John Plamenatz, *Ideology* (London, 1970), p. 141.

76. Quoted by Gregor, *Contemporary Radical Ideologies*, p. 74.

77. Ibid., p. 79. Emphasis omitted.

78. Lenin, *CW*, 5: 492ff.

79. Ibid., pp. 508ff. *See also* Haimson, op. cit., pp. 135ff. Emphasis added.

80. Nicolas Berdyaev, *The Origin of Russian Communism* (London, 1937), p. 125.

81. For an analysis of the voluntaristic legacy bestowed by Lenin upon Soviet thought, *see* ibid., pp. 12ff., and Daniels, "Soviet Power and Marxist Determinism," pp. 12ff.

82. Ernst Fischer and Franz Marek, *Was Lenin Wirklich Sagte* (Vienna, Munich, 1969).

83. *See* references, especially to the first work, in Note 1 above.

84. Henri Lefebvre, *La pensée de Lénine* (Paris, 1957). Translated into Swedish as *Lenins tänkande* (Stockholm, 1971). *See* pp. 74f. of the latter version for the above statements.

85. *See*, e.g., Maurice Cornforth, *The Open Philosophy and the Open Society* (London, 1968), pp. 17ff. and his major work, *Dialectical Materialism, An Introduction*, vols. 1-3 (New York, 1953-1954).

86. *See* the previous discussion of Ollman's book, pp. 63, 64 above.

87. Alisdaire MacIntyre, *Against the Self-Images of the Age* (London, 1971), p. 46.

88. Labedz, ed., op. cit. p. 26.

89. Lichtheim, *Marxism*, p. 330. *See also* Wetter, *Der dialektische Materialismus*, pp. 138ff., and on the break between Lenin and his associates, ibid., pp. 77ff., Haimson, op. cit., pp. 182ff., Carr, op. cit., pp. 26ff., Schapiro, *The Communist Party in the Soviet Union*, pp. 54ff.

90. Lichtheim, *Marxism*, p. 331.

91. Louis Althusser, *Lénine et la philosophie* (Paris, 1968), translated into Swedish as *Lenin och filosofi* (Stockholm, 1969). The reference is taken from p. 10 of the Swedish translation.

92. Ibid.

93. "Lenin," Plamenatz writes, "was not a philosopher or social theorist of even secondary importance. To think otherwise is quite to mistake the nature of his genius. His more theoretical works, had anyone else written them, would now be read by no one; he never understood the intelligible parts of dialectical and historical materialism, and so—despite his good intentions—was never able to defend them except by quoting their authors and abusing their critics." Plamenatz, *German Marxism and Russian Communism*, p. 221.

94. E. H. Carr, *What Is History* ? (London, 1962), pp. 132f.

95. Ernest Nagel, *The Structure of Science* (New York, 1961), p. 492.

96. Karl R. Popper, *Conjectures and Refutations*, rev. ed. (London, 1972), p. 98. *See also* pp. 97ff.

97. Ibid., pp. 98f. Emphases added.

98. *See* ibid., p. 98.

99. Ibid., pp. 98f.

100. Jordan, *Evolution of Dialectical Materialism*, p. 236; *see also* pp. 235f.

101. Ibid., p. 236.

102. Ibid.

103. *See* Gregor, *A Survey of Marxism*, pp. 75f.

104. *See* Popper, op. cit., p. 99, fn. 5.

105. Ibid., p. 104.

106. Lenin, *CW*, 14: 104f. Author's emphases.

107. Ibid., p. 136.

108. Ibid., p. 103.

109. Jordan, *Evolution of Dialectical Materialism*, p. 217. *See also* Anton Pannekoek, *Lenin as Philosopher* (New York, 1948), pp. 48ff.

110. Jordan, *Evolution of Dialectical Materialism*, p. 221. *See also* pp. 230f. from which I have taken these arguments.

111. Ibid., pp. 220, 221. *See also* Gregor, *A Survey of Marxism*, p. 80. Berkeley's arguments in this matter are most clear-cut in *Principles of Human*

Knowledge, vol 17, p. 80: *see*, e.g., the collection edited by Edwin A. Burtt, *The English Philosophers from Bacon to Mill* (New York, 1939), in which these paragraphs can be found, respectively, on pp. 528, 550. The point which appears to have escaped Lenin is that being a materialist entails being a realist, while realism does not necessarily entail materialism. See Jordan, *Evolution of Dialectical Materialism*, pp. 217, 231.

112. *See* Jordan, *Philosophy and Ideology*, p. 331.

113. Ibid.

114. Bertrand Russell, *The Analysis of Matter* (London, 1954), p. 218.

115. Jordan, *Evolution of Dialectical Materialism*, p. 212.

116. Lenin, *CW*, 14: 130.

117. *See* Gregor, *A Survey of Marxism*, p. 85.

118. Gregor refers specifically to Maurice Cornforth and D. V. Caplin, two well-known British Marxist-Leninists. *See* ibid., p. 65.

119. Lenin, *CW*, 14: pp. 232, 234ff. In these pages Lenin gives the reasons for his rejection of Helmholtz's theory, which he finds to be an inconsistent materialism suffused with Kantian notions. It is interesting to note, however, that Plekhanov accepted the 'theory of hieroglyphs,' for which he was criticized in *Materialism and Empirio-Criticism*, and for which he still suffers official disapprobation. *See* Wetter, *Der dialektische Materialismus*, p. 116.

120. *See* Jordan, *Philosophy and Ideology*, p. 327.

121. *See* ibid.

122. Ibid. This is just as much a criticism of the causal theory of perception, on which the copy theory builds. *See* ibid., p. 337.

123. In addition to Jordan's arguments in ibid., pp. 326ff., *see* Gregor, *A Survey of Marxism*, pp. 83ff., and G. A. Paul's "Lenin's Theory of Perception," *Analysis* 5, no. 5 (1938): 65ff., which constitutes a short, typically British, and exhaustive refutation of Lenin's copy theory of perception.

124. Quoted in David Joravsky, op. cit., p. 18.

125. Quoted in Jordan, *Philosophy and Ideology*, p. 327.

126. Ibid. It should perhaps be noted that Cornforth has criticized the early Wittgenstein on precisely this account, that is, of presenting a pictorial and thus solipsistic theory of propositions. He appears not, however, to accept a similar criticism of Lenin's copy theory of perception, presumably because he does not subscribe to it but interprets Lenin's position in terms of causal representationalism. Cornforth, *Marxism and the Linguistic Philosophy* (London, 1965), pp. 121ff.

127. It is very interesting to note how Lenin's 'copy' or 'transcript' theory of *epistemological materialism* leads him to reinterpret one of Marx's most salient theses of *historical materialism*. Thus Lenin claims that "Social consciousness *reflects* social being—that is Marx's teaching. . . . Consciousness in general *reflects* being—that is a general thesis of all materialism." *CW*, 14: 323. Marx, of course, claimed something quite different, viz., that man's social being *determines* his consciousness. Emphases added. *See* Karl Marx and Friedrich Engels, *Selected Works*, vol. I (Moscow, n.d.), p. 356. In addition, Peter Berger and Stanley Pullberg have rightly stressed the nondialectical character of Lenin's claim, and appreciatively quote Carlos Astrada: "To consider the dialectical

process of knowledge as a mere reflection, copy or photograph of real processes, is to surreptitiously reify the fluidity of the processes themselves, and to forget the structural unity of subject and object that is supposed by the dialectic." Peter Berger and Stanley Pullberg, "Reification and the Sociological Critique of Consciousness," *History and Theory* 4, no. 2 (1965): 205fn. As the reader will remember, this is the same general point that Lichtheim has made about Lenin's epistemology. *See* Lichtheim, *Marxism*, p. 331.

128. *See* Popper, op. cit., pp. 103f.

129. *See* Gregor, A Survey of Marxism, pp. 92ff. and Popper, op. cit., pp. 104f. This argument is formally similar to the one employed to confute Marx's historicism in the previous chapter.

130. Popper, op. cit., p. 106. *See also* pp. 105ff.

131. Ibid., p. 115. Emphases added.

132. Lenin, *CW*, 14: 137.

133. Ibid.

134. Ibid.

135. Ibid., pp. 335f. Emphases added.

136. Ibid., p. 356.

137. Ibid.

138. *See* Jordan, *Evolution of Dialectical Materialism*, p. 224.

139. *See* Gregor, *Survey of Marxism*, pp. 77ff., Jordan, *Evolution of Dialectical Materialism*, p. 213, and Pannekoek, op. cit., pp. 48ff. *See also* Russell, op. cit., pp. 8, 26, and Werner Heisenberg, *Physics and Philosophy* (London, 1959), and *Philosophical Problems of Nuclear Science* (London, 1952).

140. It is interesting to note that Cornforth, in the foreword to his *Marxism and the Linguistic Philosophy*, admits that his earlier account (in *Science vs. Idealism*) of the legitimacy of the Leninist dichotomization was mistaken. "The chief fault," he thus writes, "in that earlier book was . . . that I had equated bourgeois empiricist philosophy with subjective idealism. That equation is not correct, because since the nineteen-fourties the linguistic philosophy has succeeded in ridding itself of subjective idealism." Ibid., pp. 12f. In a later book, *The Open Society and the Open Philosophy*, he appears, however, to have reverted to his old position, and that in a rather crude fashion. This is perhaps inevitable, since as long as one sticks to Lenin's position, any standpoint which is not that of epistemological materialism is, ipso facto, idealism. Thus there is no difference between 'bourgeois empiricist philosophy' and 'linguistic philosophy' on this score.

141. Jordan, *Philosophy and Ideology*, p. 320.

142. Jordan, *Evolution of Dialectical Materialism*, p. 221.

143. Ibid. *See also* Pannekoek, op. cit., pp. 48ff.

144. *See* Jordan, *Evolution of Dialectical Materialism*, p. 321 and Wetter, *Der dialektische Materialismus*, pp. 134ff.

145. N. V. Valentinov, one of Lenin's main philosophical opponents, writes in his memoirs that Lenin believed "knowledge of the laws of social life . . . precisely because epistemology, the theory of knowledge, is a party science—can be only the privilege of the Party headed by Lenin." Quoted by Joravsky, op. cit., p. 24. Similarly, M. B. Mitin, writing in 1930 (when he had established himself as one of

the leading Soviet philosophers) inferred from *Materialism and Empirio-Criticism* that "There is not and cannot be a philosophy that wants to be considered Marxist-Leninist philosophy while denying the necessity of ideational-political and theoretical leadership on the part of the Communist Party and its leading staff." Also quoted in ibid.

146. *See* Jordan, *Philosophy and Ideology*, p. 333. *See also* Wetter, *Der dialektische Materialismus*, p. 174.

147. For a recent discussion of the debate on philosophic partisanship in Soviet and East European philosophy, *see* the excellent review by Dahm, op. cit., pp. 45ff. and especially 60ff. Emphases added.

148. Robert E. MacMaster, "In the Russian Manner: Thought as Incipient Action," *Harvard Slavic Studies* 4 (1957): 290f.

149. Leon Trotsky, *Lenin* (London, 1925), pp. 223f.

150. Berdyaev, op. cit., pp. 138f.

151. Daniels, op. cit., p. 342.

152. Lenin, *CW*, 14: 326.

153. Lenin, *CW*, 1: 142.

154. Ibid.

155. C. J. Friedrich, *Man and His Government* (New York, 1963), p. 89; Daniel Bell, *The End of Ideology* (New York, 1962), p. 400.

156. Feuer, "Lenin's Fantasy," p. 25.

157. Berdyaev, op. cit., p. 139. This view of a one-sided preoccupation on Lenin's part with revolutionary praxis is not, however, shared by all commentators. *See*, e.g., Meyer, op. cit., pp. 4f. Meyer does admit, however, that "Lenin's own manipulative attitude towards philosophy has been established fairly well." Ibid. *See also* Wetter, *Der dialektische Materialismus*, pp. 132ff.

158. Jordan, *Philosophy and Ideology*, p. 445.

159. Lenin, *CW*, 14: 325. Emphases added.

160. Ibid.

161. Ibid., p. 326

162. For the definitive confutation of historicism, see Karl R. Popper, *The Poverty of Historicism* (New York, 1961). *See also* Gordon Leff, *History and Social Theory* (London, 1969) and *The Tyranny of Concepts* (London, 1969).

163. Quoted by Costello, op. cit., p. 396. *See also* Jordan, *Philosophy and Ideology*, p. 446.

164. E. J. Hobsbawm, "Marx's Contribution to Historiography" in Robin Blackburn, ed., *Ideology and Social Science* (London, 1972), p. 275.

165. For an extensive critique of Marxist-Leninist historicism, *see* Jordan, *Philosophy and Ideology*, pp. 433ff and *The Evolution of Dialectical Materialism*, pp. 353ff.

166. Lenin, *CW*, 5: 370.

167. Ibid., pp. 368f.

168. Ibid., p. 355.

169. Ibid., pp. 367, 369.

170. Ibid., pp. 355, 386, respectively. Emphases added.

171. Berdyaev, op. cit., pp. 139f.

172. Daniels, op. cit., pp. 344f. Emphases added.

173. Jordan, *Evolution of Dialectical Materialism*, p. 238.

174. Ibid., p. 238.

175. *See*, e.g., Lieber, op. cit., pp. 154ff.

176. Feuer, "Lenin's Fantasy," p. 25. Joravsky adds that *"Materialism and Empirio-Criticism* was clearly a step towards the frightful style of quote and club that would dominate Soviet philosophical writing for a generation following 1930." Joravsky, op. cit., p. 36.

177. For a short analysis of this aspect of Leninism in Soviet Marxism, *see* H. Marcuse, *Soviet Marxism: A Critical Analysis* (1958; reprint ed., London, 1971), pp. 101ff.

178. Mannheim, in his description of the 'utopian' character of Marxism, has made this point very cogently: "It becomes the task of the political leader deliberately to reinforce those forces the dynamics of which seem to move in the direction desired by him, and to turn in his own direction or at least to render impotent those which seem to be to his disadvantage. Historical experience becomes thereby a truly strategic plan. Everything in history may now be experienced as an intellectually and volitionally controllable phenomenon." Karl Mannheim, *Ideology and Utopia* (London, 1936, reprinted 1972), p. 222.

179. Robert K. Merton, *Social Theory and Social Structure* (Glencoe, 1957), p. 423. Emphases added. *See also* Erich Hahn, "Zur Kritik des bürgerlichen Bewusstseins" in Kurt Lenk, ed., *Ideologie: Ideologiekritik und Wissenssoziologie* (Berlin, 1967), pp. 144ff.

180. Quoted in Merton, op. cit., p. 421.

181. Ibid., pp. 421f.

182. Heisenberg, *Physics and Philosophy*, pp. 71ff.

183. Quoted in Jordan, *Philosophy and Ideology*, p. 470.

184. Quoted in ibid., p. 483.

185. *See* Marcuse, op. cit., pp. 16f.

186. Lenin, *Selected Works* (Moscow, 1967), 1: 644. Emphasis added.

4

MANNHEIM, THE SOCIOLOGY OF KNOWLEDGE AND THE CONCEPT OF IDEOLOGY

THE NATURE OF MANNHEIM'S CONCEPTION OF IDEOLOGY

INTRODUCTION: HISTORIOGRAPHY, HISTORISM, AND THE ROOTS OF IDEOLOGY

One of the more symptomatic vicissitudes of the concept of ideology in modern intellectual history is to be found in the progression of historiography itself, and particularly in the development of the relationship between it and that aspect of the historian's concern which, since the days of Voltaire and Herder, is known as the 'philosophy of history.' This name is, of course, neither clear-cut in meaning nor entirely uncontroversial in the designation of a legitimate subject matter. Although not everybody has gone as far as Jacob Burckhardt, the eminent nineteenth-century Swiss historian, who simply pronounced it to be meaningless, a 'centaur' in the form of a *contradictio in adjecto*, many have, nevertheless, expressed a deep discomfort with the conjunction of the philosophical with the historical modalities of thought—with the marriage between what is perceived as a purely analytical or abstract universe of discourse and that of a factual or empirical discipline.[1] But if we define the 'philosophy of history' as encompassing the attempt to determine, in one way or another, the meaning or significance of the historical process as a whole, including the methodological implications and metatheoretical feasibility of such an intendment, then it does constitute an intellectual tradition of the first order, not only within historiography itself but also in European history of ideas as such.[2] It is a rich, complex, and variform body of thought which stretches from Vico's once long-neglected *Scienza nuovo* to not only Toynbee's massive *A Study of History* and Spengler's brooding *The Decline of the West* (two of this century's least optimistic and at the same time most discredited 'philosophies of history'), but also to the more positive and methodological contributions of, for example, such distinguished philosophic historians as Benedetto Croce, Wilhelm Dilthey, and R. G. Collingwood.[3] It is also within this tradition that we have to place not only Hegel, the great synthesizer of the contributions to the philosophy of history of Voltaire and Kant, as well as the scattered historical notions of the German romantic school of Herder, Schiller, Fichte, and Schelling, but also Marx, whose transformation and extension of Hegel's logic of history has left us with what to this day remains the most consistent and adamant effort in interpreting human history not simply as a series of small-scale events of varying magnitude and importance but, on the contrary, as a self-sustaining and intelligible whole.[4]

However, despite the scope and suggestiveness of this post-Enlightenment body of historicophilosophical thought, and notwithstanding the immense influence of Hegel and Marx in other areas of the history of ideas, the impact of the philosophy of history on nineteenth-century historiography was not of any great consequence. On the contrary, what characterizes the intellectual development of this age is above all the upsurge during it of an immense antispeculative thrust and a profound criticism of all metaphysical or projective propositions about historical phenomena.[5] In Collingwood's words, this was a time when the "ideal of universal history was swept aside as a vain dream, and the ideal of historical literature became the monograph."[6] This is true in particular of the great German school of critical historians, whose 'historical realism' became the dominant model for almost all historical scholarship in Europe during and after the middle of the century.

Leopold von Ranke set the tone with what has been called his rigorous objectivism, the sole purpose of which was to show "how it actually happened" —a goal which he pursued to such an extent that, as Ernst Cassirer has written, "he would have preferred 'to blot out his own self likewise,' so to speak, in order to let only the historical events and mighty forces of the centuries be heard."[7] Similarly, if perhaps to even greater effect, Theodor Mommsen stressed and perfected the accurate ascertainment of facts through the treatment of literary sources by means of philological criticism, a method which emphasized the decomposition of historical narrative into its component parts, the more trustworthy of which were then submitted to the even severer test of internal criticism.[8] The quintessence of the historiographical tenets submitted by these two historians—by many regarded as the two most eminent of their century—has been summarized by Collingwood as consisting of two cardinal rules, both of which were to secure and thus serve the objectivity of historical facts: the first is that knowledge of historical events can only be acquired by the separate ascertainment of each fact by itself; and, secondly, once determined, each such independent fact is to be regarded without judgment by the historian, that is, it has to be viewed as existing by itself and therefore apart from the knower's cognition or evaluation of it.[9] The ultimate norm for the historian's craft thus became the objective analysis of the facticity of history by means of the most rigorous, discriminative, and critical methods available to historical scholarship. In consequence, although the criteria propounded for it came short of treating the study of history as a 'science' in the full positivistic sense prevalent at the time (no 'laws' of history were to be sought, only 'facts'), they are as far removed from the projective, holistic, and inherently normative concerns of the philosophy of history as it is possible to get.[10]

"Ranke," E. H. Carr writes with his characteristic and keen irony, "piously believed that divine providence would take care of the meaning of history if he took care of the facts," and adds that the nineteenth-century historians following in his footsteps continued in being generally indifferent to the philosophy of history simply because the facts so taken care of "were on the whole satisfactory," and therefore the "inclination to ask and answer awkward questions about them was correspondingly weak." In his picturesque words, this "was the age of innocence, and historians walked in the Garden of Eden, without a scrap of philosophy to cover them, naked and unashamed before the god of history."[11] However, this faith in the facts of history and the optimism fostered by them was not to be sustained for long after the turn of the century. There were various reasons, both historical and methodological, for this somewhat abrupt reawakening to philosophical questions on the part of German historians.

Historically, World War I had given a tremendous jolt to the nineteenth-century belief in material progress and divine providence, and this was particularly keenly felt within a country and a culture which had been shattered to its roots by that great conflagration. Facts were no longer as satisfactory as they previously seemed to have been, and it was difficult if not impossible to see—or at least to accept—the meaning of it all as one looked over the fields and crosses of Verdun. "We no longer theorize under the protection of a stable order," Ernst Troeltsch, the eminent German historian and theologian, intoned painfully and pondorously, shortly before his death in 1923, " . . . but in the midst of a storm of changes, within which each and every familiar word is tested for its practical utility, with the result that much which previously was real or at least was viewed with utter seriousness, has now become meaningless."[12] He was certainly not alone in holding these doom-filled sentiments about a crisis in historiography, nor was he the only one to advocate a return, on the part of historians, to the philosophical analysis of history and its meaning.[13] Indeed, so profound was this change of heart that Wilhelm Bauer, a German historian writing about his colleagues shortly after the war, felt compelled to reflect openly on the fact that in his time the philosophy of history was being much more actively pursued than the writing of history itself.[14]

But if historically it was the nature and outcome of the war which made the renewed inquiry into the 'meaning' of history a seemingly ineluctable task, it was nevertheless a reevaluation of historiography which methodologically had been presaged by a set of earlier and different challenges to historiographical orthodoxy, coming to the fore already before the turn of the century. We may for the sake of convenience categorize these challenges as the emergence of antipositivism which, although as a movement it was by no means homogeneous (nor confined to historiography), had as its main theme the rejection of the methodological monism of positivistic thinking and the view, long advocated by positivists and increasingly accepted by historians, that the natural sciences exemplified the only viable norm for—or that it had a monopoly on—the rational understanding of reality in all its manifold aspects. [15]

Wilhelm Windelband, the distinguished neo-Kantian historian of philosophy, gave the first reverberating repudiation of the notion of the unity of the sciences in his rectorial address at Strassbourg in 1894, claiming two significantly different and equally legitimate purposes for the natural sciences and the historical disciplines respectively. The nature of the first, he insisted, was 'nomothetic,' that is, its essence lies in the search for, and formulation of, general and universal laws. However, the nature of history as a 'science' (*Wissenschaft*) necessarily is 'ideographic' in that it concerns itself solely with the descriptive analysis of individuality and the individual origin of phenomena. [16] This distinction and its implications became a basic tenet of antipositivism, and we find it in the works of such diverse and distinguished German scholars as Wilhelm Dilthey, George Simmel, Heinrich Rickert, and Max Weber. A further new distinction, first introduced by J. G. Droysen in 1858 but not fully worked out until Dilthey explored it toward the end of the century, concerns the nature of explanation and how it differs between the natural sciences and—to use a term of his which came into vogue rapidly—the *Geisteswissenschaften* (human sciences). The dichotomy here brought to the fore is that between *Erklären* and *Verstehen*, of which only the latter (which refers to the notion of 'understanding' as an interpretative activity involving a reflective and intuitive diagnosis of the meaning of events as distinguished from 'explanation' in terms of a subsumption-theoretic model) is said to be appropriate within the human sciences. [17] A third attack on the prevalent historiography came from Rickert, a neo-Kantian philosopher of the so-called Baden school who, while he accepted Windelband's view, added to it a second distinction: that between valuing and nonvaluing understanding. History, in his view, is concerned not only with the descriptive study of individuality but also with the normative aspects which characterize all of historical reality in its individual existence.[18] The method of the natural sciences cannot apprehend this aspect, since it can lead only to arbitrary, nonevaluative constructions of the mind, which give us no understanding whatsoever of the "immense multiplicity" of human existence.[19]

What we have here is thus a complete repudiation of the quasi-positivistic trends (and especially the identification of historical scholarship with the objective ascertainment of facts) which had characterized the German school of critical history, and the positing in its place of the *Geisteswissenschaften* as an autonomous scholarly enterprise, defined in terms of its own distinct methodology, subject matter, and set of goals. More specifically, what came to be propounded was what has been called a 'hermeneutic' approach to historical studies, a model of interpretation and understanding which, although it has obvious neo-Kantian (and even some neo-Hegelian) roots, should be perceived not so much as a resuscitation of 'idealism' contra the historical 'realism' of the previous century but rather as a statement regarding the sui generis and 'humanistic' character of the *Geisteswissenschaften* as against the positivistic and 'naturalistic' notion of the unity of science.[20] The issues raised by this early challenge to the supremacy of the method of the natural sciences were only the beginning of a controversy which has continued to rage to this day, not only within the narrower confines of historiography itself, but also, and indeed more intensely, in the field of scientific methodology in general and in the philosophy of the social sciences in particular.

One of the more significant facets and consequences of this challenge to what has variously been called the underlying 'positivism,' 'naturalism,' or 'scientism' of the nineteenth-century historiography, coupled with the demand that the question regarding the 'meaning' of history both as a subject matter and as a discipline be reopened, was the emergence of queries directed at the epistemological status and methodological implications of the 'hermeneutic' method of the *Geisteswissenschaften*. This was inevitable inasmuch as the criteria for objective knowledge in the 'monothetic' sciences were no longer regarded as appropriate for such putatively 'ideographic' and normative areas of analysis as history. One of the results of this was the introduction of a doctrine and movement which became widely known in the early 1920s (although the word itself was coined a few decades earlier) as 'historism' (*Historismus*).

Much has been written about this term, but there is little agreement on its meaning except that it became a weapon for defending or denigrating a host of different and often contradictory positions. "The concept of historism is new," one German scholar wrote in the 1940s, in one of the most extensive and thorough treatments of this question," and its meanings contradictory; it is a conceptual battle-axe which has emerged from, and is continually being affirmed, negated and reinterpreted in the turmoil of uncountable discussions and polemics of the recent past."[21] However, despite the highly divergent connotations and factious character of this term, it can for our purposes here be said to represent the general notion—in itself anything but uniform in its content and consequences—that historical knowledge is in one sense or another the only basis for understanding and evaluating human problems and intellectual standpoints; or more particularly, that only by admitting the *historicity* inherent in these and by treating them primarily in terms of their historical origin and development—rather than with reference to 'rationalistic' categories—can we hope to find the appropriate yardstick for determining their truth, meaning, and/or value.[22] Thus 'historism' not only recognizes the fact that we experience different epochs differently, but also involves (and this is even more important) an emphasis on the genetic point of view, that is, as one dictionary of philosophy has defined it in its purest form, on the "view that the history of anything is sufficient explanation of it, that the values of anything can be accounted for through the discovery of its origins, that the nature of anything is entirely comprehended in its development."[23] What we have here is, in short, the notion that history is the magistra or arbiter of human knowledge and values, and that it itself can only be understood through its own 'historicization,' that is, by treating history in terms of its own genetic unfolding, a process in which the historian's contribution to understanding can never be anything but a temporal achievement of a given historical period.[24]

Two main forms of historism emerged during the first decades of this century. The first is preeminently represented by Ernst Troeltsch in the unfinished torso of his *Der Historismus und seine Probleme*, published in 1923. In it he stresses the centrality of the *evaluational* factor inherent in the historian's work, that is, his existential beholdenness to his own time and culture, and proffers a solution to the problem of relativism—the main problem of the title of his book—by positing the notion of a historical and monistic value-continuity in the form of a series of cultural syntheses, each of which is appropriate for a given age, and with reference to which it should be examined and judged in order to assure a maximum of 'objectivity.'[25] He does admit, however, that this poses great difficulties for the historian; and in the final analysis he is forced to resort to an appeal to 'faith'—both to a metaphysical faith in the existence of such a value-continuity (in order to counter a resignation to an "anarchy of values" on the historian's part) and to an intellectual faith in the ability of the historian to overcome his own predilections and values when confronted with history, both past and present.[26]

The historism propounded by Troeltsch is an example of what Maurice Mandelbaum has called the doctrine of the 'historicity of values,' that is, the belief that cultural values (in the widest sense of the term) are relative to the age or group in which they find their most dominant and widespread acceptance.[27] The second type of historism is in a sense an extrapolation from the first, and came to the fore as a direct answer to the generally recognized failure of the former to escape the tentacles of historical relativism. It is also this form of the historistic doctrine which provides the most important conceptual baseline for that meaning of 'ideology' which will be discussed in this chapter. To distinguish it from the above type we may refer to it as the doctrine of the 'historicity of knowledge,' that is, the broad claim that no statement can be considered 'true' or 'false' except with reference to the time period and socio-historical roots of its formulation.

This doctrine is most forcefully argued by the young Karl Mannheim in an extensive essay titled "Historism," published only one year after Troeltsch's book in the influential journal *Archiv für Sozialwissenschaft und Sozialpolitik*. The analysis presented in it bears directly on Troeltsch's discussion of the same topic, to which Mannheim also gives detailed and sympathetic attention before proceeding to state his own point of view. "No historical propositions are possible," he writes in his introduction, in full agreement with Troeltsch, "which are not historicophilosophically penetrated by the observer."[28] This is an inescapable and at the same time a profound fact, and as a result we have to accept the nature of historism as "a sprititual power, which has to be faced, whether one likes it or not."[29] The imperativeness of this task follows from the recognition that historism has become "the true bearer of our *Weltanschauung*, a principle which, with an invisible hand, organizes not only all human studies, but also everyday life."[30] Having established his acceptance of Troeltsch's standpoint in this respect, he proceeds, however, to draw conclusions from these premises which clearly go beyond, and at certain decisive points oppose, those which Troeltsch had presented only a year earlier.

The most crucial of these is his insistence on the fact that the central issue which has to be faced, once the basic validity of the thesis of the existential beholdenness of historical thought is accepted, is not in the first place the crisis of *values* with which it confronts the *Geisteswissenschaften*, but a deeper crisis pertaining to *rationality*. Troeltsch, by accepting the doctrine of the preeminence of values in historical understanding (and in this he had followed in Rickert's footsteps), was unable to perceive this consequence, and as a result also failed not only in 'thinking through' historism, but also in escaping the dead-end street of relativism. "Historism is a *Weltanschauung*," he argues against Troeltsch, "and as such not only penetrates the centers of our outer and inner lives, but also governs our thinking, and therefore affects science and scientific methodology, logic, epistemology and ontology."[31] As a historiographical claim this is certainly the reintroduction, with a vengeance, of philosophy into the historian's chambers, at the same time as it is an 'historicization' of philosophy which lacks nothing in boldness and extensity.

Two seminal aspects of this doctrine are of immediate importance to the present discussion. The first is Mannheim's explicit emphasis on the dialectical and holistic nature of the dynamism of man's intellectual development and historical consciousness. Indeed, the Hegelian roots of his conception of the dialectical movement of not only history but of thought itself are clearly recognizable; and we know that Mannheim came to be nurtured by them through his association with Georg Lukács (a fellow Hungarian) and especially through his reading of the latter's *History and Class Consciousness*, published the same year as Troeltsch's work, to which he gives a glowing reference towards the end of his essay.[32] The second important element is closely connected with the first; indeed, it provides the former with its logical and epistemological rationale, at the same time as it contains his specification of the consequences of historism for the concept of rationality itself. As such it also constitutes his counterargument to the charge of relativism levelled against historism along all points of the intellectual spectrum of his time.

Mannheim's basic response to this charge is that it is based on a conception of reason which is no longer philosophically tenable or intellectually defensible in view of the advancement achieved by man's contemporary historicophilosophical insights. In barest outline, his argument is that the principle of the autonomy of the cognitive spheres so typical of the Enlightenment and the nineteenth century is no longer valid; only as long as this axiom and its corollaries are unquestionably accepted has the traditional concept of relativism (and that of absolute truth) any application. It is, furthermore, totally unacceptable and indeed a begging of the question "to negate or refute a new philosophy—based on a new analytic foundation—in terms of the premises of a previous system, simply because it contradicts the assumptions grounded in the latter."[33] On the contrary, he insists, any argument for or against a theoretical system has to go beyond the cognitive delimitations of thought and refer to its existential and historical roots.

We also have the introduction if not development of a third theme in this early essay, one which would become increasingly dominant in the subsequent growth of Mannheim's thought. For Lukács not only introduced Hegelian aspects to Mannheim's thinking; more importantly and equally unsurprisingly, he led Mannheim to assimilate certain Marxist notions as well, leading him to extend the implications of historism beyond the confines of historiography. This extension lies in the introduction of sociopolitical factors into his analysis; and although it is already in-cipient in the above essay, it receives its most explicit and thorough explication in *Ideology and Utopia*. This study, Mannheim's first book and major work, not only immediately established his repu-tation in the scholarly world, but also made him known as being foremost an innovative sociologist rather than a philosopher of history. This extension of historism to the sociological analysis of the nature, causes, and consequences of the inherent variability of thought became the task of what he first called (in a following essay) "Die Soziologie des Wissens," and thereafter simply "Wis-senssoziologie" (not entirely unambiguously translated into Eng-lish as the "sociology of knowledge").[34] It is, as we shall see very shortly, in his elaboration of this new discipline, to which his analysis of historism had led him, that he develops that conception of ideology with which his name is closely associated in the history of ideas.

'IDEOLOGY' AND THE 'SOCIOLOGY OF KNOWLEDGE'

"What unites historism and Marxism from the point of view of German sociology," Kurt Lenk has written in his extensive analy-sis of *Marx und der Wissenssoziologie*, "is the comprehension of mental categories and images as expressions of underlying onto-logical realities."[35] The essays contained in Mannheim's *Ideology and Utopia* probably constitute the most prominent analytic work in which this theme is presented and the differing traditions of historism and certain Marxian tenets are fused and synthesized into a new theoretical configuration.[36] In more specific terms, the proposition which Mannheim took over and developed from these two sources is the view that human thought can arise and function only in a specific sociohistorical milieu, a phenomenon which he also refers to as the "existential determination of thought,"or more succinctly—following in Marx's rather than in Lenin's footsteps—as "ideology."

However, and this is important to notice immediately, while for Marx this discovery of the 'ideological' nature of thought had primarily a *concrete* import, leading to the call for deep-rooted societal changes involving the radical dissolution of the ubiquitous reificatory structures affecting both knowledge and human existence in capitalist society, Mannheim's predominating response to it (at least up to *Ideology and Utopia*) was not political in the above sense but was quite clearly *methodological* in essence. Instead of the *Theses on Feuerbach* of Marx's critique of ideology (in which he had presented us with the famous call to philosophers to rise up and change the world rather than to indulge in the contemplative life with its sedentary lucubrations over its nature) Mannheim insists on the resolute 'thinking through' of the philosophical and cognitive implications of the phenomenon of ideology, since in his view it is these in the first place which lie at the heart of the contemporary predicament of thought, and not the 'alienating' structures of a noncognitive or 'material' nature.[37] Since this predicament is central to *Verstehen*, it is vital that before anything else we turn to an analysis of those factors "which are inevitably forcing more and more persons to reflect not merely about the things of the world, but about thinking itself and even here not so much about truth in itself, as about the alarming fact that the same world can appear differently to different observers."[38] As the reader will notice, this is the same issue which Mannheim had tackled some years earlier in his analysis of Troeltsch's historism; but whereas he there posed the methodological question regarding the possibility and validity of *historical* knowledge in view of the inevitable beholdenness of the historian's principles, criteria, and viewpoints to his existential situation, he here extends this historiographical problem into a much broader realm: to the relationship between knowledge and social existence per se.[39] "What we are concerned with here," he writes, "is the elemental perplexity of our time, which can be epitomized in the symptomatic question 'How is it possible for man to continue to think and live in a time when the problems of ideology and utopia are being radically raised and thought through in all their implications?' "[40] At the same time he posits a query which directs itself as much to Marx's analysis of ideology and sociopolitical reality as to the contemporary flux of politics: the question how a *science* of politics is "possible in the face of the inherently ideological character of all thought."[41] This is the main theme of his book as a whole, and as such it is also an explicit specification of the 'noological' (to use his terminology) and methodological rather than politicoeconomic character of 'ideology'—an emphasis which decisively propels him beyond the Marxian conception, at the same time as it is a development in his thought which his previous grappling with historism had made all but inevitable.

In what way, then, does Mannheim's conceptualization of "ideology" lead him beyond Marx at the same time as he fuses the Marxian concept with the historistic tenets highlighted above? Mannheim gives his answer to this question on the first pages of the second essay in *Ideology and Utopia*—an essay so central to his argumentation as whole that it bears the same title as the book itself. True to his historistic past, he proceeds not by simply defining 'ideology' but rather by tracing the historical development of its meaning—a procedure which he had previously justified on the basis that the very "ontology of the concept is involved in its historical changes."[42]

In this historical transmutation of 'ideology' he finds, first of all, a distinction between what he calls the 'particular' and the 'total' conception or usage of the term. Briefly, the distinction presented here is between a psychological and a noological meaning of "ideology," between ascribing sociohistorical determination to, on the one hand, the *motives* behind the given ideas of a person and, on the other, to his total *Weltanschauung*, including the conceptual foundations underlying it. Thus, while the 'particular' conception of ideology operates with a psychology of interests (albeit that these are viewed as a function of the 'social situation'), the "total conception uses a more formal functional analysis, without reference to motivations, confining itself to an objective description of the structural differences in minds operating in different social settings."[43] While the attribution of 'ideological' motives to the ideas of somebody does not entail the impossibility or rejection of a commonly shared frame of reference, including commonly shared criteria of validity, the total conception posits "fundamentally divergent thought-systems" and thus the structural impossibility of a common noological basis for discourse.[44]

Historically, Mannheim writes, the 'particular' conception antedates the 'total' conception, and this for very good historico-philosophical reasons. Thus, while the notion of ascribing 'ideological' motives to particular ideas or doctrines is already incipient in, for example, Bacon's theory of the 'idols' and in Machiavelli's trenchant observation that the "thought of the palace is one thing, and that of the public square another," the total conception—that is, the introduction of 'ideology' to the ontological and noological levels—only became possible when the notion of a dynamically changing historical and holistic consciousness emerged, treating ideas not as abstract and unchanging, atomistic entities but as products of a synthesizing and dynamic 'national spirit.'[45] This was accomplished by the concomitant emergence of the nation-state (and nationalism) and the Hegelian fusion of Kant's epistemology with the romantic movement of the early nineteenth century. However, it was Marx who, by translating Hegel's conception of the 'national spirit' as the dynamic bearer of a collective consciousness into the concept of *class consciousness*, gave the total conception its philosophically most developed and comprehensive form. Indeed, Mannheim submits, what Marx accomplished was the fusion of the particular with the total view of ideology, which now became exclusively associated with the 'false consciousness' of the bourgeoisie as against the putatively nonideological nature of the consciousness of the proletariat.[46]

However, Mannheim continues, this attribution of 'ideology' only to the bourgeois class can no longer be sustained in the face of post-Marxian changes in sociohistorical understanding. He here clearly has in mind primarily the movement of the *Geisteswissenschaften*, and particularly the emergence of the notion, which he had previously analyzed in his article on historism (and subsequent papers), of the existential determination of thought. "As a result," he notes, "we are entering upon a new epoch in social and intellectual development," in which the "analysis of thought and ideas in terms of ideologies is much too wide in its application and much too important a weapon to become the permanent monopoly of any one party."[47] On the basis of this view of the transformation of the applicability of 'ideology' he then introduces his *second* important distinction:

As long as one does not call his own position into question but regards it as absolute, while interpreting his opponents' ideas as a mere function of the social positions they occupy, the decisive step forward has not yet been taken. It is true, of course, that in such a case the total conception of ideology is being used, since one is interested in analyzing the structure of the mind of one's opponent in its totality, and is not merely singling out a few isolated propositions. But since, in such an instance, one is interested merely in a sociological analysis of the opponent's ideas, one never gets beyond a highly restricted, or what I should like to call a *special*, formulation of the theory. In contrast to this special formulation, the *general* form of the total conception of ideology is being used by the analyst when he has the courage to subject not just the adversary's point of view but all points of view, including his own, to the ideological analysis.[48]

With this ascertainment Mannheim also comes to his main subject-matter, namely, the methodological consequences which have to be drawn from what has been described above. The most important of these, he enjoins programmatically, is that with "the emergence of the general formulation of the total conception of ideology, the simple theory of ideology develops into the sociology of knowledge. What was once the intellectual armament of a party is transformed into a *method of research* in social and intellectual history generally." To which he adds that this "sociologically oriented history of ideas is destined to provide modern man with a revised view of the whole historical process."[49] This view is, of course, that of historism.

In outline, the general theory of ideology *qua* sociology of knowledge entails a framework for analyzing the relationship between given structures of thought or knowledge, on the one hand, and the structures of the sociohistorical situation to which all thought-systems are bound, on the other. It is, furthermore, a theory of ideology which, as he insists, involves the *nonevaluative* analysis of this interdependence, in distinction to the 'special' theory—and particularly the Marxian—which by necessity is partisanly evaluative in that it does not recognize the universality of ideology, but reserves it only for the thought of adversaries.

But by what methodological procedure does Mannheim propose to describe or demonstrate objectively the concrete ideological relationship between cognitive structures, on the one hand, and the structures of sociohistorical relationships, on the other? This is an important query with regard to the concept of ideology as a whole, since in effect it seeks a specification of the empirical referents and the applicability of the concept. Mannheim here takes a different and more painstaking road than either Marx or Lenin (and in this he was deeply influenced not only by Max Weber but once again by Lukács—also at one time a pupil of Weber's—who in his *History and Class Consciousness* clearly saw the problematic nature of Marx's theory of ideology).[50]He calls this the procedure of *imputation*, of which he says the following (and I shall quote him at some length, since we here have one of the central facets of the general theory of ideology):

There are two levels on which the task of imputation may proceed. The first (*Sinngemässe Zurechnung*) deals with general problems of interpretation. It reconstructs integral styles of thought and perspectives, tracing single expressions and records of thought which appear to be related back to a central *Weltanschauung*, which they express. It makes explicit the whole of the system which is implicit in the discrete segments of a system of thought. . . . Even after this has been done, the problem of imputation on this level is not yet completely solved.

Even if, for instance, we were successful in showing that in the first half of the nineteenth century most intellectual activities and products could, from the standpoint of their meanings, be subsumed under and imputed to the polarity of "liberal" and "conservative" thought, the problem would still arise whether this explicit reference to a central outlook which proceeds purely on an intellectual level actually corresponds to the facts. . . .

The second level of imputation (*Faktizitätszurechnung*) operates by assuming that the ideal types built up through the process described above are indispensable hypotheses for research, and then asking to what extent liberals and conservatives actually did think in these terms, and in what measure, in individual cases, these ideal-types were actually realized in their thinking. . . .

When the structures and the tendencies of two styles of thought have been worked out, we are faced with the task of their sociological imputation. As sociologists we do not attempt to explain the forms and variations in conservative thought, for example, solely by reference to the conservative *Weltanschauung*. On the contrary,we seek to derive them firstly from the composition of the groups and strata which express themselves in that mode of thought. And secondly, we seek to explain the impulses and direction of the development of conservative thought through the structural situation and the changes it undergoes within a larger, historically conditioned whole (such as Germany, for instance), and through the constantly varying problems raised by the changing structure.[51]

This is a passage very central to Mannheim's doctrine of ideology and its analysis, containing the essence of his historism as well as its development into a sociological analysis of thought. We shall therefore have good reason to return to it when turning to a critique of his contribution to the history of our concept.

Mannheim does not, however, rest content with merely a non-evaluative, empirical, and objective analysis of the phenomenon of ideology. Thus he notes that although the sociology of knowledge is "on the one hand a theory, and on the other hand an historical-sociological method of research," he also adds that as "theory it may take two forms," of which only the first is non-evaluative, namely, the "theory of the social determination of knowledge."[52] For in addition to this first and empirical form of the theory there is a second and *evaluative* type of inquiry which, although it is not necessarily connected with the first, tends to follow from it in terms of an "invisible shift" which "is typical of the whole development of contemporary thought."[53] The "purely empirical investigation through description and structural analysis of the ways in which social relationships . . . influence thought . . . may pass . . . into an epistemological inquiry concerned with the bearing of this relationship upon the problem of validity."[54] What we have here is Mannheim's *third* major distinction in his discussion of 'ideology': the distinction between, on the one hand, a *substantive* sociology of knowledge (to use Robert Merton's term) and, on the other, what has been variously called his *epistemological* 'sociology of knowledge' or *sociological* 'theory of knowledge.'[55] The substantive theory can be said to consist of what Mannheim has referred to above as the 'first' form of the theory and the 'method of research' connected with it (the method of imputation), while in the second category can be placed all his statements on the epistemological consequences of the general conception of ideology.

Which, then, are the epistemological consequences which Mannheim draws from the sociology of knowledge? Briefly, his argument can be put in terms of the following propositions: (a) The sociology of knowledge "has made certain discoveries which have more than mere factual relevance, and which cannot be adequately dealt with until some of the conceptions and prejudices of contemporary epistemology have been revised."[56] (b) The most important of these discoveries is, on the one hand, the fact that when the sociologist of knowledge points out "a relationship . . . between an assertion and a situation, there is contained in the very intent of this procedure the tendency to 'particularize' its validity," and, on the other, the further empirical discovery, on a higher level of analysis, that "the position of the observer" himself also influences "the results of thought," that is, that the existential determination of thought operates not only on the level of the observed object but is equally operative on the level of the observer himself. The consequence of these two facts, empirically ascertained by the sociology of knowledge, is that we can "attribute only partial validity to particular assertions," including the assertions posited by the sociologist of knowledge himself; and it is in this "fact . . . that . . . we find that new element which compels us to revise the fundamental pre-suppositions of present-day epistemology."[57] (c) In view of this, it becomes clear that we "are dealing here with a case in which the pure determination of a fact (the fact of the partiality of a perspective which is demonstrable in concrete assertions) may become relevant to determining the validity of a proposition and in which the nature of the genesis of an assertion may become relevant to its truth. . . . "[58] With regard to contemporary epistemology, this ascertainment of the "factuality of cognitive norms" (to use Thelma Lavine's phrase) "furnishes an obstacle to the construction of a sphere of validity in which the criteria of truth are independent of origins."[59] (d) Thus the *philosophical* consequences of an empirical sociology of knowledge are genuine and substantial, since they not only call into question a fundamental tenet of methodological orthodoxy, namely, the doctrine of the "primacy of epistemology over the special sciences," but also force us to displace any and all "a priori certainties" from our theories of knowledge, in the place of which we have to put the insight that epistemology, like any other aspect of knowledge, grows and develops dynamically in tune with the growth of the special sciences rather than the other way round. Or as Mannheim also puts it, "revolutions in methodology and epistemology are always sequels and repercussions of the revolutions in the immediate empirical procedures for getting knowledge," with the result that an epistemological doctrine can never possess more than 'particularized' validity.[60]

One of the consequences of this evaluative import of the sociology of knowledge is, as we have already noted, that not even the sociology of knowledge itself can lay claim to being more than partially valid. "The function of the findings of the sociology of knowledge," Mannheim admits quite frankly, "lies somewhere in a fashion hitherto not clearly understood, between irrelevance to the establishment of truth on the one hand, and entire adequacy for determing truth on the other."[61] As an analysis it can merely be "a first preparatory step leading to direct discussion, in an age which is aware of the heterogeneity of its interests and the disunity of its basis of thought, and which seeks to attain this unity on a higher level."[62] In this goal lies the second and positive aspect of Mannheim's evaluative conception of the sociology of knowledge; that is, in the attainment of a 'noological' basis for the sociological understanding of social life which, although it can no longer be predicated in terms of a "sphere of truth itself," can still escape the cluches of radical relativism.[63] For it is not enough, in his view, to refute the charge of relativism leveled against the sociology of knowledge by merely showing that the charge itself is based on epistemological premises which no longer can be accepted as philosophically tenable. Rather, he believes that new premises for validity have to be posited, and that despite the inherently ideological character of all thought, there are ideational perspectives which, although sociohistorically determined, are cognitively superior to others. "As in the case of visual perspectives," he thus notes, "where certain positions have the advantage of revealing the decisive features of the object, so here pre-eminence is given to that perspective which gives evidence of the greatest comprehensiveness and the greatest fruitfulness in dealing with empirical material."[64] As the reader will remember, Mannheim's starting point was the fundamental question of how to attain a valid methodological basis for understanding, given the ideological nature of knowledge, and more particularly, of how to create and to justify the possibility of objectively (or 'scientifically') being able to analyze politics, given the inherent existential beholdenness of all thought (especially political thought). In the last passage quoted above he gives us a formal, epistemological criterion for attaining such a basis—a perspective possessing the greatest 'comprehensiveness' and empirical 'fruitfulness'—but he still has to show just how, in concrete terms, this is possible.

As Merton has correctly noted in his classic analysis of the sociology of knowledge, Mannheim gives us three answers to how to escape a view which (as Mannheim writes in a footnote) "sees in intellectual activity not more than arbitrary personal judgments and propaganda," and to place in its stead "the type of inquiry which is seriously concerned with an objective analysis" despite the "irreducible residue of evaluation inherent in the structure of all thought."[65] In Merton's terminology, these solutions can be presented under three headings: dynamic criteria of validity, relationism, and structural warranties of validity.[66] We shall briefly take a look at all three, although not in the order presented by Merton.

Mannheim's doctrine of relationism in his most famous answer to the charge that his conceptualization of the ideological character of thought ineluctably leads to radical relativism. Since we have already seen in what epistemological manner he repudiates this charge (by repudiating the philosophical basis for it) we need not dwell on that aspect; but we have yet to see what criteria of validity he proffers in its stead. He does this first of all by sketching three possible positions which one can take with reference to the problem of the genetic factor in ascertaining the validity of an assertion.

The first of these is what we can call 'radical relativism.' The second is the opposite of this response; it denies that the imputations established by the substantive sociology of knowledge between a statement and its assertor tell us anything "concerning the truth-value of the assertion, since the manner in which a statement originates does not affect its validity." The third position, which is that opted for by Mannheim, lies somewhere between the other two:

It differs from the first view in that it shows that the mere factual demonstration and identification of the social position of the assertor as yet tells us nothing about the truth-value of his assertion. It implies only the suspicion that this assertion might represent merely a partial view. As over against the second alternative, it maintains that it would be incorrect to regard the sociology of knowledge as giving no more than a description of the actual conditions under which an assertion arises (factual-genesis). Every complete and thorough sociological analysis delimits, in content as well as structure, the view to be analyzed. In other words, it attempts not merely to establish the existence of the relationship, but at the same time to particularize its scope and the extent of its validity.[67]

This is the position of *relationism*, which, while rejecting the applicability of the 'genetic fallacy,' does not thereby imply that "there are no criteria of rightness or wrongness in a discussion," or that validity is arbitrary; rather, it insists "that it lies in the nature of certain assertions that they cannot be formulated absolutely, but only in terms of the perspective of a given situation."[68] In short, relationism is a view which stresses the importance, fundamental to epistemology, of the perspectival structure characterizing all assertions. And the 'perspective' of a thinker is, as Mannheim has previously indicated, a notational equivalent of 'ideology.'[69] It should be noted, in addition, that by tying 'relationism' as a principle of validity to 'imputation' as a method of substantive analysis, Mannheim indicates how closely intertwined these two aspects of this theory of the sociology of knowledge in fact are; and this he also explicitly admits when he notes that 'relationism' is a combination of a nonevaluative analysis with a specific epistemology.[70]

But Mannheim realizes that relationism can only be of relevance to the question of validity *within* a given perspective or 'ideological' context and therefore does not solve the problem of how to mediate between, or to evaluate the relative merits of, different perspectives or ideological standpoints. Furthermore, he still has to show how to arrive at that 'comprehensive' viewpoint which he has advocated in his formal criteria for validity, or what he also calls the "dynamic synthesis" of all perspectives at a given point in time.[71] What is thus called for, in addition, is a treatment of the problem of validity on a higher level of analysis, and this Mannheim does by positing an argument for the existence of *structural warranties* of validity, inhering not in thought itself but in the structural dynamics of the social matrix.

"One of the most important facts about modern life," he accordingly argues, "is that in it, unlike preceding cultures, intellectual activity is not carried on exclusively by a socially rigidly defined class, such as a priesthood, but rather by a special stratum which is to a large degree unattached to any social class and which is recruited from an increasingly inclusive area of social life."[72] The significance of this fact—that 'intellectuals' belong to an "unanchored, *relatively* classless stratum"; that they constitute a group which is highly "differentiated" in terms of their social origins and roots; that this group's membership is characterized by great "heterogeneity" and a "multiplicity of... component elements" and so forth—is directly determined by the emergence of a "unifying sociological bond" of a different and more inclusive kind than the traditional structures of social identity (with their ascriptive tendencies) are able to provide.[73] This new bond which unites the "socially unattached intelligentsia"—the *freischwebende Intelligenz*, as Mannheim also calls it, following Alfred Weber—is education (or *Bildung*), or more specifically, the participation, on the part of an increasing number of people from all stations in life, in a "common cultural heritage."[74] The effect of this social factor, and the cultural nexus which it creates, is not only that it "progressively tends to suppress differences of birth, status, profession, and wealth," but that it also fosters a broad recognition of "the conflicting purposes and tendencies which rage in society at large."[75] As a consequence of this 'cultural' rather than 'class' attachment, Mannheim insists, the socially unattached intelligentsia achieves not only "an intimate grasp of the total situation," but because of this is also constantly forced to arrive at a "dynamic synthesis" of the conflicting totality of the social life confronting it at a given point in time. And in so doing the intelligentsia increasingly overrides the influence of any particular standpoint or perspective, since it leads it to think in terms of categories which are characterized, on the one hand, by its decreasing beholdenness to any one sociohistorical location, and on the other, by its synthesizing openness to the manifold aspects of social existence as a whole. The result is the emergence of a body of thought which becomes less and less 'ideological' as it becomes increasingly immune to any one-sided sociohistorical determination. The less 'ideological' thought becomes in this sense, the more extensive becomes its scope of validity.[76]

Mannheim's third and last argument for how to determine the nonrelativistic validity of thought despite its existential beholdenness is presented in terms of certain *dynamic criteria* of validity which he considers highly relevant in judging given ideas or intellectual standpoints. It can at once be stated that this argument is, of the three which he presents, the most *historistic* of his veridical claims for the sociology of knowledge. His argument is, in very succinct terms, that an intellectual standpoint is 'true' or 'right' only when and if it allows its bearer to adjust himself 'correctly' to his historical and social situation, that is, only if his praxis is in tune with the realities surrounding him. Or to put it negatively, a "theory . . . is wrong if in a given practical situation it uses concepts and categories which, if taken seriously, would prevent man from adjusting himself at that historical stage."[77] It is thus a criterion based on the notion of adaptation, and is as such a translation—in its negative form—of Marx's concept of 'false consciousness.' This latter concept, Mannheim writes, in fact takes "on a new meaning. Viewed from this standpoint, knowledge is distorted and ideological when it fails to take account of the new realities applying to a situation, and when it attempts to conceal them by thinking of them in categories which are inappropriate."[78] What we have here is a criterion resting on the notion of cognitive adjustment or adaptation to a sociohistorical situation, defined in terms of the notion of praxis as the epistemological nexus. It is a dynamic and an evaluative criterion because, as Mannheim notes, it presupposes certain judgments regarding the reality and structure of ideas and because these judgments are inextricably tied to a social and historical reality which is in constant flux.[79]

Taken as a whole, this last argument for the nonrelativistic nature of the epistemological judgments of the sociology of knowledge has a certain peculiarity which sets it somewhat apart from the first two arguments offered by Mannheim. We can perhaps best express this difference by noting that while his 'relationism' and his trust in the socially unattached intelligentsia are expressed in *structural* terms in one way or another, this last argument is in essence based on a *normative* predication rather than on a brief for the epistemological necessity of exploring structural relationships between cognitive and sociological factors.[80] This distinction can also be described by noting that while the emphasis in the first two arguments is placed on the *interpretation* of social and cognitive structures and of their relationships, the stress in the last argument explicitly lies on the *judgment* of cognitive patterns and their existential function within a given sociohistorical situation.[81] Indeed, the very notion of 'false consciousness' is deeply normative in essence; and Mannheim quite clearly employs it with such a connotation in mind. This is not surprising, however, since he himself repeatedly emphasized his preoccupation with the basic issues of moral and intellectual order in a contemporary world replete with normative uncertainty and intellectual disorientation. This strong identification with what one scholar has referred to as the 'moral-philosophic syndrome' is also clearly in evidence in both his earlier and later work, as has been noted by almost all of his commentators, both sympathetic and critical, many of whom have tried to explain it—and probably with some justice—with reference to the intellectual turbulence characteristic of the Weimar Republic.[82]

However, it is not the normative character of Mannheim's sociology of knowledge which is of primary interest here, but rather the fact that closely connected with this aspect of his thought we also find a *fourth* and final important distinction with regard to the meaning of the concept of ideology. While it is a very important distinction in itself, it is also a rather perplexing one, since it is prima facie not compatible with the meaning of 'ideology' as discussed above. For the sake of convenience I shall refer to it as his *diagnostic* conception of 'ideology' as distinguished from his *general* definition of the concept.

Although this additional conception is in evidence in certain passages of the first essays of his book, it comes into its own only in the fourth, in which he addresses himself to the nature of what he calls the 'Utopian Mentality.'[83] What we find here is a differentiation between 'ideology' and 'utopia' presented in terms of two further analytical distinctions: the distinction, firstly, between thought which is either congruous or incongruous with reality, and secondly, the distinction between two forms of incongruity. Both 'ideology' and 'utopia' are said to belong to the second category above, that is, to the class of cognitive categories characterized by incongruence, while they differ from each other in terms of the *type* of transcendence from the immediate situation in which they partake.[84] In other words, what Mannheim has given us here is a tripartite division of ideas defined in terms of their functionality within what he calls a 'topia,' that is, "every actually existing and ongoing social order."[85] 'Ideologies' are the most prevalent and, although situationally transcendent, tend to preserve the status quo; 'utopias,' while equally transcendent, have the opposite import, in that they offer 'revolutionary possibilities'; while 'topian' thought (as I shall call it here) is the least common, entailing a mentality which is in harmony with a given situation, thus providing it with a praxis which is required by that situation.[86] Mannheim does not, however, dwell much on this last type of thought, although one gets the impression that it is this form of mentality which reflects 'true consciousness' and which the sociology of knowledge seeks to foster. (But he does, in the final paragraph of this chapter—which is also the final chapter in the original, German version of the book—raise the question of the desirability of such a mentality and gives an answer which is both deeply felt and probingly ambivalent.)[87]

But what, in terms of this definition of ideology as the antithesis of utopia, are the more specific characteristics of 'ideology,' and in what concrete terms does it present itself to us, both in contemporary thought and in that of the past? Mannheim gives us three examples, adding in clarification that these are just typical cases of 'ideology,' since there "is an endless number of transitional stages ranging all the way from good-intentioned, situationally transcendent mentality through 'cant mentality' to ideology in the sense of conscious lies," and then in a footnote refers us back to the second essay for further details and clarification.[88] This last suggestion is not very helpful, however, since we are, as I will try to show, quite obviously there dealing with a different conception of the term than is presented here.

First of all, while Mannheim's 'general' conception of ideology is a *fundamental* category of *Wissenssoziologie* (the noological baseline for his substantive, methodological, and epistemological concerns with the nature and consequences of the link between thought and its sociohistorical genesis) we here have a conception which is little more than a *residual* category of, or a foil for, his discussion and conceptualization of 'utopia.' Furthermore, while 'ideology' in its 'general' meaning is in essence a *structural* configuration, as we have previously seen, we have here a utilization of it which is primarily *functional*, both in a purposive and a systemic sense. In the third place, while here the existence of 'ideology' as a phenomenon is determined by means of a process of *diagnostication* (and more particularly, by diagnosing the putative function and de facto outcome of ideational systems ex post facto), Mannheim's previous conception of the ideological factor is *imputational*, that is, it refers to a procedure which, premised on the socio-gnostic tenet of the existential determination of thought, gives content to a particular historical configuration of the ideological structure in terms not of an input-output and temporal chain, but in terms of 'ideal types' imputed by the analyst to given groups or epochs. Fourthly, while we here have a conception which is *variable*, in the sense that what is 'utopia' today may become an 'ideology' tomorrow (though apparently not vice versa), Mannheim's previous discussion does not allow for such semantic fluidity, since the ideological factor as a structural relationship entails a *constant* meaning of the term, the applicability of which does not vary in terms of how ideas relate to the sociohistorical reality in which they have their genesis and from which they obtain their meaning. That is, although the ideological structure of thought *qua* existentially determined ideation may become weakened—as it ostensibly does with the emergence of the socially unattached intelligentsia—it does not disappear, since this weakening of ideology is a result not of the congruence or incongruence with reality of the thought of the intelligentsia, but of its decreased beholdenness to any particular sociohistorical grouping. Also, while in his previous discussion Mannheim's concern with the ideological phenomenon to a large extent revolves around the question of the epistemological and methodological validity of the sociology of knowledge *qua* theory of ideology, 'ideology' as here defined has no such implications. The notion of ideology conceived of as a body of distorted ideas or as a distortive mentality with reference to its congruity or incongruity with reality, serving de facto to preserve the status quo rather than changing it, has only diagnostic consequences, not *metatheoretical*.

The fact is that we are here—as Mannheim clearly shows in his discussion—dealing with the notion of *mentality* and not, as in his previous analysis of ideology, with the *cognitive* nexus between the structure of our ideas, on the one hand, and the structure of sociohistorical reality, on the other. The difference between these two is of course fundamental, and yet more than a few commentators have either treated both conceptions of ideology as one, or they have ignored the one in favor of the other. This latter mistake, while debilitating, need not necessarily lead to confusion but merely to an incomplete understanding of Mannheim's contribution. However, the former error is outright pernicious in its consequences, betraying (as for example in the case of Virgil Hinshaw's critique) a lack of attention to the text and a bias against Mannheim which is very unjust in the face of the complexity and probing nature of Mannheim's analysis of the ideological phenomenon.[89]

We can now summarize the conceptions of ideology which are associated with the name of Mannheim and the sociology of knowledge of which he is the originator. First of all, we have a notion of ideology which can be called the *general formulation*, which consists of two different but interrelated subclasses, both flowing from the sociology of knowledge as a method and field of research. The first of these is the conception of ideology expressed in terms of Mannheim's substantive or empirical explication of the sociology of knowledge, while the second flows from the epistemological or evaluative branch of that discipline. The second formulation presents us with a much more restricted notion, explicated not in terms of the cognitive structures which the sociology of knowledge lays bare, but with reference to the nature and content of thought-systems and especially with reference to their function within the social context of thought. Since the second formulation gives us a notion which is based on an analysis of how given ideas are used rather than how they originate—what their practical edge is, so to speak—I have called it Mannheim's *diagnostic formulation* of the ideological phenomenon. Let us now turn to a critical look at each of these in the order presented above.

CRITIQUE OF MANNHEIM'S CONCEPTIONS OF IDEOLOGY

THE GENERAL CONCEPTION OF IDEOLOGY

'Ideology' and Mannheim's Substantive Sociology of Knowledge

The linchpin around which the sociology of knowledge revolves is the proposition that thought is existentially determined. According to Mannheim this relationship between knowledge and its sociohistorical setting—the ideological relationship—"may be regarded as demonstrated fact" in those areas of thought

in which we can show (a) that the process of knowing does not actually develop historically in accordance with immanent laws, that it does not follow only from the "nature of things" or from "pure logical possibilities," and that it is not driven by an "inner dialectic." On the contrary, the emergence and the crystallization of actual thought is influenced in many decisive points by extra-theoretical factors of the most diverse sort. These may be called, in contradistinction to purely theoretical factors, existential factors. This existential determination of thought will also have to be regarded as a fact (b) if the influence of these existential factors on the concrete content of knowledge is of more than mere peripheral importance, if they are relevant not only to the genesis of ideas, but penetrate into their forms and content and if, furthermore, they decisively determine the scope and the intensity of our experience and observation, i.e. that which we formerly referred to as the "perspective" of the subject.[90]

Our first question concerns the kind of relationship Mannheim seeks to demonstrate: what is the precise character of the connection which he posits as the "concrete fact" of the existential determination of knowledge. Here we immediately encounter one of the major difficulties with his substantive sociology of knowledge or theory of ideology, since he never makes it unequivocally clear what he regards as the central and empirically ascertainable fact of the phenomenon of ideology. In a footnote to his definition above he writes that "we do not mean by 'determination' a mechanical cause-effect sequence: we leave the meaning of 'determination' open, and only empirical investigation will show us how strict is the correlation between life-situation and thought-process, or what scope exists for variations in the correlation."[91] But if a strictly causal relationship is precluded (and thereby any taint of vulgar Marxism), and if in addition the form of determination is left 'open,' that is, if a specification of the types or modes of relationship between knowledge and social structure which are said to hold is not given, then it would seem that one thereby (in Merton's words) "precludes the possibility of formulating problems for empirical investigation."[92] But of course Mannheim does have certain notions about this relationship, as both his theoretical statements on the subject matter indicate and his empirical investigations make clear.

Merton, after quoting a number of passages in which the posited relationship is expressed in various ways, finds no fewer than five different types of assumptions regarding this connection, ranging from that of causation (despite Mannheim's denial) to emanationist notions of a Hegelian kind.[93] Thelma Lavine notes, on her part, that in trying to avoid the notion of social causation (though frequently lapsing into causal terminology), Mannheim speaks interchangeably of the empirical 'correlation,' 'structural correspondence,' 'congruence' or 'isomorphism' between knowledge and the socioeconomic situation.[94] Elsewhere she indicates the prevalence of a 'structural' nomenclature, as well as the usage of the term "function" in its mathematical meaning.[95] Mannheim's 'functionalist' interpretation of the above relationship is also stressed by both Werner Stark and Hans-Joachim Lieber, although the latter adds that Mannheim did not merely stay within a 'functional' framework of the correlative kind, but also stressed the interdependence and reciprocity of the relationship between thought and society.[96] In addition, he points to Mannheim's Marxian notion that the "content of knowledge and its structure are 'expressions' of social life, which, by means of intellectual categories, are expressed in this manner."[97] Similarly, if much earlier, Ernst Grünwald had recognized in Mannheim's idea of existential beholdenness not only a functional aspect (in which social reality forms the *ens realissimum* of the relationship between it and thought) but also the notions of "emanation" or "manifestation," or more succinctly, the idea of an "emanatory manifestation."[98] Max Horkheimer, in reviewing Mannheim's book shortly after its appearance in Germany, writes (and quotes from it) that he "wishes 'to substitute structural-analytic or morphological categories—existing between man's existential condition and his epistemological forms'—for psychological findings." To which he immediately adds that "what he means with this is never made clear."[99] Frank Hartung similarly emphasizes the nebulous character of Mannheim's central proposition and is especially struck (and annoyed) by the prevalence of "no accident" and "in accord with" phrases in *Ideology and Utopia* (of the first kind a cursory count left him with no fewer than twenty-one passages in which it is used).[100] Finally we can cite Alexander von Schelting, who in his extensive critique of Mannheim notes not only the " 'functionalization' of thought in terms of social existence," but also the notions of " 'outer' correspondence of changes within the mental and social spheres," as well as that of an " 'inner' correspondence" between cognitive and social structures.[101]

We are thus given a multiplicity of notions regarding the nature of *Seinsverbundenheit*, almost all of which are neither precise nor easily demonstrated empirically and some of which are clearly contradictory. This is, of course, a state of affairs which makes this notion easily impugnable and is particularly noteworthy since this concept forms the mainstay for Mannheim's whole substantive sociology of knowledge as well as constituting the basis for his general definition of the concept of ideology. Now it is true that Mannheim was not totally unaware of these problems affecting his conceptual baseline, nor did he pretend to offer a cut-and-dried "prospectus of the new discipline of the Sociology of Knowledge" (to quote the final and programmatic words in his introductory chapter).[102] In a letter written shortly before his death, he defended himself against charges of ambiguity and vagueness by stating that if there are contradictions and inconsistencies... this is, I think, not so much due to the fact that I overlooked them but because I make a point of developing a theme to its end even if it contradicts some other statements. I use this method because I think that in this marginal field of human knowledge we should not conceal inconsistencies, so to speak covering up the wounds, but our duty is to show the sore spots in human thinking at its present stage.[103]

But is this recognition of, and justification for, a lack of clarity and consistency enough? Or to put it differently, does the grave charge of conceptual ambiguity and vagueness—the admitted 'openness' of 'existential determination'—lose its edge once its assumptions are put to empirical test, as Mannheim himself seems to indicate in the footnote referred to earlier? The answer to this query hinges on the resolution of the second major issue confronting us when reading the extensive passage quoted: the question of *how* Mannheim proposes to establish *empirically* the putative relationship— whatever kind it may be—between thought and its social anchorage. If we assume for the moment that thought in fact is "influenced in many decisive points by extratheoretical factors," and if this influence "is of more than peripheral importance," then how does Mannheim propose to demonstrate this beholdenness of both the "forms and content" of knowledge and ideas to their social genesis?

As we have noted previously, Mannheim's answer to this is the procedure of *imputation*. He speaks of three levels of imputation: the level of *interpretative imputation* which deals with general aspects of interpretation and the construction of whole and ideal systems of thought or ideational structures (*Weltanschauungen*); the level of *factual imputation*, on which the ideal types previously constructed are related to the actual thoughts, ideas, or notions of particular individuals or historical groups; and finally, the level of *sociological imputation*, from which dynamic and thus proper sociological explanations of the relationship of cognitive or ideational structures to sociohistorical factors can proceed.[104] Let me immediately say that this procedure or method of research and analysis as further explicated and utilized by Mannheim is thoroughly infused with methodological problems of major importance, despite his claim that it "offers the maximum reliability in the reconstruction of intellectual development," leading to a "systematic comprehension of the relationship between social existence and thought."[105] Imputation, while as such not necessarily a suspect concept in the sociological analysis of ideas, in fact becomes a double-edged sword in Mannheim's hands which effectively cuts off the delicate branch—the conception of the "existential determination of thought"—on which he is perched.

The first major problem with Mannheim's utilization of the method of imputation is contained in the premises of the notion of interpretative imputation. What is the purpose of this procedure, and how does Mannheim go about attaining it? As to its purpose, he clearly states in the central passage previously quoted that this method "reconstructs integral styles of thought and perspectives, tracing single expressions and records of thought which appear to be related back to a central *Weltanschauung*, which they express." That is, "it makes explicit the whole of the system which is implicit in the discrete segments of a system of thought." Furthermore, in "styles of thought which are not avowedly a part of a closed system, it uncovers the underlying unity of outlook."[106] In a passage in a previous chapter of *Ideology and Utopia* he describes this procedure in somewhat more detail. "If we confine our observations to the mental processes which take place in the individual and regard him as the only bearer of ideology," he writes there,

we shall never grasp in its totality the structure of the intellectual world belonging to a social group in a given historical situation. Although this mental world as a whole could never come into existence without the experiences and productive responses of the different individuals, its inner structure is not to be found in a mere integration of these individual experiences ... Every individual participates only in certain fragments of this thought-system, the totality of which is not in the least a mere sum of these fragmentary individual experiences. As a totality the thought-system is integrated systematically, and is no mere casual jumble of fragmentary experiences of discrete members of the group ... As soon as the total conception of ideology is used, we attempt to reconstruct the whole outlook of a social group, and neither the concrete individuals nor the abstract sum of them can legitimately be considered as bearers of this ideological thought-system as a whole. The aim of the analysis on this level is the reconstruction of the systematic theoretical basis underlying the single judgments of the individual.[107]

In short, the purpose on this level of imputation is the ideal-typical 'reconstruction' of 'thought-systems' in their 'totality' as '*Weltan-schauungen*,' and relating these to 'particular groups' in 'given historical situations.' It is thus a combination of a Weberian concept (the 'ideal type'), a Dilthian emphasis (the explanatory centrality of 'Weltanschauungen' in the understanding of history), and a methodological orientation inspired by Lukács' neo-Marxism (the imputation of 'ideal' thought-systems—in the case of Lukács, 'consciousness'—to sociohistorical, and equally 'ideal,' 'groups'). But despite this eminent pedigree, Mannheim's conception of interpretative imputation must be regarded as a highly unsatisfactory synthesis of what are essentially incompatible elements (of which at least the last two are also problematic in themselves).

First of all, while Weber introduced the notion of 'ideal types' as a heuristic device in the form of an abstract construction without empirical reference, Mannheim here clearly uses it—as he writes himself—in the reconstruction of ideational entities *qua Weltanschauungen*, while at the same time admitting that "neither the concrete individuals nor the abstract sum of them can legitimately be considered as bearers of this ideological thought-system as a whole."[108] But if these integrated totalities of thought exist in no individual person, then how can Mannheim submit that they exist at all—that is, what evidence does he proffer that the construction of ideal types in this manner is a reconstruction of ideational (and thus empirical) reality? In this question Arthur Child surely is correct in saying that far "from being a reconstruction of reality, this type of integrated totality would seem to exist solely in the mind of the investigator."[109] And to a point Mannheim admits this; yet at the same time he submits that the aim of his analysis "on this level is the reconstruction of the systematic theoretical basis *underlying* the single judgments of the individual."[110] This is obviously yet another instance of the reification of abstract constructions—of Whitehead's fallacy of misplaced concreteness—so prevalent in the history of 'ideology': a methodological sin which, as I have previously indicated, consists in the illicit traversal of levels of analysis and abstraction, in which concepts which properly belong to the analytic and abstract domain are at the same time treated as if they had empirical reference or application.[111]

The way in which this fallacy is committed in the case of Mannheim is not difficult to ascertain. It is clear, first of all, that from the "casual jumble of fragmentary experiences of discrete members of the group" in question his method intends neither to compile the "mere sum of these fragmentary individual experiences," nor to achieve "a mere integration" of them. On the contrary, and on the basis of these individual or discrete ideational elements, his aim is to *construct*—that is, to *abstract* onto a higher level of analysis—the "structure of the intellectual world belonging to a social group," thereby (in the manner of Troeltsch's cultural synthesis) making "explicit the whole of the system which is implicit in the discrete segments of a system of thought." The result is an abstracted *Weltanschauung* which neither "the concrete individuals nor the abstract sum of them can legitimately be considered bearers of," since we are here dealing with holistic thought-systems "integrated systematically" in terms of their 'totality.' Secondly, however, Mannheim then turns around and maintains that the integrated abstraction which this procedure yields at the same time constitutes the "reconstruction of the systematic theoretical basis underlying the single judgments of the individual." But this he certainly cannot do. The "basis *underlying* the single judgments of the individual" can only be *empirically* ascertained, not 'reconstructed' in terms of an observer's interpretative—and highly abstract and synthesizing—extrapolations from a host of discrete and individual ideational elements. This methodological fallacy also explains how Mannheim can maintain, on the one hand, that a reconstructed thought-totality does not exert an influence on individual judgments (how can they, since individuals "participate only in certain fragments of such thought-systems"?), while on the other he can also insist that this same totality "underlies" such judgments.[112] This absurdity is a typical example of the result to which the reification of abstract constructs can and often does lead. As such it is a product of the synthesis of two highly incompatible as well as doubtful notions: Lukács' transubstantiation of Weber's ideal types into real or ontological entities constituting sociohistorical reality (in his case, 'class' and 'class-consciousness'), and Dilthey's normative notion of *Weltanschauung* as the historical and holistic emanation of actual sociohistorical groups, a concept which Mannheim transformed into a Lukáscian ideal type, thereby shearing it of its immanentalist nature, for which he substituted the characteristics of a 'reconstructed' and 'integrated totality.'[113] The result is reified and ontological holism in its purest form—the kind which Popper has so effectively castigated for its lack of both empirical relevance and methodological legitimacy.[114]

This brings us to the second level of imputation—the procedure of factual imputation. The question here is that if the reconstructed thought-systems produced on the first level of imputation do not exist in the minds of individuals, and if they, in addition, cannot be predicated in terms of the "abstract sum" of their thoughts and ideas, how then can Mannheim (as Child notes correctly) speak of imputation at all?[115] The answer is that he cannot, given the nature of interpretative imputation. It is quite beside the point to ask, as Mannheim does in describing this form of imputation, "in what measure, in individual cases, these ideal-types were actually realized" in the thought of concrete individual.[116] And equally pointless are the following two claims: "The consistent carrying out of this task of imputation will finally produce the *concrete* picture of the course and direction of development which has *actually* taken place. It will reveal the *actual* history of . . . styles of thought. This method offers the maximum reliability in the reconstruction of intellectual development . . . and . . . makes possible a reconstruction of *reality*."[117] To believe this is to equal Baron Munchhausen's celebrated feat of extricating both himself and his horse from a quagmire simply by an exerted tug on his pigtail.

The same judgment applies to what Mannheim calls *sociological imputation*, which stands or falls on the validity of the previous two—and especially the first—forms of imputation. For it is obvious that if he is unable on methodologically sound grounds to either construct imputable thought-systems or to prove their 'facticity' with reference to empirically identifiable individuals or groups, then any sociological explanation of the dynamic interrelationship between, and concatenated development of, ideational and sociohistorical structures becomes a meaningless venture. Such 'explanations' lack empirical reference and thus are but arbitrary hypotheses, equal as "views from above" (to use Ernst Grünwald's terminology) to any other hypothesis on the relationship between thought and its genetic anchorage.[118] In consequence, any 'determination' which such a method claims to lay bare is defensible only in terms of the presuppositions of the hypothesis itself, thereby revealing its arbitrary nature. "Whether this a factual or ideal attribution," Raymond Aron writes with reference to an example of the imputational method in Mannheim's work, "it does not conceal the arbitrary character of a method which assumes as its basis a correspondence between ideas and social situation, and which then regards as a confirmation of this dogma constructions which are only justified in terms of the dogma itself."[119] Furthermore, as Dietrich Rüschemeyer has shown in a critical study of the problems of the sociology of knowledge, the notion of the 'existential determination of knowledge' in Mannheim's analyses appears by its very nature to be not only empirically an inherently unprovable hypothesis but is also a predication which to a large measure is tautological in nature. In his analysis of Mannheim's essay on "Conservative Thought" ("Das konservative Denken")—the main study in which the latter attempted an empirical analysis of his main thesis by means of the imputational method—this scholar has found that the groups to which thought-totalities are imputed are to a large extent defined in terms of the imputed structures themselves.[120] In other words, not only are 'thought-systems' themselves reified and holistic structures, but so too are the 'groups' to which they are imputed; and since both are defined in terms of each other, it is easy to see how any statement about the relationship which is said to hold between the two becomes true simply by definition.[121]

From all these criticisms it thus seems clear that not only does Mannheim's method of imputation in all its ramifications fall by the wayside, but so a fortiori does his claim that the sociology of knowledge is able *empirically* to demonstrate the assumptions of the existential determination of thought. If this is the case, then it is also very difficult to see how his *substantive* claims for the sociology of knowledge can be accepted on their own merits. And, more important for our purposes, it also follows from the above that Mannheim's conception of 'ideology' as an empirically ascertainable total system of thought defined in terms of its existential beholdenness to a given sociohistorical and existential situation loses its significance for an empirically grounded social science.

As I have already intimated, this criticism of Mannheim's method of imputation (and the notions underlying it) is not to be taken as a criticism of the imputational procedure as such. On the contrary, it is my belief that any useful discussion and viable conceptualization of "ideology" will have to include a methodologically acceptable answer to the problem of how 'ideas' can be imputed to individuals or social groups. Mannheim's mistake lay not in stressing 'imputation' as a central instrument of analysis, but rather—to use Child's characterization—in putting the cart before the horse.[122] Methodologically it just will not do first to 'discover' or to 'reconstruct' abstractly a thought-system (or 'ideology') from scattered ideational elements and then to proceed to its imputation to some 'fitting' social group. To do so is to equate 'imputation' with 'imposition,' which in any form of analysis claiming empirical reference is a sin of the first order. Rather, what is called for is a procedure in the reverse order: we have to place *first* not abstract reconstructions but empirical investigations of ideas, beliefs, and so forth, in *direct* conjunction with the groups or individuals which can be said to hold them; only after this has been done can we legitimately proceed to the higher level of sociological imputation and, hopefully, fruitful explanation. Once this is realized it will become clear why the scope of 'ideology' will have to become much more circumscribed than is generally the case, and why the social groups to which a given form of it can legitimately be imputed will also have to be limited.

'Ideology' and the Epistemological Consequences of the Sociology of Knowledge

"It is important to notice," Mannheim writes of the two forms of analysis to which the general definition of ideology can lead, "that these two types of inquiry are not necessarily connected and one can accept the empirical results without drawing the epistemological conclusions."[123] But although he does not say the converse (that one can reject the empirical results while still accepting the epistemological relevance of the sociology of knowledge) it is clear that given the methodological premise that there exists no *logical* entailment between the two, we cannot dispose of the epistemological propositions simply by refuting Mannheim's substantive theory. As a consequence we will have to judge the epistemological propositions explicated in terms of his general definition on their own merits.

While the tenet that there exists no logical entailment between empirical facts and epistemological principles may seem unproblematic at first, it becomes less so the closer we look at the nature of Mannheim's arguments for a sociological theory of knowledge. For it is a fact, and a very central fact, that he explicitly rejects this tenet, and quite openly, at the most crucial junctures of his argumentation, refers to elements of his substantive theory in order either to substantiate or to reject epistemological claims. We are thus faced with something of a dilemma and with a choice between two options: the first is to reject outright, on the basis of general philosophical principles, any epistemological claims adduced on empirical grounds; the second is to give Mannheim the benefit of his own logic and to follow it wherever it may lead—although, we should add, within reasonable limits. The former option is the easy way out, and has in my opinion been too readily embraced by most of his critics. The second is less axiomatic and thus more difficult; but it is, to my mind, the one which is called for if we are to do full justice to Mannheim's assertion, made late in his life, that his thought is a product of an intellectual's inherent and deeply felt duty "to show the sore spots in human thinking at its present stage."[124] If there indeed are such 'sore spots,' nothing can be lost by analyzing his recommended embrocations; and if there are none, or at least not those to which he has pointed, then we can perhaps breathe with relief and relegate Mannheim to that well-inhabited repository reserved for philosophical idiosyncracy and intellectual aberration.

To accept the first option above is indeed to beg the fundamental question which forms the quintessence of Mannheim's whole epistemology: his rejection, with respect to large areas of human knowledge (apparently only the axiomatic fields of formal logic and mathematics are excluded), of the legitimacy of the genetic fallacy. The fact is that Mannheim was very well aware that his critics would charge him for falling prey to this fallacy, and by preempting them on this point he also effectively neutralized any facile attacks based on this principle.[125] Thus it will simply not do to use *contra* him the very doctrine which is at issue and which he challenged with such vehemence. Rather, if we want to hold on to the methodological legitimacy of the dictum that the genesis of a proposition is irrelevant to its validity, then we will have to challenge Mannheim's arguments *against* it, not make use *of* it.[126]

As we have seen above, the thesis that the genesis of thought or of a proposition is relevant to its validity is first presented in Mannheim's article on "Historism." Indeed, his whole attack there on the 'static' epistemology of post-Enlightenment philosophy is an argument against the validity of the genetic (or historical) fallacy and for the fundamental historicity of human knowledge. As one dictionary of philosophy has put it succinctly, historism is in essence the "doctrine which discounts the fallaciousness of the historical fallacy." And since it is also, in Mannheim's own words, a new "universal, metaphysical and methodological principle," he maintains that it is impossible "to negate or refute" it "in terms of the premises of a previous system, simply because it contradicts the assumptions grounded in the latter."[127] Thus to reject it simply on the axiomatic grounds that "the genesis of the principal assumptions of a systematic science has nothing to do with their validity" is, according to him, to miss the whole point of the historical and noological development of the *Geisteswissenschaften* away from the positivistic and 'static' (or 'mechanical') model of science as posited by nineteenth-century philosophical orthodoxy, which in decisive points has been replaced by a 'dynamic' recognition of the genetic and historistic point of view (or *Weltanschauungen*).[128] In other words, what Mannheim offers us here is an argument in terms of what today is known as a 'paradigmatic revolution,' that is, the emergence of a new universe of discourse, involving a radical shift in philosophical and metaphysical axioms or premises.

But Mannheim also gives us a different line of argumentation against the above doctrine. In *Ideology and Utopia* he opposes it by referring to *empirical* findings rather than to the emergence of radical shifts in scientific *Weltanschauungen*. That is to say, while he once again presents the same epistemological proposition (that the "nature of the genesis of an assertion may become relevant to its truth"), his argument is inductive rather than deductive, since the emphasis here is placed not on philosophical premises but on the epistemological consequences which, in his view, necessarily flow from the empirical findings of a substantive sociology of knowledge.[129] To recapitulate his argument: he states that once "the actual relations of knowledge to the social situation" have been ascertained by the sociologist of knowledge, and once he has found, as a result of this analysis, that "we always attribute only partial validity to particular assertions," he is thereby forced (once he faces up to the philosophical consequences flowing from his empirical work) to draw the conclusion that not only is the validity of his own assertions equally partial, but also that knowledge in general can never be true 'as such' but only with reference to a given perspective.[130] In other words, we here have (according to Mannheim) an empirical ascertainment which "furnishes an obstacle to the construction of a sphere of validity in which the criteria of truth are independent of origins."[131] It suggests not only that the doctrine of the primacy of epistemology over the special sciences is invalid, but also that epistemology itself is but a "correlate of a particular mode of thought," that is, that the 'existential beholdenness of thought' applies not only to particular assertions but to all theories of knowledge as well.[132] In essence, therefore, Mannheim's arguments against the genetic fallacy are based on an empirical appeal and, more specifically, on the facts provided by the 'new science' of the sociology of knowledge. In a sense, therefore, the epistemological consequences which Mannheim draws from the sociology of knowledge do hinge, after all, on the linchpin of his substantive theory; they do not do so because of any logical relationship, but simply as a result of the nature of his argument in support of the former doctrine and against the dictum that facts and their genesis are irrelevant to the validity of statements about them.

We can now turn to a consideration of the strength of these various arguments in support of Mannheim's rejection of the validity of the genetic fallacy (and the principle underlying the latter, that empirical factors have no bearing on epistemological questions). I think that it can be shown that in both their forms these arguments are anything but adequate and that this can be done without any way invoking the doctrine of the genetic fallacy itself. We shall first turn to his empiricist argument as presented in *Ideology and Utopia* and then to the 'paradigmatic' arguments contained in "Historism."

The crucial question with regard to Mannheim's empiricist argument is not whether empirical findings have or do not have epistemological consequences, but whether he has been able to show that his own specific findings have such consequences. The answer must be that in his case they do not have epistemological consequences, for the simple reason that we lack the empirical facts to which he has appealed. To put it succinctly, Mannheim has not, as I have argued above, given us an *empirical* demonstration of the main proposition of his substantive sociology of knowledge, that is, of the existential determination of knowledge as defined by him. Indeed, as we have already seen, he has not even been able to make clear in what manner it can be said that there empirically exists a significant relationship between thought and sociohistorical situations. In addition, he has failed in constructing an empirical method for imputing thought-systems to social categories, as well as in proving their 'facticity' with reference to such empirically identifiable groups. In short, the 'facts' to which he has pointed are but unsubstantiated hypotheses with no empirical anchorage in concrete research. This being the case, his whole argument for the facticity of cognitive and epistemological norms falls flat on its face: for if the 'special science' of the sociologist of knowledge cannot empirically demonstrate the "actual relations of knowledge to the social situation," then it can only draw one inference from its findings, namely, that since there are as yet no epistemologically relevant facts to appeal to, no epistemological consequences can be drawn from them. Mannheim's contention may indeed be valid; but he has signally failed to demonstrate this in terms relevant to his own argument.

In turning to Mannheim's first argument against the fallaciousness of the genetic fallacy, we get into a more intricate and difficult area of disputation. While the proposition which he posits in it is essentially the same as the one above, it is couched in wholly different and stickier terms, involving the fundamentals not only of philosophic discourse but of the history of philosophy and of science as a whole. As I have indicated above, it is an argument which is 'paradigmatic' in essence, and as such involves us in a philosophical dispute about the fundamentals of the scientific method which perhaps today is more heated than ever.

Although to my knowledge Mannheim never used the word "paradigm" itself, it is not difficult to recognize that his intention in positing historism as the new "universal, metaphysical and methodological principle" governing the pursuit of knowledge was the ascertainment and explication of what in his day was called a new *Weltanschauung*, and what today is known, ever since the celebrated publication of Thomas Kuhn's *The Structure of Scientific Revolutions* in 1962, as a 'paradigmatic' change or shift in the cognitive world of science and philosophy.[133] Indeed, the parallels between the two are so obvious—though rarely recognized—that I shall not further justify the assertion that Mannheim's case for the validity of historism is an argument which is quintessentially 'paradigmatic' in the sense explicated by Kuhn and his followers.[134] What does need to be shown, however, is that precisely because of this 'paradigmatic' character of his arguments, they lose both their methodological force and philosophical standing. In my view, they do this primarily for three reasons, each sufficient to refute Mannheim's case as a whole.

The first argument against his 'paradigmatic' claims is the most straightforward in that it consists simply of an ex post facto refutation of historism *qua* paradigm. By positing historism as a prima facie paradigmatic map of the scientific world, Mannheim was necessarily forced to submit it to the vote of the scientific community constituting this universe. It is a historical fact that the scholarly community has at least until now not given historism the requisite mandate; thus historism as defined by Mannheim was at best a spurious paradigm, one among many ostensive but unsuccessful *Weltanschauungen* littering the highway of the history of philosophy and science.

Although not as simple, the second argument is equally clearcut; at the same time, it can be said to explain why historism was never to root itself 'paradigmatically' in the soil of scientific and philosophical discourse. Since this argument rests on the nature of, and reasons for, paradigmatic changes as explicated by Kuhn, I shall very succinctly try to summarize his views. In his words, paradigmatic or scientific revolutions "are inaugurated by a growing sense ... that an existing paradigm has ceased to function adequately in the exploration of an aspect of nature to which that paradigm itself had previously led the way."[135] They are the result of a 'crisis' in the normal scientific puzzle-solving activity, of 'anomalies' discovered in ongoing research, of unforeseen gaps in the cumulative process of exploration characterizing science as it is usually done.[136] They become inevitable at certain crucial points in the growth and development of science when these crises, anomalies, or gaps demand major theoretical revisions; and the result is the introduction of fundamentally new theories or paradigms, in terms of which 'normal science' again can proceed as a cumulative rather than a revolutionary process. Kuhn explicitly uses the metaphor of 'political revolution' in describing these breaks in the scientific process, since in both instances we have a situation which is not amenable to ameliorative measures or compromises of one kind or another, but a crisis which is so fundamental in nature that only the imposition of a new dispensation can settle the issues involved and thus bring back order to an inflamed state of affairs. Kuhn gives many examples of such paradigmatic revolutions in the history of science, but the most clear-cut and illustrative is perhaps the Copernican revolution, which involved a complete refutation of Ptolemaic astronomy, including the whole scientific 'paradigm' underlying it. The cut between the two was neat, involving the introduction of a new scientific world view wholly incommensurable with the previous, which was lain to rest in the same manner as the Russian revolution had buried the ancien régime of czarist Russia in one decisive process of eradication.

The crucial issue in paradigmatic revolutions is thus the existence of fundamental problems which are perceived to be insoluble in terms of existing theoretical frameworks. Mannheim, as we have seen in some detail, believed that such a 'crisis' had indeed arisen after the turn of the century, and that it was a consequence of the emergence of the antipositivistic movement of the *Geisteswissenschaften* which not only rejected the unified model of science of the previous century but which also pointed to the preeminence of normative considerations in the pursuit of knowledge, especially the existential beholdenness of all thought. In his view, this development had brought forth a fundamental crisis in the conception of reason itself, since it seemed inevitably to lead to the rocks of radical relativism, with consequences which were as significant as they were immediate and intellectually shattering. "What we are concerned with here," we have already noted in his introduction to *Ideology and Utopia*, "is the elemental perplexity of our time, which can be epitomized in the symptomatic question 'How is it possible to think and live in a time when the problems of ideology and utopia are being radically raised and thought through in all their implications?" The *Geisteswissenschaften* had inaugurated a break with previous orthodoxy, but it had not been thought through to the end, with the result that it was stuck in a cul-de-sac from which only a totally new *Weltanschauung* could liberate it. His cure, as we have seen, is to readmit the philosophy of history to a central position and, more particularly, to acquire the radical historical consciousness which historism offers as the only adequate paradigm in a time of deep intellectual crisis.

But why, then, did historism not gain a paradigmatic foothold in the *Geisteswissenschaften* in particular and in contemporary intellectual life in general? The answer, I believe, is to be found in a fundamentally wrong diagnosis on the part of Mannheim. The fact is that the problems surrounding the normative or evaluative element in thought, the existential beholdenness or determination of the scholar's work, the 'existential determination of thought,' or whatever we wish to call the value element inherent in all thinking, were not so crucial in nature that they needed a paradigmatic resolution. Indeed, even before Mannheim the question had been squarely faced by Weber, his erstwhile teacher, who gave an answer to it which was not only commensurable with the 'normal science' of his time but which in one form or another is still central to this discussion as a whole.[137] I need not at this point go into the details of Weber's answer, except to note that he fully recognized the existential beholdenness of scholarly work, while at the same time insisting that this value-relation—the intellectual's beholdenness to his existential situation and his own particular values—should be clearly distinguished from the value-freedom (*Wertfreiheit*) of the intellectual's scientific work, that is, the objectivity of the scientific endeavor.[138] The simple fact, he noted, that two scholars (say historians) approach the same subject matter in terms of different values and perspectives does not, by itself or as such, impugn the objectivity or validity of the respective statements which they may make about that subject matter. Such predications are true or false depending not on the values implicitly held or explicitly professed by the scholar concerned, but on criteria which hold irrespective of the basic valuational baseline underlying them. These criteria, if they are to be afforded scientific status, must be intersubjectively accessible to any competent observer or scholar; or as Weber also puts it, the characteristics of science and logic are precisely such that a Chinaman can be brought to accept their results insofar as the facts or data permit it without thereby accepting—or having to accept—the values of Occidental cultures, or indeed any particular value (except, of course, the value of these criteria).[139] In short, Weber's point is that wholly irreconcilable values can be compatible with the acceptance of the same sets of facts (or of a scientific explanation of them).[140]

My intention here is not to defend or to dispute Weber's argument but merely to show that there was an answer available within 'normal science' during Mannheim's time to the issues surrounding relativity and values and that, insofar as this was the case, he had no basis for insisting on a 'crisis' of such magnitude that a 'paradigmatic' revolution was called for. Indeed, the only reason for such an insistence would have been an effective demonstration that Weber's doctrine of objectivity could be controverted on its own grounds, that is, a demonstration that matters of fact and matters of value are not logically distinguishable after all.[141] As we have seen above, Mannheim signally failed in giving us such a demonstration. All that he was able to show was the palpable fact, clearly pointed to by Weber in his conception of 'value-relation,' that 'values' of one kind or another do play an important role in the scholar's approach to a subject matter and in his formulation of hypotheses with regard to it; but to do this is by no means to controvert the doctrine of the objectivity of the scientific enterprise.[142] In short, the facts here clearly speak against Mannheim's own personal perception of a paradigmatic crisis; and as such they undermine his whole historistic viewpoint as effectively as any other argument.

The third and last argument against Mannheim's paradigmatic claims for historism is an argument against the notion of 'paradigm' itself. To understand it we have to recapitulate the case which Mannheim has made for the inapplicability of 'normal' or 'ortho-dox' refutations of historism, especially for the inapplicability of arguments building on the doctrine of the genetic fallacy. What he states, in effect, is that since historism is a wholly new *Weltan-schauung*, a new 'paradigm' in the Kuhnian sense of the word, any arguments against it emanating from the 'paradigm' which it has superseded are without effect, simply because the new 'paradigm' —*Historismus* in his case—is a totally new theoretical and philo-sophical system predicated on new axiomatic premises. In other words, he is saying that historism and the paradigm which it has replaced are theoretically and cognitively incommensurable since they belong to two entirely different universes of discourse. Thomas Kuhn, significantly enough, has given a similar argument for the incommensurability of different 'paradigms' in the history of science. Although in his "Postscript" to the second edition of his book he denies that he has maintained that "proponents of incom-mensurable theories cannot communicate with each other at all," he at the same time admits that if, in a debate, two proponents possessing different points of view "discover that they differ about the meaning or application of stipulated rules . . . their prior agree-ment provides no sufficient basis for proof. . . and the debate continues in the form it inevitably takes during scientific revolu-tion."[143] What happens to two such proponents as a result of a 'scientific' or 'paradigmatic' revolution? "They speak," Kuhn answers, ". . . from what I have called incommensurable view-points."[144] By 'incommensurability' he here means that the only recourse left for reciprocal argumentation—indeed for meaning-ful communication—once two disputants have landed in a 'para-digmatic' impasse is the extratheoretical instrument of persuasion: and the only outcome of such a process is 'conversion' (or 'Gestalt switch,' as he also calls it) or a recalcitrant adherence to either of two incommensurable and incomparable systems of thought. 'Good reasons,' in the scientific or philosophical sense of the word, do not enter directly into such 'scientific' changes of attitude or standpoint; nor is the mere 'translation' of terms across paradigmatic boundaries enough to settle issues of this nature.[145] Such a translation is indeed impossible, since adherents of two different 'paradigms' speak two totally different languages, even though they may use the same words and concepts. It is in view of this thesis that Kuhn, Paul Feyerabend, N. R. Hanson, and Stephen Toulmin have been called 'radical meaning variance theorists,' since they hold, in one way or another, that "transitions from one scientific tradition to another force radical changes in what is observed, in the meanings of the terms employed, and in the metastandards involved." They, Carl R. Kordig continues, ". . . claim that total replacement, not reduction, is what does and should occur during scientific revolutions."[146] This is, of course, precisely what Mannheim maintained when he claimed that historism had superseded the old, 'static' premises of philosophy by means of the introduction of a new universal, metaphysical, and methodological principle, which because of its very paradigmatic nature cannot be refuted in terms of older principles.

It seems obvious to me, however, that entirely convincing arguments have been put forward against Kuhn et al., showing that not only is this notion of a 'paradigm' riddled with contradictions and a logic which leads to absurdities, but that it gives a fallacious picture of the nature of the scientific enterprise. Not only have Kuhn and other 'paradigmatic' theorists failed to demonstrate their own arguments; they have also been unsuccessful in refuting the view that there in fact exist meaningful ways of comparing and judging different scientific theories and frameworks on the basis of standards which remain invariant in the process of scientific change.

The arguments against the Kuhnian concept of 'paradigm' and 'paradigmatic' change are many; but since I am not concerned with the intense debate which ensued upon the publication of Kuhn's monograph, I shall only refer to a few of these, namely, those that bear most directly on Mannheim's arguments for the radical nature of shifts in *Weltanschauungen*. The most important of these arguments has been offered, I feel, by Popper in the following passage, in which he argues against what he calls 'The Myth of the

Framework': "I believe that at any moment we are prisoners caught in the framework of our theories; our expectations; our past experiences; our language. But we are prisoners in a Pickwickian sense: if we try, we can break out of our framework at any time. Admittedly we shall find ourselves again in a framework, but it will be a better and roomier one; and we can at any moment break out of it again."[147] As long as no persuasive counterargument can be offered against this view, the notion of 'paradigm' as posited by Kuhn—and Mannheim—remains at best spurious. I cannot find that any such arguments have been forthcoming. As to arguments against the radical meaning variance position, the most persuasive and fundamental is what, ironically enough, is commonly known as the Mannheimian Paradox, or the so-called self-referential problem. When Kuhn maintains that no two paradigms are commensurable, or when Mannheim claims that a new *Weltanschauung* such as historism cannot be evaluated in terms of a preceding one, they are advocating—and at least in the case of Mannheim, explicitly so—that no invariant standards exist, that is, that objectivity is a delusion. But there is of course a fundamental contradiction involved in this, since if this proposition is to be taken as true, in the sense that it is put forward in all seriousness as inviting our evaluation and acceptance, then it purports to be a cognitive claim presupposing objective validity; but if so, then it itself is false. As Israel Scheffler writes, "to put forth *any* claim with seriousness is to presuppose commitment to the view that evaluation is possible, and that it favors acceptance; it is to indicate one's readiness to support the claim in fair argument, as being correct or true or proper. For this reason, the particular claim that evaluation is a myth and fair argument a delusion is obviously self-destructive."[148] It is here, I believe, in arguing against the notion of 'paradigmatic' relativism, against the view, as Martin Landau has phrased it, that in our accounts of reality we cannot but "plagiarize the *Zeitgeist*," that the following critique by Merton is in place: "Mannheim's conception of the general total ideology . . . leads at once, it would seem, to radical relativism with its familiar vicious circle in which the very propositions asserting such relativism are *ipso facto* invalid."[149] As Kordig has argued, such circles are inevitable as long as we do not allow for both first-order and second-order invariance—that is, invariance in both observational terms and meaning of concepts, as well as in metatheoretical standards—in the growth of science.[150] Furthermore, it is only when we accede to this requirement that we can speak at all about scientific progress, something which both Mannheim and Kuhn have stressed as a central concern of their analyses, but which the paradigmatic nature of their arguments in principle cannot allow for.[151] In summary, the argument here is that if we wish to make the claim that one paradigm cannot be used to controvert another, or cannot be understood in terms of another, yet at the same time insist that the one is superior to the other, then we need—logically—a 'supra-paradigm'; but once we admit that, the notion of 'paradigm' loses all its force. So much for the 'paradigmatic' nature of Mannheim's argument against the fallaciousness of the genetic fallacy.

The remaining arguments offered by Mannheim with regard to the epistemological consequences of his general definition of ideology are those for determining the validity of given statements despite their existential beholdenness. As the reader will remember, they are posited in terms of relationism, certain structural warranties, and, lastly, dynamic criteria for validity. I shall consider the first two immediately and the last one in the next and final section of this chapter, since it properly belongs to Mannheim's diagnostic conception of ideology.

The first argument hinges on the procedure of imputation; and since, as we have already seen, this method is not able to establish what Mannheim thinks it does, his notion of relationism consequently falls by the wayside. It does so also because it is either trivial or irrelevant: trivial, if by relationism is meant the truistic notion that certain ideas are more acceptable to some people than to others, or that there exist more than one universe of discourse according to which ideas can be 'particularized'; irrelevant, as long as he is unable to demonstrate the primacy of social determinants in the process of knowledge. It is probably true to say, as a scholar has recently done, that Mannheim mistook pluralism for relativism and thus confused the fact that people see reality differently with the view that they see different realities.[152] Had he not done so, he would possibly not have come up with the dubious, if seductive, notion of 'relationism.'

Mannheim's failure to give grounds for adducing this primacy also invalidates his arguments for the special role of the unattached intelligentsia. Furthermore, he gives us no reason to assume that elite education does not produce a singularly 'perspectival' or 'particularist' *Weltanschauung*, despite the putative social heterogeneity of intellectuals. For as a scholar has recently noted in this connection, such a world view can prima facie be considered to be as "situationally specific as all other worldviews."[153] It is probably because of this that Lenk writes that the unattached intellectuals appear to be nothing more than "a kind of sociological 'deus ex machina'."[154] Furthermore, as Hans Speier noted long ago in his review of Mannheim's book, the "very process of recognizing the inferior 'truth-value' of the various views as well as the selection of the most valuable elements for purposes of attaining a synthesis presupposes criteria which cannot be derived from these views. In other words, any synthesis postulates 'non-ideological' knowledge rather than multiple social determination."[155] We are in fact back again at the paradox underlying the basic and radical relativistic thesis inhering in Mannheim's general definition of ideology. Or as Mandelbaum has written of this solution of Mannheim's, if "you are truly bound by your own perspective it seems difficult to believe that this procedure is possible."[156] Also, given Mannheim's 'paradigmatic' argument as analyzed above, Bhiku Parekh's more recent judgment is surely correct:

As each perspective is a self-enclosed world and no one can get out of it, the possibility of a dialogue is foreclosed. This applies to the sociologist of knowledge as well who, despite Mannheim's rather naive theory of 'socially unattached intellectuals,' is as much a prisoner of his existentially determined perspective as anyone else, and therefore cannot have the ability to reconstruct other perspectives faithfully or to relate them to their adherents' life situation or provide a 'common denominator' between them.[157]

In short, given the nature of the existential beholdenness of thought, an appeal to a social grouping—or to what Popper calls the procedure of 'sociotherapy'—with regard to the question of validity is doomed to fail for plain logical reasons; it is as much a cul-de-sac (and probably even more so) as was Troeltsch's appeal to values and value-continuities as expressed in cultural syntheses.[158]

The only valid social (or 'intellectualist') appeal in this connection is surely Popper's, in his argument for what he refers to as the "public character of scientific method."[159] I. C. Jarvie has paraphrased this argument as follows:

Science does not consist in a mind (or consciousness) directly perceiving the true or real. Science consists in a body of theories and procedures which are the outcome of a friendly-hostile co-operative endeavour among scientists to propose solutions to problems and subject them to the check of free criticism. This process is maximized by organizing it within a framework of institutions: rules of debate, emphasis on the appeal to intersubjective arguments from experience. . . . It is precisely because science has more sharply focused its problems and more carefully organized and orchestrated discussion of them (in laboratories, journals, conferences, seminars, etc.) that it has the best claim to represent mankind's knowledge.[160]

As against Mannheim's method for attaining optimal objectivity, Popper himself notes that

the sociology of knowledge is not only self-destructive . . . it also shows an astounding failure to understand precisely its main subject, the *social aspects* of knowledge, or rather, of scientific method. It looks upon science or knowledge as a process in the mind or 'consciousness' of the individual scientist, or perhaps as the product of such a process. If considered in this way what we call scientific objectivity must indeed become completely ununderstandable, or even impossible; and not only in the social and political sciences, where class interests and similar hidden motives may play a part, but just as much in the natural sciences.[161]

Here, I feel, we indeed have the strongest argument not only against Mannheim's appeal to structural warranties of validity but also against his conception of what constitutes objectivity per se.

THE DIAGNOSTIC CONCEPTION OF IDEOLOGY

Mannheim's notion of 'utopia' is perhaps his most un-Marxian idea at the same time as it comes very close to Lenin's conception of a 'mobilizing ideology.'[162] It is also, in distinction to the doctrine of the existential beholdenness of thought (in the discussion of which, as we have seen, he is in his most Marxian mood), an eminently 'idealistic' notion, since it places a heavy stress on the dynamic, causal efficacy of 'ideas' in social change. "The existing order," he writes, "gives birth to utopias which in turn break the bonds of the existing order, leaving it free to develop in the direction of the next order of existence."[163] In a sense, therefore, his conception of 'utopia' is the opposite side of his dynamic and dialectical view of social existence: instead of speaking of man's ideational beholdenness to his sociohistorical environment, he here directs his attention to how ideas can affect it. Obviously, however, not all ideas can be 'utopian' in this sense; for we also have 'ideologies,' which are the converse of 'utopias' in that they do not contain "revolutionary possibilities," or do not "tend to shatter, partially or wholly, the order of things" prevailing at a given time and in a given society.[164]

In Mannheim's diagnostic conception of ideology his central concern with politics shines through at its clearest. Because of this the conception at first sight appears to be an idea which suffers much less from the problem of 'cognitive location' than his previous conceptualizations, since neither epistemology nor empirical science *qua* science plays a role in it. But a closer look at it will reveal that we are here, once again, drawn into a web of methodological and semantic conundrums. The first problem confronting us is that although Mannheim purports merely to diagnose the function of different types of ideas in social systems and historical epochs, he does this in terms of two concepts—ideologies and utopias—which are extremely fluid in meaning, since they denote phenomena which can only be fitted into these conceptual containers as the result of a process of ex post facto determination. Consequently, contemporary ideas cannot, as he explicitly admits, be classified in terms of these categories; for we cannot know if these are to be regarded as 'ideological' or 'utopian' until we have observed their particular function or effect over time. We thus have a delimitation that makes this conception of ideology extremely problematic to the social sciences, which by their very nature are committed to the understanding and explanation of the present, as well as to the prediction (when and if possible) of future states of affairs. But prima facie the concept may still have value as a historian's tool of analysis and thus be available indirectly to the social scientist in that limited capacity. This, however, depends on the acceptability of Mannheim's arguments for the ex post facto verification of 'ideological' and 'utopian' mentalities. The question here is if his definitions allow for such cognitive specifications of the sociohistorical function of ideas, given his premises; and the answer is, I am afraid, that they do not. Let us briefly see why this is the case.

After noting why it is inappropriate to use these two terms in the characterization and analysis of contemporary ideas, Mannheim writes that "if we look into the past, it however seems possible to find a fairly adequate criterion of what is to be regarded as ideological and what is utopian. This criterion is their realization. Ideas which later turned out to have been only distorted representations of a past or potential social order were ideological, while those which were adquately realized in the succeeding social order were relative utopias."[165] In such a diagnosis the "point of departure . . . is a *concrete* historically and socially determined reality which is in a constant process of change"; and more specifically, with regard to mentalities, "we have in mind concrete, discoverable structures . . . as they are to be found in living, individual human beings. We are not thinking here of some purely arbitrary constructed entity . . . or a metaphysical entity which is to be posited beyond the *concrete* minds of individuals . . . Rather we mean the *concretely* discoverable structures of mentality as they are demonstrable in individual men. Therefore we will be concerned here with *concrete* thinking, acting, and feeling and their inner connections in *concrete* types of men."[166] To which he adds, almost as an afterthought, that the 'ideal-types' utilized for such analyses of mentalities "are intended in addition for the understanding not only of psychological facts, but also for the comprehension, in all their 'purity,' of the structures which are historically unfolding and operating in them."[167] What we have here is a four-step movement from (i) "concrete . . . reality" to (ii) "concrete . . . thinking" to (iii) 'ideological' and 'utopian' consequences defined in terms of the historically dynamic relationship between these two factors, and from this to (iv) 'pure' structures "unfolding and operating" in the process constituting sociohistorical change as determined by the interrelationship between concrete forms of ideas and concrete reality (or 'social orders').

What immediately strikes us is Mannheim's stress on the 'concrete' nature of these steplike determinations (hence my emphases above), a prominence which is omnipresent in all except the last step; but by emphasizing *its* 'purity,' it too highlights the putative concreteness of his diagnostic method as postulated in the first three steps. In addition, he makes it quite clear that this determination is possible only on the basis of the former, concrete ascertainments, since it is only after the previous steps have been taken that we can achieve—on a 'higher' level of abstraction—the 'pure' picture of the 'pure' and dynamic structures of thought contained in history. He is in fact at pains to stress that his diagnosis here of the function of ideas—of the function of "mentalities in their social-historical differentiations"—is neither Kantian nor Hegelian in nature; it is an analysis based not on "consciousness as such" or on "metaphysical entities . . . beyond the concrete minds of individuals" but on "each individual mind in its concreteness."[168] But is Mannheim in a position to proffer such 'concrete' claims for this method of analysis? I think not, given the basic premises of his whole methodology and the philosophy of history underlying it.

The fact is that he here operates very consciously on the basis of the historism previously described and analyzed. That is to say, the procedure of determining if ideas are 'realized' or not, if they are 'adequate' or 'inadequate' to a given historical reality, presumes that the 'meaning' of the historical process—or at least its 'direction'—is knowable; and furthermore, that one can ascertain that a given historical 'step' is a 'logical,' 'meaningful,' or 'expected' stage in this dynamic development of history.[169] Now Mannheim does not deny this; to do so would be to nullify his assertion that the 'realizability' of a given idea—and thus its 'adequacy' or 'inadequacy,' its 'congruity' or 'incongruity': indeed its 'truth'—is a question of *historical* ascertainment. But given the historistic nature of this criterion for determining which ideas are 'distorted' or 'distortive' and which are not, in addition to the epistemological postulates of his sociology of knowledge, it is difficult to see how one in fact can determine the *concrete* nature of ideas as they existed in *concrete* individuals acting in the *past*. Such an ascertainment presupposes a criterion for determining *objective* truth, that is, the traditional concept of truth previously rejected by Mannheim. Or in von Schelting's words:

There would obviously be no meaning at all in basing the value of social conceptions upon their role in the social process, unless it is presupposed that this very role can be ascertained, in a way that necessarily carries conviction, on the basis of historical facts, and by means of logic. Without this presupposition the new 'truth' concept lacks any real foundation, *even if* we should take for granted its metaphysical implications concerning the 'meaning' of the historical process. This presupposition carries the assertion that there is a possibility of objective cognition of historical facts and their relationship. Mannheim himself explicitly declares that it is possible to ascertain the contribution to historical development of every 'utopia,' every 'social-historical conception'."[170]

William E. Connolly makes the same point when he writes that "Mannheim's concept of ideology and utopia assume a background of recognized knowledge against which to measure the distortion of a given political interpretation."[171] This explicit declaration or assumption cannot be accepted, however, as long as Mannheim at the same time retains the epistemological and 'paradigmatic' claims of his sociology of knowledge. There is no reason for us to assume that he had abandoned these in this chapter of his book, especially since he concluded the English edition of *Ideology and Utopia* with a chapter reiterating the previous claims of his sociology of knowledge. Nor is Mannheim's substantive method of any help here; as we have seen, it rests on the procedure of imputation, and our criticism of this procedure was precisely that it was unable to ascertain *concrete* ideas in *concrete* historical individuals. In short, given his basic methodological and epistemological premises, steps (i) to (iii) remain beyond his analytic grasp. As Mandelbaum has written, "it is doubtful whether the perspectives of another age can enter into our own perspectives, on Mannheim's view of the matter. Even if we consider the conflicting historical accounts of other ages as part of our own situation

(*Seinslage*) it can only be these accounts perspectively seen by us (not their own perspective) which enter into our judgments."[172] Thus to write, as Mannheim does, that to "carry . . . out this diagnostic method, one must necessarily participate in the feelings and motives of the parties struggling for dominance over historical reality," is to state a requirement (that of *Verstehen*) which the basic philosophical standpoint espoused by him cannot in principle fulfill.[173] As a consequence of this, the last step above also falls by the wayside, since it depends on the former three. It is also, I believe, a highly revealing step, for although it is presented almost as an afterthought, and ostensibly is a step of abstraction building upon prior concrete ascertainments, *it* and not concrete reality appears to provide the baseline for his whole diagnostic method. "Constructive abstractions," Mannheim writes in an interesting passage early in this chapter, "is a prerequisite for empirical investigation, which, if it fulfils the anticipations implicit in the concept or, more simply, if it supplies evidence for the correctness of the construct, gives to the latter the dignity of a reconstruction."[174] Although this statement has certain merits, I think that he here lets the cat out of the bag, revealing in the process that far from being a final step building on concrete facts, the 'pure' structures of thought "historically unfolding and operating in" the 'ideal-types' of the mentalities presented in his analysis are nothing but historic reifications. It was precisely against this use of abstractions that Weber had inveighed; and although Mannheim appears to heed him in the sentence just preceding that in which step (iv) is contained, he then immediately seems to have forgotten this and speaks about ideational structures historically 'unfolding' and 'operating in' his 'ideal-types.'[175] The reason why he did this is undoubtedly his adherence to a historiographical viewpoint which is thoroughly metaphysical and as such untenable. Why his historism is unacceptable need not be spelled out here: almost every point of criticism leveled against Mannheim's doctrines above has been a criticism of the historistic point of view underlying his sociology of knowledge.

But what if Mannheim had disowned his sociology of knowledge and its historiographical mainstays: would his diagnostic method and his definition of ideational functionality (and thus of 'ideology') then be more acceptable? This too is highly doubtful, for various reasons. For one, as von Schelting has noted, ideas that 'break down' or 'shatter' one social order need not necessarily be the same as those that are 'realized' in the subsequent one.[176] In fact, we cannot a priori be sure ex post facto of ideational connectivity between successive social orders. Furthermore, Mannheim speaks indiscriminately of ideas, beliefs, notions, and so on, without differentiating in any way between *cognitive conceptions* and *norms* with reference to what is 'true,' 'valuable,' 'congruent,' and so forth. It is obvious that it is one thing to speak, for example, of the 'correspondence' between norms and social action, on the one hand, and of such a correspondence in terms of cognitive conceptions, on the other hand. In addition, with regard to norms, these have to be distinguished in terms of what function they serve in social action: some necessarily sanction an actual situation, while others necessarily put demands on it and therefore cannot 'correspond' to it.[177] Mannheim gives us no independent criteria for distinguishing between these; nor does he differentiate between norms which actually, in concrete individual beings, are being acted upon and norms sanctioning a social system on a higher level of analysis (including the particular norms acted upon). Indeed, his whole discussion of the notions surrounding the concept of mentality is so filled with vague formulations and ambiguous statements that it is on the whole meaningless.

But we need dwell no longer on Mannheim's contribution to the usage and function of the concept of ideology. Its greatest merit is that it contains a resolute unfolding—to their ultimate logical limits—of the various conceptions of the term prevalent at his time, including his own. As such it reveals the cul-de-sac to which all philosophical, epistemological, and metaphysical specifications of it lead. Indeed, Mannheim can be said to stand at the logical end of an almost Hegelian and dialectical development of the concept, a progression in which Marx can be considered as having provided the thesis, Lenin the antithesis, and Mannheim the synthesis. In having closed this circle Mannheim at the same time has made the concept available for a new lease on life, one freed from the pitfalls of a meaning and conceptualization not grounded on empirical reality.

NOTES

1. *See* Walter Hofer, *Geschichtschreibung und Weltanschauung* (Munich, 1950), p. 10. *See also* Ernst Cassirer, *The Problem of Knowledge* (New Haven, 1950), pp. 275ff.

2. The literature on the philosophy of history is vast, and therefore can only be hinted at here; *see*, however, the relevant essays and bibliographies in, e.g., Patrick Gardiner, ed., *Theories of History* (Glencoe, Ill., 1959), *The Philosophy of History* (London, 1974); Sidney Hook, ed., *Philosophy and History* (New York, 1963); Hans Meyerhoff, ed., *The Philosophy of History in Our Time* (New York, 1959); William H. Dray, ed., *Philosophical Analysis and History* (New York, 1966). Two excellent introductory texts are William H. Dray, *Philosophy of History* (Englewood Cliffs, N.J., 1964), and W. H. Walsh, *Philosophy of History: An Introduction* (New York, 1960), while E. H. Carr's *What Is History?* (New York, 1962) is witty as well as sensible. *See also* the posthumous papers published in R. G. Collingwood, *The Idea of History* (Oxford, 1946) and Karl Löwith's quite different *Meaning in History* (Chicago, 1949), and the somewhat disappointing symposium published on "*What Is a Philosophy of History*," in *Journal of Philosophy* 49, no. 10 (1952).

3. A work (which, incidentally, includes no references to either Vico, Croce, or Collingwood, and only passing remarks on the derivativeness of Spengler's and Toynbee's morphological ideas) on the essentially Greek and Roman origin and the thematically limited and repetitive nature of all 'material' philosophies of history *qua* metaphors, is Robert A. Nisbet's perplexing *Social Change and History* (New York, 1969). For a view that the 'philosophy of history' in its modern guise is merely a secularization of the ancient eschatalogical beliefs of the Hebrew and Christian faiths, *see* Löwith, op. cit., pp. 1ff.

4. On the influences on Hegel's philosophy of history, *see*, e.g., Collingwood, op. cit., pp. 113ff. and W. H. Walsh, *An Introduction to Philosophy of History* (London, 1951), pp. 137ff. For an excellent and succinct discussion of Hegel's philosophy of history and of its influence on Marx's historicism, *see* H.-J. Lieber, *Wissen und Gesellschaft* (Tübingen, 1951), pp. 30ff.

5. *See*, e.g., Carr, op. cit., pp. 1ff.

6. Collingwood, op. cit., p. 127.

7. Cassirer, op. cit., p. 224.

8. *See* Collingwood, op. cit., p. 130.

9. Ibid., p. 131.

10. On the quasi positivism of the historical school, *see* Collingwood, op. cit., pp. 126ff. For a description and definition of 'positivism' as it pertained to this period, *see* G. H. von Wright, *Explanation and Understanding* (London, 1971), pp. 3ff.

11. Carr, op. cit., pp. 20f. Picturesque as this imagery is, Carr was, incidentally, not the first to use it in speaking about Ranke and the historiographical school fostered by him. Karl Mannheim, in fact, two decades before Carr, said the same thing and employed the same imagery. *See* Karl Mannheim, *Ideology and Utopia* (London, 1936), p. 94.

12. Ernst Troeltsch, *Der Historismus und seine Probleme* (Tübingen, 1923), p. 6. Author's translation.

13. *See*, e.g., Hofer's excellent book on the development of Ernst Meinecke's thought, and particularly of the great influence on it of World War I, op. cit., pp. 25ff.

14. Referred to in Collingwood, op. cit., p. 175.

15. *See* von Wright, op. cit., pp. 4ff.

16. *See*, e.g., ibid., p. 5, and Collingwood, op. cit., pp. 166f. For a classical refutation of this distinction, *see* Carl Hempel, "The Function of General Laws in History," reprinted in Gardiner, *Theories of History*, pp. 344ff.

17. For a short but clear discussion of this distinction, *see* von Wright, op. cit., pp. 5ff. and 29ff.

18. *See* Collingwood, op. cit., pp. 168ff. and Maurice Mandelbaum, *The Problem of Historical Knowledge* (New York, 1938), pp. 119ff. Rickert's main work is entitled *Die grenzen der naturwissenschaftichen Begriffsbildung*, published in 1896.

19. *See*, e.g., H. H. Bruun, *Science, Values and Politics in Max Weber's Methodology* (Copenhagen, 1972), pp. 84ff. Quotation on p. 85. Author's translation.

20. *See* von Wright, op. cit., pp. 5ff., 29ff. A classical critique of the historical realism of the German school is George Simmel, *Die Probleme der Geschichtsphilosophie* (Munich, 1922).

21. Hofer, op. cit., p. 322. Author's translation. *See also* the discussion by Dwight E. Lee and Robert N. Beck on "The Meaning of Historicism," *American Historical Review* 59 (1953-1954): 568ff, in which principally five different categories of 'historicism' are presented. On the roots of the term, *see* Karl Heussi, *Die Krisis des Historismus* (Tübingen, 1932), pp. 2ff. It should be noted that I will be using the word "historism" rather than "historicism" to designate *Historismus* as defined above. This seems appropriate not only because it is the natural translation of "Historismus," while "historicism" comes from the Italian word "storicismo" (as used, e.g., by Croce), but also because I have previously used "historicism" in a different sense, i.e., as defined by Popper, viz., as "an approach to the social sciences which assumes that *historical prediction* is their principal aim. . . ." Karl Popper, *The Poverty of Historicism* (New York, 1957), p. 3. Emphases added.

22. *See* the twofold definition suggested by Lee and Beck, op. cit., p. 577.

23. *See* Charles A. Beard and Alfred Vogts, "Currents of Thought in Historiography," *American Historical Review*, 42, no. 3 (1937), p. 466, while the definition comes from Dagobert D. Runes, ed., *Dictionary of Philosophy* (London, 1942), p. 127, as quoted in Lee and Beck, op. cit., p. 568.

24. Friedrich Engel-Janosi uses the above characterization—where, however, "historicism" means something different from my usage—in his *The Growth of German Historicism,* John Hopkins University Studies in History and Political Science, ser. 62, no. 2 (1944): 13.

25. *See* Troeltsch, op. cit., p. 169ff. *See also* Heinrich Rickert, *Probleme der Geschichtsphilosophie* (Heidelberg, 1924), pp. 129ff.

26. Troeltsch, op. cit., p. 175.

27. Mandelbaum, op. cit., pp. 88ff.

28. This article is published in Kurt H. Wolff, ed., *Karl Mannheim: Wissenssoziologie* (Berlin, 1964), p. 246. For Wolff's excellent comments on this essay *see* ibid., pp. 28ff. An English version of this introduction is contained in Kurt H. Wolff, ed., *From Karl Mannheim* (New York, 1971), pp. xxviiiff. Author's translation.

29. Wolff, *Karl Mannheim* . . . p. 250. Author's translation.

30. Ibid., Author's translation. Mannheim adds in a footnote that the interconnectedness of history and the philosophy of history has been pointed out most forcefully by Croce; but it is clear that his and Croce's respective positions on this question diverge in important respects.

31. Ibid., p. 252. Author's translation.

32. Ibid., p. 296. Mannheim also clearly states that his dialectical method is a modification of Hegel's; *see* ibid., p. 296.

33. Ibid., p. 253.

34. According to Georges Gurwitch, the coinage of the term "Wissenssoziologie" was claimed by Wilhelm Jerusalem, an Austrian philosopher who died the same year as Troeltsch's book was published. However, it was used by him as a new nomenclature for designating an epistemological synthesis of positivism and neo-Kantian philosophy. Gurwitch, "Wissenssoziologie" in G. Eisermann, ed., *Die Lehre von der Gesellschaft* (Stuttgart, 1958), p. 410. *See also* Wolff, "A Preliminary Inquiry into the Sociology of Knowledge from the Standpoint of the Study of Man," *Scritti di Sociologia e Politica in onere di Luigi Sturzo* (Bologna, 1953) 3:585. *See also* Wolff, "The Sociology of Knowledge and Sociological Theory" in L. Gross, ed., *Symposium on Sociological Theory* (Evanston, 1959), pp. 567ff. Max Scheler's usage of the term must not, of course, be forgotten, especially since Mannheim takes issue with him precisely with reference to this subject matter. *See* Scheler's *Die Wissensformen und die Gesellschaft* (Leipzig, 1926).

35. Kurt Lenk, *Marx in der Wissenssoziologie* (Neuwied, 1972), p. 43. *See* Lieber, op. cit., pp. 23ff. for a penetrating discussion of the Marxian antecedents of the sociology of knowledge. Author's translation.

36. In the original German version, *Ideologie und Utopie* (Bonn, 1929), Mannheim only presented Parts II-IV of the English version. Part I of the latter was especially written for the English edition, while the last part was originally published as "Wissenssoziologie" in A. Vierkandt, ed., *Handwörterbuch der Soziologie* (Stuttgart, 1931). *See* the foreword and Louis Wirth's preface in Mannheim, *Ideology and Utopia*, pp. xiff. Since this English edition is not simply a translation but a separate book from the German edition, I shall henceforth quote only from it.

37. Ibid., pp. 5, 273.

38. Ibid., p. 5.

39. Wolff, *Karl Mannheim* . . . , p. 270.

40. Mannheim, *Ideology and Utopia*, p. 28.

41. Ibid., p. 48.

42. Ibid.

43. Ibid., p. 51.

44. Ibid. *See also* pp. 238ff.

45. Ibid., pp. 56, 57ff.

46. Ibid., pp. 61ff.

47. Ibid., p. 67.

48. Ibid., pp. 68f. Emphases added.

49. Ibid., p. 69. Emphases added.

50. *See* Morris Watnick's excellent essay on "Relativism and Class Consciousness" in L. Labedz, ed., *Revisionism* (New York, 1962), pp. 142 ff., and especially pp. 155ff. Cf. also Arthur Child, "The Problem of Imputation in the Sociology of Knowledge," *Ethics* 51 (1940-1941): 202ff., as well as his critique of Lukács in "The Existential Determination of Thought," *Ethics* 52 (1941-1942): 160ff.

51. Mannheim, *Ideology and Utopia*, pp. 276ff.

52. Ibid., p. 239.

53. Ibid., p. 80.

54. Ibid., p. 239.

55. *See* Robert K. Merton, *Social Theory and Social Structure* (Chicago, 1957), p. 494. *See also* Virgil Hinshaw, "The Epistemological Relevance of Mannheim's Sociology of Knowledge," *Journal of Philosophy* 40, no. 3 (1943): 59ff.; Gerard de Gre, "The Sociology of Knowledge and the Problem of Truth," *Journal of the History of Ideas* 2 (1941): 110 (in which the author also suggests the substantive sociology of knowledge be named "gnosio-sociology"); and Alexander von Schelting, *Max Weber's Wissenslehre* (Tübingen, 1934), p. 150.

56. Mannheim, *Ideology and Utopia*, p. 257.

57. Ibid.

58. Ibid., pp. 257f.

59. Thelma Z. Lavine, "Sociological Analysis of Cognitive Norms," *Journal of Philosophy* 39 (1942): 355; Mannheim, *Ideology and Utopia*, p. 258.

60. Ibid., pp. 259f.

61. Ibid., p. 256.

62. Ibid.

63. Ibid., p. 274.

64. Ibid., p. 271.

65. Ibid., p. 89fn.

66. Merton, op. cit., p. 503.

67. Mannheim, *Ideology and Utopia*, pp. 254f.

68. Ibid., p. 254.

69. Ibid., p. 239.

70. *See* ibid., pp. 69ff.

71. *See* ibid., pp. 130ff. For a short and clear discussion of Mannheim's notions of 'synthesizing interpretation,' 'synthetic comprehensiveness,' and a 'comprehensive total view,' *see* Thelma Z. Lavine, "Knowledge as Interpretation: An Historical Survey, Part II," *Philosophical and Phenomenological Research* 2 (1950-1951): 96ff.

72. Mannheim, *Ideology and Utopia*, p. 139.

73. Ibid., pp. 137f.

74. Ibid., p. 137.

75. Ibid., p. 138.

76. *See* Lavine, "Knowledge as Interpretation . . ." pp. 96f.

77. Mannheim, *Ideology and Utopia*, p. 85.

78. Ibid., p. 86.

79. Ibid.

80. For a discussion of Mannheim's 'structuralism' *see* Thelma Z. Lavine, "Karl Mannheim and Contemporary Functionalism," *Philosophical and Phenomenological Research* 25 (1964-65): 560ff.

81. On Mannheim's 'interpretationism' as distinguished from his 'normativism,' see Lavine, "Knowledge as Interpretation . . ." pp. 93ff.

82. David Kettler, "Sociology of Knowledge and Moral Philosophy: The Place of Traditional Problems in the Formation of Mannheim's Thought," *Political Science Quarterly* 82 (1967): 402; *see also* ibid., pp. 399ff. Cf. Wolff, "The Sociology of Knowledge . . ." pp. 567ff., "A Preliminary Inquiry . . ." pp. 585ff., and *From Karl Mannheim*, pp. xiff.

83. *See*, e.g., Mannheim, *Ideology and Utopia*, pp. 84ff.

84. Ibid., pp. 173, 175.

85. Ibid., p. 174.

86. Ibid., pp. 173f.

87. Ibid., pp. 235ff.

88. Ibid., pp. 175f.

89. *See* Hinshaw, op. cit., pp. 59ff. Strangely enough, Hinshaw does not quote from the original source to which he refers, but from an article on Mannheim by Merton.

90. Mannheim, *Ideology and Utopia*, pp. 239f.

91. Ibid., p. 239.

92. Merton, op. cit., p. 498.

93. Mannheim, *Ideology and Utopia*, p. 239.

94. Lavine, "Knowledge as Interpretation . . ." p. 96.

95. Lavine, "Karl Mannheim . . ." pp. 562ff.

96. Werner Stark, *The Sociology of Knowledge* (London, 1958), pp. 261ff., and Lieber, op. cit., pp. 94ff. Emphasis added.

97. *See* Lieber, op. cit., p. 195. Author's translation.

98. Ernst Grünwald, *Das Problem der Soziologie des Wissens* (Vienna, 1934), pp. 63ff. Author's translation.

99. Max Horkheimer, "Ein neuer Ideologiebegriff?" reprinted in Kurt Lenk, ed., *Ideologiekritik und Wissenssoziologie* (Neuwied, 1967), p. 296. Author's translation.

100. Frank Hartung, "Problems of the Sociology of Knowledge," *Philosophy of Science* 19 (1952): 26.

101. Von Schelting, op. cit., pp. 100ff. Author's translation. *See also* the excellent discussion in D. Rüschemeyer, *Probleme der Wissenssoziologie* (Cologne, 1958), pp. 57ff.

102. Mannheim, *Ideology and Utopia*, p. 48.

103. Quoted by Wolff in his "Sociology of Knowledge . . ." p. 571.

104. *See* pp. 185f. above and Mannheim, *Ideology and Utopia*, pp. 276ff.

105. Ibid.

106. Ibid., p. 276.

107. Ibid., p. 52.

108. H. H. Bruun, in his excellent treatise on Weber's methodology, writes of the Weberian conception of 'ideal types': ". . . the ideal type is an *intellectual abstraction* ("Gedankenbild") constructed by means of theoretical *intensification* ("Steigerung") of certain selected, one-sided ("einseitige") *aspects* of reality, and consequently *unreal* ("Utopie")," to which Bruun adds the footnote that "In Weber's view, an intellectual abstraction, a concept, is of course always unreal in the sense that it cannot *reproduce* reality; but the unreality referred to here is, so to speak, of the second degree, in that the concept has no actual correlate in empirical reality: it is a *construction*, as well as being characterized by *internal consistency* ("widespruchslos")."Brunn, op. cit., p. 203. *See also* pp. 201ff.

109. Child, "The Problem of Imputation . . ." pp. 205f. *See also* Hartung, op. cit., pp. 25f. Incidentally, Hartung's critique of Mannheim on this score is almost a verbatim account of Child's; yet nowhere does he refer to the latter in his article. Emphases added.

110. Mannheim, *Ideology and Utopia*, p. 52.

111. *See also* Mandelbaum, op. cit., p. 81.

112. Mannheim, *Ideology and Utopia*, p. 52.

113. *See* Watnick, op. cit., pp. 115f. *See also* Child's critique of Lukács in "The Problem of Imputation . . ." pp. 213ff.

114. *See* Popper, op. cit., pp. 76ff. *See also* Gordon Leff, *History and Social Theory* (London, 1969), pp. 167ff.; Horkheimer, op. cit., pp. 296ff.; Lieber, op. cit., pp. 126ff.; Grünwald, op. cit., pp. 89ff.; and I. C. Jarvie, *Concepts and Society* (London, 1972), pp. 155ff.

115. *See* Child "The Problem of Imputation . . ." p. 206 and Hartung, op. cit., p. 26.

116. Mannheim, *Ideology and Utopia*, p. 277.

117. Ibid. Emphasis addded.

118. *See* Grünwald, op. cit., pp. 74ff.

119. Raymond Aron, *German Sociology* (London, 1965), p. 59.

120. Rüshemeyer, op. cit., pp. 50, 41ff. Thus, as Wagner correctly notes, "Mannheim's sociology of knowledge cannot be viewed as a frame of reference for empirical inquiry as long as we understand the latter term to mean procedures based on nominalistic considerations, such as have been developed by Max Weber, or on pragmatic approaches, such as may be traced to John Dewey, or on any currently recognized ways of selecting, collecting, appraising, and interpreting data according to research hypotheses which are thereby subjected to empirical test." Helmut R. Wagner, "Mannheim's Historicism," *Social Research* 19 (1952): 302.

121. Grünwald, op. cit., p. 75.

122. Child, "The Problem of Imputation . . ." p. 206.

123. Mannheim, *Ideology and Utopia*, p. 239.

124. *See* Note 103 above.

125. Thus on p. 22 in *Ideology and Utopia* Mannheim writes: "The dogmatic exponents of classical logic and philosophy are accustomed to maintain that the

genesis of an idea has nothing to say concerning its validity or meaning. They always evoke the hackneyed example to the effect that our knowledge of the life of Pythagoras and of his inner conflicts, etc., is of little value in understanding the Pythagorean propositions." *See also* pp. 256ff.

126. A typical and beautiful example of the question-begging described above—chosen because it is both clear and succinct—is de Gre, op. cit., pp. 110ff.

127. Quoted in Lee and Beck, op. cit., p. 568; the quotations from Mannheim are in Wolff, *Karl Mannheim* . . . pp. 250, 253. Author's translation.

128. Ibid., p. 255. Author's translation.

129. Mannheim, *Ideology and Utopia*, p. 257.

130. Ibid.

131. Ibid., p. 258.

132. Ibid., p. 260.

133. *See* Thomas Kuhn, *The Structure of Scientific Revolution*, 2d ed. (Chicago, 1970).

134. *See* Alan Ryan's excellent " 'Normal' Science or Political Ideology" in Peter Laslett, W. G. Runciman, and Quentin Skinner, *Philosophy, Politics and Society, Fourth Series* (Oxford, 1972), pp. 86ff.

135. Kuhn, op. cit., p. 92.

136. *See* ibid., pp. 92ff.

137. "Whatever disagreement there may continue to be among Weber's interpreters on points of detail," Runciman writes in his short critique of Weber's philosophy of social science, "it can safely be agreed that the arguments which he put forward are fundamental to the philosophy, or if you prefer the methodology, of the social sciences. Indeed, in the half century since Weber's death it has come to be increasingly widely held that with perhaps the sole exception of Book VI of Mill's *System of Logic* . . . there is still no other single work of comparable importance in the academic literature on these topics." W. G. Runciman, *A Critique of Max Weber's Philosophy of Social Science* (Cambridge, 1972), p. 1.

138. *See* Bruun, op. cit., pp. 16ff., 78ff., 145ff.

139. *See* Runciman, op. cit., p. 55.

140. Ibid., p. 57.

141. Ibid., p. 58.

142. *See* von Schelting, op. cit., pp. 157f. *See also* pp. 117ff., 309ff.

143. Kuhn, op. cit., p. 199.

144. Ibid., p. 200.

145. Ibid., p. 204.

146. Carl R. Kordig, *The Justification of Scientific Change* (Dordrecht, 1971), p. vii. For a good bibliography on the 'radical meaning variance theorists,' *see* ibid., pp. 166ff. For a famous collection of essays on and against Kuhnian analysis, *see* Imre Lakatos and Alan Musgrave, eds., *Criticism and the Growth of Knowledge* (Cambridge, 1970).

147. Karl Popper in ibid., p. 56. *See also* Martin Landau, "Comment: On Objectivity," *American Political Science Review* 66, no. 3 (September 1972): 848ff.

148. Israel Scheffler, *Science and Objectivity* (Indianapolis, 1967), p. 21.

149. Merton, op. cit., p. 503; Landau, op. cit., p. 847. Ben Walter has put this argument as follows:

"S-1: All empirical propositions about social life are (a) perspectively conditioned, and (b) therefore lack objectivity.
But it is also the case that
S-2: S-1 is an empirical proposition about social life. . . . Thus do the epistemological claims for the sociology of knowledge collapse in one inescapable and baffling contradiction."
Benjamin Walter, "The Sociology of Knowledge and the Problem of Objectivity," in L. Gross, ed., *Sociological Theory: Inquiries and Paradigms* (New York, 1967), p. 349. For a number of arguments against Kuhn et al., including this one, *see* Kordig, op. cit., pp. 50ff.

150. *See* Kordig, op. cit., pp. 85ff.

151. *See* ibid., pp. 70ff.

152. Bhikhu Parekh, "Social and Political Thought and the Problem of Ideology," Robert Benewick, R. N. Berki, and Bhikhu Parekh, eds., *Knowledge and Belief in Politics* (London, 1973), p. 68.

153. Peter Hamilton, *Knowledge and Social Structure* (London, 1974), p. 128.

154. Lenk, *Marx in der Wissenssoziologie*, p. 82.

155. Hans Speier, *American Journal of Sociology* 43 (1937-1938): 162.

156. Mandelbaum, op. cit., p. 79.

157. Parekh, op. cit., pp. 72ff.

158. *See* Popper, *The Open Society and Its Enemies, Vol. II* (London, 1962), p. 215.

159. *See* ibid., pp. 216ff.

160. Jarvie, op. cit., p. 133. *See* also Anthony Arblaster, "Ideology and Intellectuals," in Benewick, Berki, and Parekh, op. cit., p. 117f.

161. Popper, *The Open Society and Its Enemies*, pp. 216f. Emphases added.

162. As to the latter, *see* especially his discussion of 'party schools' in Mannheim, *Ideology and Utopia*, pp. 131, 141, 152, 163.

163. Ibid., p. 179.

164. Ibid., p. 173.

165. Ibid., p. 184.

166. Ibid., pp. 179, 189. Emphases added.

167. Ibid., p. 189. Emphases added.

168. Ibid., pp. 189f.

169. *See* von Schelting, op. cit., pp. 120ff and his review of Mannheim's book in *American Sociological Review* 1 (1936): 668.

170. Ibid. Emphases added.

171. William E. Connolly, *Political Science and Ideology* (New York, 1967), p. 76.

172. Mandelbaum, op. cit., p. 81.

173. Mannheim, *Ideology and Utopia*, p. 176.

174. Ibid., p. 182.

175. Ibid., p. 190.

176. Von Schelting in *American Sociological Review*, p. 669.

177. *See* ibid., pp. 670f. *See also* von Wright, op. cit., pp. 151ff.

5
CONCLUSION

"Karl Mannheim," Martin Seliger writes in his important book on *Ideology and Politics*, " . . . produced the first and so far the last comprehensive elaboration of a theory of ideology."[1] Hence it is perhaps both natural and proper that we end this critical analysis of our concept with his historic contribution. However, before definitely terminating this study, I would like to point out some of the major conclusions to be drawn from the preceding analysis.

It is obvious that historically the meaning of "ideology" has had a troublesome journey, one during which the only constant factor seems to have been its chameleonlike change of coloration. It is not surprising that today the major problem with the term is its opaque and pliable nature: like a kaleidoscope, it can be revolved to render an almost continuous series of different meanings and refractive patterns; and perhaps because of this inherent unsettledness the most popular meanings of the word are also the vaguest and most encompassing—those building on the notion of "ordinary" or "common usage" (and the principle of the semantic golden mean underlying it) rather than on conceptual and explanatory desiderata. It seems clear that this contemporary condition—forcefully defended in Seliger's distinguished analysis—is a consequence of the fact that the various meanings given to the term by Marx, Lenin, and Mannheim are still with us today, albeit often in diluted forms and interwined permutations. In view of this I have treated these major conceptions from the past in depth rather than engaging in an analysis of the plethora of current usages built mainly on the foundations laid by these three thinkers. Furthermore, there seems to have been an intrinsic need to examine critically and extensively the function of "ideology" as contained in these classic writings, rather than treating them merely as antecedents to conceptions prevailing today. Indeed, before commencing with this study but after a perusal of much of the contemporary literature, it became obvious to me that what was lacking was not so much an examination of current usages—of which we have quite a few classificatory and other studies—as a serious and critical reconsideration of the classics in this field.[2] The result has not only been a reconfirmation of the serious problems surrounding the concept as reposited in the past, but also a reemphasis of the caveat that 'ideology' is a concept which cannot be treated in a facile manner or used indiscriminantly without regard for its historical usages and their considerable methodological deficiencies.

The first and perhaps the most important conclusion which we can (and perhaps must) draw is the failure, on the part of our classical authors, to justify a general philosophical, and more particularly, an epistemological or normative raison d'être for the concept of ideology. This state of affairs is certainly not due to a failure of nerve or for lack of trying; on the contrary, all three affirmed—in diverse ways, for various purposes, and with varying depths of commitment—the preeminent *philosophical* nature and function of the concept. Equally clearly, all three have failed to sustain their arguments in the face of the fundamental methodological and philosophical objections which their conceptualizations call for. Marx's critique of ideology is philosophically as dubious as Mannheim's theory of ideology; and Lenin's attempts to 'ideologize' philosophy left him with mighty little philosophy but an abundance of quasi-metaphysical—if politically potent— rhetoric. Consequently, we will do well not to admit the concept of ideology into philosophic discourse, within which it seems to serve no other function that that of obfuscation. This applies as much to current neo- or quasi-Marxist debates as to the more common discussions to be found in non-Marxist political philosophy. If for no other reason than this, I agree with the title of Dante Germino's book, *Beyond Ideology: The Revival of Political Theory*.[3] For a similar reason I cannot accept Seliger's conceptualization of the term, which makes it more or less coterminous with—or at least subsumes it under—political philosophy.[4] There is in any case no historical justification for a definition of ideology which equates the 'ideologicalness' of political thought with its 'moral texture.' Why give a new name for something that is as old as Socrates, Plato, and Aristotle? There is also another reason why 'ideology' should not be given a meaning which has philosophical or epistemological relevance, or be used in dealing with questions raised by normative political theory: only if we dislodge it from these universes of discourse can it, I believe, be made available for *empirical* inquiry within political science. Also, only in doing this can it escape the heat and the mutually recriminatory charges of the tail-eating kind which almost invariably seem to accrue from the normative or philosophical usages of the term. With regard to this point, an example from the contemporary literature is more than superficially illustrative.

In a debate, initiated in the mid-1950s by among others Raymond Aron, Daniel Bell, Seymour Martin Lipset, and Edward Shils, a thesis was put forward claiming the 'end of ideology' or, more correctly, the 'decline of ideology.'[5] In general terms, this hypothesis sought to establish an inverse correlation between the degree of economic development and the intensity of ideology in a given society. It soon generated keen criticism on the part of more than a few eminent scholars; and the debate appears by no means to be over yet, some twenty-five years after this hypothesis was first propounded.[6] One of the main reasons why this thesis is still controversial today is that whereas the 'decline of ideology' hypothesis was posited as an *empirical* thesis, its critics have, in the main, treated it as if it pertained to questions belonging to the realm of *political philosophy*.

In this respect two of the main critics, Henry David Aiken and Joseph LaPalombara, are particularly illustrative.[7] The former, in a debate with Bell, insisted that "political ideology is nothing but political discourse . . . in its most general, formative level."[8] Hence, and this is the crucial point according to Aiken, to declare the 'end (or decline) of ideology' is tantamount to claiming the end of politics itself; and thus as a thesis it is nothing but an "anti-ideological ideology."[9] Similarly, LaPalombara provides a definition which is couched essentially in normative political terms; for in his view ideology "involves a philosophy of history, a view of man's present place in it, some estimate of probable future development, and a set of prescriptions regarding how to hasten, retard, and/or modify that developmental direction."[10] On the basis of this conception he then goes on to assert that the "irony attaching to arguments in and against these 'findings' [of the above proponents] is that they have themselves taken on many of the undeniable earmarks of *ideological* conflict. Thus, I wish to acknowledge that my own effort in this paper may be in part—and quite properly—identified as ideological."[11] Now it is clear that if there is any irony involved here, it strikes at the critics rather than at the proponents of the decline of ideology thesis; and this irony lies in the fact that as long as 'ideology' is given a broadly politico-philosophical meaning, nobody—least of all critics like LaPalombara—can win this argument. To a degree he admits this when he acknowledges that "the underlying theme of my argument here is that we have not, in fact, resolved the Mannheim Paradox"; but the point which he seems to miss completely is that Bell, Lipset, and others, have not—in proclaiming their decline hypothesis—raised any arguments at all for or against the social scientist's ability to escape (to quote LaPalombara's definition of this paradox) "the narrow focus and distortions implicit in ideological thought."[12] They have been speaking in terms of, and with reference to, empirical phenomena far removed from the methodological self-doubts—certainly justified—of the social sciences. Thus I fully concur with the judgment that "the most alarming attribute of the antidecline writers is their apparent willingness to disregard the empirical significance of the hypothesis in question and to rely, instead, on semantic justification."[13] Clearly, therefore, such rubrics in the literature as "The End of Ideology as Ideology" (to take but one example from this debate) cannot but immediately indicate a use of the concept of ideology which, as I have tried to argue in this whole study, is inherently self-defeating and unfruitful.[14] Similarly, the following charge, also made by LaPalombara, is surely dubious as a bona fide criticism: "It is abundantly clear that those who write about ideology's decline, with few exceptions, intend a pejorative denotation and connotation of the term."[15] Surely, if 'ideology' is defined not in philosophical terms but as a concept pertaining to empirical reality and its analysis, 'pejorativeness' does not enter into the picture. Here, once again, the distinction made by Ernest Nagel between 'characterizing' and 'appraising' concepts is relevant; and my point is that 'ideology' can only be a prima facie fruitful concept as long as it is posited in terms of the former rather than the latter category.[16]

Our second conclusion is partly related to the first, but goes beyond it since it relates to the *scope* of the meaning of ideology and not merely to the nature of its contents. Here, once again, Seliger's analysis is pertinent. His basic definitional standpoint is that all usages of "ideology" can, in general, be divided into two mutually exclusive categories. "I propose," he notes in his introduction,

to call one the restrictive conception, because it comprises the definitions which, like the original Marxian conception of ideology but on different grounds, confine the term to specific political belief systems. The other category comprises those conceptions which stipulate the applicability of the term 'ideology' to all political belief systems. I will call this category of definitions the inclusive conception.[17]

He goes on to describe the hallmarks of these two types of notions.

What defines the inclusive use of ideology in the context of social and political theory and science is that it covers sets of ideas by which men posit, explain and justify ends and means of organized social action, and specifically political action, irrespective of whether such action aims to preserve, amend, uproot or rebuild a given order. [On the other hand, in] the restrictive use of the term, 'ideology' is reserved for extremist belief systems and parties; or ideological factors are held to be present in some and absent from other belief systems; or at least, they are assumed to be more important in some than in others.[18]

On the basis of this definitional baseline, Seliger goes on to argue against the 'restrictive' and for the 'inclusive' conception for over three hundred pages, availing himself not only of his extensive scholarship but arguments which prima facie seem to be as persuasive as they are incisive. And yet I aver, particularly in view of my previous analysis, that it is precisely a 'restrictive' rather than a broad and omnibus definition of ideology which we should aim at.

There are various reasons for arguing against the inclusive conception. First of all, as I have maintained above, any definition which is couched in broad philosophical or normative terms is bound to be self-defeating, and can, in addition, find no methodological (as distinguished from historical) justification in the pages of the classics. It is clear that Seliger has such a specification of the term in mind in his elaborate definition of the concept.[19] Secondly, if such an intendment is not implied, then it appears to me that we inevitably end up with a definition which is merely notational, thus possessing no substantive and even less any significant value. It is with reference to this latter aspect that I feel that Seliger is off on the wrong road when he writes:

we can check the adequacy of the connotations of the term 'ideology' by referring to the articulated perspectives and the specific attributes and kinds of behaviour with which the concept is associated . . . Thus, in order to disclose the shortcomings of the restrictive conception and argue the case for the inclusive conception . . . reference will be made, first of all, to the contents of known political belief systems adopted and propagated by political parties and movements, but also to systems developed by social and political thinkers.[20]

"How something functions or is meant to function," he adds on the following page, clarifying his methodological conception of how we discover fruitful conceptualizations, "determines what it can be said to be."[21] Certainly these statements deserve a closer look.

First of all, I do not see how the "adequacy of the connotations of the term 'ideology' " can be determined—particularly for explanatory purposes—by means of the method posited above. For if the touchstone of 'adequacy' is to be the "articulated perspectives," etc., as contained in "known political belief systems," etc., "with which the concept is associated," then it follows almost by definition that an 'umbrella' or omnibus concept will emerge, that is, one covering—on the principle of the least common denominator— the whole gamut of meanings given to 'ideology' both in the specialist literature and in common parlance. In short, given this methodological baseline, it is not surprising that Seliger feels obliged to defend an 'inclusive' conception. But as I have previously argued, it is precisely the fact that 'ideology' is used so indiscriminately by most scholars that makes it so problematic for analytic and particularly explanatory purposes. In this sense Seliger's conception bears all the characteristics of what Giovanni Sartori has castigated as 'conceptual stretching.'[22] It is also due to this method that Seliger can make a claim with which we are already familiar, namely, that "politics can become entirely unideological only if they become completely incoherent," from which he also draws the conclusion that "since such incoherence in party and/or national politics is extremely unlikely, politics will remain ideological."[23] If this is not question-begging, it is certainly a claim which can be upheld only if "ideological" is nothing but a notational equivalent for "ideational" in one sense or another. Here we have, once again, the semantic equation (and hence confusion) which has so deeply suffused the decline of ideology debate; it is not surprising that Seliger, given his definition, explicitly takes the side of the critics of this thesis.

As to Seliger's 'functional' dictum above, let me simply say that although it may be true (or truistic) that the ontological condition of something is in some sense determined by its function, it does not follow from this that we also know—by means of the same determination—what its *name* is. Thus, for example, it is one thing to say that we know the nature of societal norms or rules by means of an examination of their societal function, and something else to claim that we know what 'ideology' is by examining its function in society and politics. In the former case we have no *terminological* problem, whereas in the case of "ideology" we most certainly do. 'Norms' in the above example can be phenomenologically determined precisely because there is no problem with regard to "norms"; but 'ideology' is problematic precisely because "ideology" means x to A, y to B and z to C (and here Stuart Hampshire's point that language "is itself a kind of behaviour interwoven with other kinds" is of little help, despite Seliger's appreciative reference).[24] Hence, he certainly skates on very thin ice when he claims that although " 'ideology' has for long been invested with a strange variety of meanings . . . [it] has always denoted sets of attitudes and ways of behaviour which can be observed in the real world."[25] Yes, certainly: but *what* has been, or is being, observed? Marx saw 'false consciousness' in various forms. Lenin perceived a philosophical partisanship which stretched back for two thousand years and which is now embodied in the revolutionary mission of the proletariat vis-à-vis the bourgeoisie. And Mannheim looked at the existential beholdenness of all thought, including his own. We can add many more such claims of 'attributes' and 'behavior' which have been 'observed' in the 'real world' (and some see 'ideology' in all thought except their own, despite Seliger's sanguine claim that "there is no necessary correlation between one's notion of ideology and one's ideology").[26] I am afraid that what is being seen in this sense is almost invariably something contained primarily in the beholder's eyes; and though 'real,' these things are more often than not real in the sense that Peter Pan's fairies were real. Obviously the only apperception in common here, given this appeal, is that somehow 'ideology' refers to 'real-world' 'ideas' in some sense or other, either to ideas held or to ideas acted upon. But of course then the concept itself has lost all but a notational function.

A third conclusion lies close at hand: it is methodologically a cul-de-sac to seek for a conceptualization basing itself on, or aiming at, either a theory of ideology or a critique of ideology. I think it is obvious, looking at past attempts to construct such edifices, that they beg more questions than they answer. Rather, our primary purpose should be to classify and delimit the concept instead of constructing 'theories' around it. That is to say, before we can explain anything, or prepare it for 'theoretical processing,' we have to engage in what F. S. C. Northrop has dubbed the 'natural history stage of inquiry.' This is best pursued in terms of what Sartori calls 'definition by analysis,' that is, "the process of defining a term by finding the genus to which the object designated by the term belongs, and then specifying the attributes which distinguish such object from all other species of the same genus."[27] This is essentially a matter of classification, or what is also called taxonomical treatment (the old hallowed Latin designation is of course analysis *per genus et differentiam*); I fully agree with Sartori (and Harry Eckstein) that its neglect in much of contemporary social science has a lot to do with our methodological and disciplinary problems in the study of politics.[28] Thus, although it may be a naive belief, as John Gunnell has claimed, that there is "a necessary and natural progression in any science from taxonomy or description and classification to explanatory theory," it is certainly not simpleminded to maintain that no explanation—or 'theories'—can be posited without being grounded in the most basic form of concept formation entailed by the method of definitional classification.[29] Although, as Arthur L. Kalleberg has noted, concept formation as "a general problem in philosophy . . . is extremely complex inasmuch as it covers questions of definition, classification, comparison, measurement, and empirical interpretation," he is surely right when he adds that the basic problem in conceptualization is the analysis of

the questions of definition and especially of the criteria of classification to be used in developing the basic concepts of political science, concepts of the attributes of political phenomena. [For] not only is it necessary to resolve this question prior to engaging in the questions of comparison and measurement, but it is precisely on this most basic level that it is possible to see most clearly the nature of the misunderstandings held by antagonists on both sides of the controversy about a behavioural science in politics.[30]

With reference to this point I feel, once again, that Seliger errs in his analysis.

"One would have expected," he writes, "a sustained effort by philosophers, sociologists, anthropologists, political scientists and psychologists to establish a generally acceptable definition of ideology, rather than that they should proceed by way of stipulative definitions."[31] One does wonder, however, how such a generally acceptable definition can be established except by means of stipulative definitions persuasive enough to warrant general scholarly assent. Seliger's answer seems to lie in the aim of creating a 'theory of ideology,' an effort which indeed forms the main goal of his book. In his own words, the "object of this study is neither exegetical nor historical. What appears initially to be exegesis, and short- or long-range historical flashbacks, is subservient to the theory that is being advanced."[32] He goes on to assert, in the substantive sections of his analysis, among other things, that the "demonstration according to an agreed criterion of the ubiquity of the justification of interests by morals furnishes, then, a firm foundation of the inseparability of all politics and ideology."[33] As a mainstay for a 'theory of ideology' this statement is, however, highly suspect. For although I have no argument with Seliger that in all politics we find a moral or normative component, I cannot understand how he is able to conclude from this generally accepted axiom that it demonstrates the "inseparability of all politics and *ideology*." The "justification of interests by morals," or the "universal ascertainability of this linkage" is surely no "*proof* of the *validity* of the inclusive conception"; at best it follows from a stipulation according to which "ideology" and "morals" (or "norms") are made' coterminous, in which case such locutions as 'validity' and 'proof' are entirely malapropos in the sense used above.[34] Here we can, once again, remind ourselves of May Brodbeck's point that to "criticize a concept on the ground that its definition is not 'really' what the concept means makes sense only if the definition is proffered as an explication of how a term is already being used. In that case we are given not a definition—which is always stipulative —but a report, which may be true or false."[35] Yet it is clear that Seliger is here not merely reporting on how the term is being used—although he does that in many places, incisively, and often with pertinent criticisms—but is presenting us with, as we have already noted, a 'theory of ideology.' This attempt is, in my view, the fundamental problem with his discussion as a whole. Certainly the classification of definitions of ideology into his two categories has great merit—but only as classifications of usage. However, instead of proceeding to construct a 'theory of ideology' à la Mannheim, he would have done better to consider the need not for *theory* but for a *conceptualization* of ideology which would make it useful for explaining political phenomena (we note, perhaps without surprise, that Seliger's book is described on the back cover as "the first since Mannheim to elaborate a comprehensive theory of ideology"). The fact is that in political science there are far too many 'theories' wandering about and too few fruitful and significant concepts taking root; we seem to want to run before we can even walk properly, to use a trite but pertinent phrase.

Since my overriding aim in this study has been to analyze critically the usage of 'ideology' in the writings of the three of the most seminal and influential historic contributors to its development, I shall not here venture to stipulate a definition of my own.

However, on the basis of this analysis, and with particular reference to the criterion of conceptual significance as discussed in the first chapter, I have come to the conclusion that if our concept has any present-day *explanatory* function in the study of empirical political phenomena it is surely not due to any Marxian contributions in terms of 'false consciousness' or 'superstructural' class notions, nor to Mannheim's resolute extension—to their logical limit—of Marxian conceptions, but because of Lenin's explications of the *politicizing* nature and function of 'ideology' as a *belief system* involving *mass action* and *organization*. By claiming this conclusion I am of course not advocating any kind of pro- or anti-Leninism; I am simply saying that of all the conceptions of ideology which we have considered in this study, his 'mobilizing' notion is the only one which has any *empirical* reference and relevance. In short, it is the only usage which can be shown to possess significance in the realm of politics as an active and genuinely *political* phenomenon.

To assert this is, however, by no means to accede to the following criticism made by Seliger contra 'restrictive' definitions (of which Lenin's mobilizing conception is a prime example): "But one shortcoming underlies all others. Most adherents of the restrictive definition who equate ideology with doctrinaire extremism equate it with totalitarianism. They have failed to ask themselves the simple question: what advantage accrues from reserving for analysis of the ideational foundations of totalitarianism the word 'ideology,' which provides no verbal clue to the phenomenon at hand?"[36] To this charge let me say, first of all, that by advocating a 'Leninist' conceptualization I certainly do *not* equate 'ideology' with 'totalitarianism.' I feel, secondly, that the above imputation is unjustified with regard to many eminent scholars who do not accept the 'inclusive' viewpoint for one reason or another. Certainly the main proponents of the decline hypothesis (and Seliger has mainly these in mind here) have not made the above equation. If they, and others, have claimed that 'totalitarian' regimes are more 'ideological' than others, or that underlying or suffusing such regimes we find some form of 'doctrinaire extremism,' or that 'totalitarianism' is primarily based on 'ideology,' and so forth, they have not done so in terms of an *'equation'* between 'ideology' and 'totalitarianism.' On the contrary, if these and similar statements are to be accorded any truth-value, this can be done only on the basis of empirical determination, not definitional or semantic subsumption. For very obvious reasons, therefore, a proponent of a restrictive definition has prima facie no reason for asking himself Seliger's 'simple' question (though he may, if in a particularly vicious mood, point to certain *historical* clues why these two notions often tend to be associated with each other). Certainly there is no "verbal clue" to be found in 'ideology' that signals 'totalitarianism;' but neither does 'ideology' presage verbally the page-long definition which Seliger submits. Indeed, to speak of "verbal clues" in this context is, as we must conclude from the previous chapters, as silly as to assume that a fully acceptable definition of our term is to be found in the venerable and etymologically rich pages of the *Oxford English Dictionary*.

With these remarks I end this analysis of what Daniel Bell, in a somber mood of Biblical resignation, calls an "irretrievably fallen word."[37] Fallen "ideology" certainly has since the days of the optimistic idéologues; and—vide Nietzsche's trenchant observation spearheading these many pages—in so doing it probably has caused a leg or two to be broken as well. But I do not deem it to be beyond some form of redeeming grace; hence the juxtaposition of the more salubrious and uplifting words from *The Shorter Catechism* with the Nietzschean indictment.

In addition to its sacerdotal locution, not out of place in the present context, this authoritative passage also suggests the conceptual wherewithal for such redemption. Appropriately translated into secular language, 'thought,' 'wish,' and 'deed' point to what seem to me to be the three most salient dimensions of the ideological phenomenon in politics, as well as to the interrelationship holding between them. Certainly, if we define 'ideology' with reference to strictly delimited *cognitive, affective,* and *action-oriented* parameters, we have a concept which is dead neither to politics nor to its analysis.[38] However, as to the question whether such belief-systems lead to everlasting salvation and happiness, no answer will even be intimated here.

NOTES

1. Martin Seliger, *Ideology and Politics* (London, 1976), p. 13. At this point I should mention that two very important books on the topic of this study came into my hands only after this study was completed. These are: Martin Seliger's book on *The Marxist Conception of Ideology* (London, 1977), and A. P. Simonds, *Karl Mannheim's Sociology of Knowledge* (Oxford, 1978).

2. *See*, inter alia, N. Birnbaum, "The Sociological Study of Ideology (1940-1960), A Trend Report and Bibliography," *Current Sociology* no. 2 (1960), J. Barion, *Was ist Ideologie?* (Bonn, 1964), P. Corbett, *Ideologies* (London, 1965), G. Lichtheim, *The Concept of Ideology and Other Essays* (New York, 1967), pp. 4ff., E. A. Shils, "The Concept and Function of Ideology" in *International Encyclopedia of the Social Sciences*, vol. 7 (1968), J. Plamenatz, *Ideology* (London, 1970), M. Rejai, "Political Ideology: Theoretical and Comparative Perspectives" in M. Rejai, ed., *Decline of Ideology* (Chicago, 1971), R. Heeger, "Vad är en ideologi?" *Statsvetenskaplig tidskrift*, no. 3 (1972), pp. 307ff., H. M. Drucker, *The Political Use of Ideology* (London, 1974). The most up-to-date and perhaps extensive bibliography on the concept of ideology is to be found in Seliger, op. cit., pp. 31ff.

3. Dante Germino, *Beyond Ideology: The Revival of Political Theory* (New York, 1967).

4. *See*, e.g., Seliger, op. cit., pp. 112ff., and his 'elaborate' definition on pp. 119f.

5. *See* in particular Chaim I. Waxman, ed., *The End of Ideology Debate* (New York, 1968) and M. Rejai, ed., op. cit.

6. *See*, e.g., S. M. Lipset, "Ideology and No End," *Encounter* 39, no. 6 (December 1972): 17ff.

7. *See* respectively, Waxman, op. cit., pp. 229ff. and 315ff.

8. Ibid., p. 251

9. Ibid., p. 276.

10. Ibid., p. 320.

11. Ibid., p. 318.

12. Ibid., pp. 316, 318.

13. M. Rejai, W. L. Mason, and D. C. Beller, "Empirical Relevance of the Hypothesis of Decline" in M. Rejai, op. cit., p. 269.

14. Waxman, op. cit., pp. 182ff; the author of this article is Robert A. Haber.

15. Ibid., pp. 318f.

16. Ernest Nagel, *The Structure of Science* (New York, 1961), p. 492.

17. Seliger, op. cit., p. 14.

18. Ibid.

19. Ibid., pp. 119f.

20. Ibid., p. 15.

21. Ibid., p. 16.

22. Giovanni Sartori, "Concept Misformation in Comparative Politics," *American Political Science Review* 64, no. 4 (1970): 1034ff.

23. Seliger, op. cit., pp. 103f.

24. Ibid., p. 15.

25. Ibid.

26. Ibid., p. 18.

27. Sartori, op. cit., p. 1043.

28. *See* ibid., p. 1033 and Harry Eckstein, ed., *Internal War* (New York, 1964), pp. 8ff.

29. John Gunnell, "Social Science and Political Reality: The Problem of Explanation," *Social Research* 35 (Spring 1968): 165.

30. Arthur L. Kalleberg, "Concept Formation in Normative and Political Studies: Toward Reconciliation in Political Theory," *American Political Science Review* 60, no. 1 (March 1969): 26.

31. Seliger, op. cit., p. 13.

32. Ibid., p. 17.

33. Ibid., p. 135.

34. Ibid. and p. 18. Emphases added.

35. May Brodbeck, "General Introduction" in Brodbeck, ed., *Readings in the Philosophy of the Social Sciences* (New York, 1968), p. 5.

36. Seliger, op. cit., p. 26.

37. Quoted in Seliger, op. cit., p. 87.

38. For two conceptualizations along these lines, *see* Giovanni Sartori's incisive and seminal article—much criticized by Seliger—on "Politics, Ideology and Belief Systems," *American Political Science Review* 63, no. 2 (1969): 398ff., and M. Rejai in Rejai, ed., op. cit., pp. 1ff. For an elaboration on their discussions and my own standpoint, *see* my book *The Comparative Study of Foreign Policy and the Conceptualization of Ideology*, forthcoming.

BIBLIOGRAPHY

Abel, T. "The Operation Called *Verstehen*" in *Readings in the Philosophy of Science*. New York, 1953.
———. "A Reply to Professor Wax." *Sociology and Social Research* 51 (1966-1967).
Adorno, T. W. "Das Bewusstsein der Wissenssoziologie" in Lenk, ed., *Ideologie: Ideologiekritik und Wissenssoziologie*.
Aiken, H. D. *The Age of Ideology*. New York, 1961.
———. "The Revolt Against Ideology" in Waxman, ed., *The End of Ideology Debate*.
Allardt, E. and Littunen, Y., eds. *Cleavages, Ideologies and Party Systems*. Helsinki, 1968.
Althusser, L. *Lénine et la philosophie*. Paris, 1968.
———. *Lenin och filosofi*. Stockholm, 1969.
Antoni, C. *From History to Sociology*. Detroit, 1959.
Apter, D. E., ed. *Ideology and Discontent*. New York, 1964.
———. "Introduction: Ideology and Discontent" in Apter, ed., *Ideology and Discontent*.
Arblaster, A. "Ideology and Intellectuals" in Benewick, et al., *Knowledge and Belief in Politics*.
Aron, R. *The Opium of the Intellectuals*. New York, 1962.
———. *German Sociology*. London, 1965.
———. *The Industrial Society*. New York, 1967.
Ashcroft, R. "Marx and Weber on Liberalism as Bourgeois Ideology." *Comparative Studies in Society and History* 14 (1972).
Avineri, Shlomo. "Marx and the Intellectuals." *Journal of the History of Ideas* 28, no. 2 (1967).
———. *Karl Marx: Social and Political Thought*. Cambridge, 1971.
Barion, J. *Was ist Ideologie?* Bonn, 1964.
Barnes, S. H. "Ideology and the Organization of Conflict: On the Relationship between Political Thought and Behavior." *Journal of Politics* 28 (1966).
Barth, H. *Wahrheit und Ideologie*. Zurich, 1945.
Beard, C. A. "Written History as an Act of Faith." *American Historical Review* 39, no. 2 (1934).

————. "That Noble Dream." *American Historical Review* 41, no. 1 (1935).

Beard, C. A., and Vogst, A. "Currents of Thought in Historiography." *American Historical Review* 42, no. 3 (1937).

Bell, D. *The End of Ideology.* New York, 1960.

————. "Ideology and Soviet Politics." *Slavic Review* 24, no. 4 (1965).

Bell, D., and Aiken, H. D. "Ideology—A Debate" in Waxman, ed., *The End of Ideology Debate.*

Bendix, R. *Max Weber: An Intellectual Portrait.* Garden City, N.Y., 1962.

————. "The Age of Ideology: Persistent and Changing" in Apter, ed., *Ideology and Discontent.*

Benewick, R., Berki, R. N., and Parekh, B., eds. *Knowledge and Belief in Politics: The Problem of Ideology.* London, 1973.

Berdyaev, N. *The Origin of Russian Communism.* London, 1937.

Berger, P. "Identity as a Problem in the Sociology of Knowledge." *Archives Européenes de Sociologie* 7, no. 1 (1966).

Berger, P. and Pullberg, S. "Reification and the Sociological Critique of Consciousness." *History and Theory* 4, no. 2 (1965).

Bergmann, G. "Ideology." *Ethics* 61 (1951).

Berlin, I. *Four Essays on Liberty.* London, 1969.

————. *Karl Marx.* Oxford, 1939.

Birnbaum, N. "The Sociological Study of Ideology (1940-60): A Trend Report and Bibliography." *Current Sociology* 9, no. 2 (1960).

Blackburn, R., ed. *Ideology in Social Science.* London, 1972.

Bober, M. M. *Karl Marx's Interpretation of History.* Cambridge, Mass., 1927.

Borger, R. and Cioffi, F., eds. *Explanation and the Behavioural Sciences.* Cambridge, 1970.

Bottomore, T. B. "Some Reflections on the Sociology of Knowledge." *British Journal of Sociology* 7 (1956).

Braude, L. *"Die Verstehende Soziologie*: A New Look at an Old Problem." *Sociology and Social Research* 50 (1965-1966).

Brodbeck, M., ed. *Readings in the Philosophy of the Social Sciences.* New York, 1968.

————. "General Introduction" in Brodbeck, ed., *Readings in the Philosophy of the Social Sciences.*

Brown, R. "The Explanation of Behavior." *Philosophy* 40 (1965).

Bruun, H. H. *Science, Values and Politics in Max Weber's Methodology.* Copenhagen, 1972.

Brzezinski, Z. B. *Ideology and Power in Soviet Politics.* New York, 1962.

Burks, R. V. "A Conception of Ideology for Historians." *Journal of the History of Ideas* 10 (1949).

Bursisch, W. *Ideologie und Sachzwang: Die Entideologisierungsthese in neueren Gesellschaftstheorien.* Tübingen, 1967.

Burtt, E. A. *The English Philosophers from Bacon to Mill.* New York, 1939.

Carlsnaes, W. "A Conceptual Analysis of African Nationalism" in Hessler, ed., *Ideer och ideologier.*

Carmichael, J. "Trotsky's Agony, I." *Encounter* 38, no. 5 (May 1972).

Carr, E. H. *The Bolshevik Revolution of the Soviet Union.* London, 1960.
——. *What Is History?* New York, 1962.
Cassirer, E. *The Problem of Knowledge.* New Haven, 1950.
Child, A. "The Problem of Imputation in the Sociology of Knowledge." *Ethics* 51 (1940-1941).
——. "The Theoretical Possibility of the Sociology of Knowledge." *Ethics* 51 (1940-1941).
——. "The Existential Determination of Thought." *Ethics* 52 (1941-1942).
——. "The Problem of Imputation Resolved." *Ethics* 54 (1943-1944).
Christensen, K. M., ed. *Ideologies and Modern Politics.* London, 1972.
Christoph, J. B. "Consensus and Cleavage in British Political Ideology." *American Political Science Review*, 59, no. 3 (1965).
Collingwood, R. G. *The Idea of History.* Oxford, 1946.
Connolly, W. E. *Political Science and Ideology.* New York, 1967.
Converse, P. E. "The Nature of Belief Systems in Mass Politics" in Apter, ed., *Ideology and Discontent.*
Corbett, P. *Ideologies.* London, 1965.
Cornforth, M. *Dialectical Materialism: An Introduction.* London, 1954.
——. *Marxism and the Linguistic Philosophy.* London, 1965.
——. *The Open Philosophy and the Open Society.* London, 1968.
Costello, D. P. "Voluntarism and Determinism in Bolshevist Doctrine." *Soviet Studies* 12 (1960-1961).
Cox, R. H., ed. *Ideology, Politics, and Political Theory.* Belmont, Mass., 1969.
Cunningham, A. "Reflections on Projections: The Range of Ideology" in Benewick et al., *Knowledge and Belief in Politics.*
Curtis, M., ed. *Marxism.* New York, 1970.
Dahl, R. A. *A Preface to Democratic Theory.* Chicago, 1956.
——. "A Critique of the Ruling Elite Model." *American Political Science Review* 52 (1958).
——. *Who Governs?* New Haven, 1961.
——. "Ideology, Conflict and Consensus: Notes for a Theory." Paper presented at the Seventh World Congress of the International Political Science Association, September 1967, at Brussels.
Dahm, H. "Der Ideologiebegriff bei Marx und die heutige Kontroverse über Ideologie und Wissenschaft in den sozialistischen Ländern." *Studies in Soviet Thought* 12, no. 1 (April 1972).
Dan, T. *The Origins of Bolshevism.* London 1964.
Daniels, R. V. "Lenin and the Russian Revolutionary Tradition." *Harvard Slavic Studies* 4 (1957).
——. "Soviet Power and Marxist Determinism." *Problems of Communism* 9, no. 3 (1960).
Delaney, W. "The Role of Ideology: A Summation" in Waxman, ed., *The End of Ideology Debate.*
DePalma, G. *The Study of Conflict in Western Society: A Critique of the End of Ideology.* Morristown, 1973.
Dicke, G. *Der Identitätsgedanke bei Feuerbach und Marx.* Cologne, 1960.

Diggins, J. P. "Ideology and Pragmatism: Philosophy or Passion?" *American Politial Science Review* 64, no. 3 (1970).

Dion, L. "Political Ideology as a Tool of Functional Analysis in Socio-Political Dynamics: An Hypothesis." *Canadian Journal of Economics and Political Science* 25 (1959).

Drachkovitch, M. M., ed. *Marxist Ideology in the Contemporary World*. New York, 1966.

Dray, W. H. *Philosophy of History*. Englewood Cliffs, N.J., 1964.

———., ed. *Philosophical Analysis and History*. New York, 1966.

———. "Singular Hypotheticals and Historical Explanation" in Gross, ed., *Sociological Theory: Inquiries and Paradigms*.

Drucker, H. M. *The Political Use of Ideology*. London, 1974.

van Duzer, C. H. *Contribution of the Ideologues to French Revolutionary Thought*. Baltimore, 1935.

Eckstein, H., ed. *Internal War*. New York, 1964.

Eisermann, G., ed. *Die Lehre von der Gesellschaft*. Stuttgart, 1958.

Emmet, D. and MacIntyre, A., eds. *Sociological Theory and Philosophical Analysis*. London, 1970.

Engelberg, E., ed. *Probleme der Geschichtsmethodologie*. Berlin, 1972.

Engel-Janosi, F. "The Growth of German Historicism." *Johns Hopkins University Studies and Political Science*, ser. 62, no. 2 (1944).

Eriksson, B. *Om den sociologiska analysen av kunskap*. Uppsala, 1972.

Eysenck, H. J. "The Dangers of the New Zealots." *Encounter* 39, no. 6 (December 1972).

Federn, K. *The Materialist Conception of History*. London, 1939.

Fetscher, I. *Von Marx zur Sowjetideologie*. Frankfurt, 1957.

Feuer, L. S. "What Is Philosophy of History." *Journal of Philosophy* 49, no. 10 (1952).

———. "Beyond Ideology" in Waxman, ed., *The End of Ideology Debate*.

———. *The Scientific Intellectual*. New York, 1963.

———. "Marxism and the Hegemony of the Intellectual Class." *Transactions of the Fifth World Congress of Sociology* 4. Brussels, 1964.

———. "Lenin's Fantasy." *Encounter* 35, no. 6 (December 1970).

———. "Ideology and No End: Some Personal History." *Encounter* 40, no. 10 (April 1973).

———. *Ideology and the Ideologists*. Oxford, 1975.

Feyerabend, P. *Against Method*. London, 1975.

Fischer, E. and Marek, F. *Was Lenin Wirklich Sagte*. Vienna, 1969.

Frankel, C. "Theory and Practice in Marx's Thought." *Marx and Contemporary Thought*. The Hague 1969.

Friedrich, C. J. *Man and His Government*. New York, 1963.

———. "Ideology in Politics: A Theoretical Comment." *Slavic Review* 25, no. 4 (1965).

Friedrich, M. *Philosophie und Ökonomie beim jünger Marx*. Berlin, 1960.

Friess, H. L. "Historical Interpretation and Culture Analysis." *Journal of Philosophy* 49, no. 10 (1952).

Gardiner, P., ed. *Theories of History*. Glencoe, 1959.

――――. *The Nature of Historical Explanation*. London, 1961.

――――., ed. *The Philosophy of History*. London, 1974.

Geertz, C. "Ideologies as Cultural Systems" in Apter, ed., *Ideology and Discontent*.

Geiger, T. *Ideologie und Wahrheit*. Stuttgart, 1953.

Germino, D. *Beyond Ideology: The Revival of Political Theory*. New York, 1967.

Geyer, D. *Lenin in der russischen Sozialdemokratie*, Cologne. 1962.

Gluck, S. E. "The Epistemology of Mannheim's Sociology of Knowledge." *Methodes* 6 (1954).

deGre, G. "The Sociology of Knowledge and the Problem of Truth." *Journal of the History of Ideas* 2 (1941).

Gregor, A. J. *A Survey of Marxism*. New York, 1965.

――――. *Contemporary Radical Ideologies*. New York, 1968.

Gropp, R. O. "Die marxistische dialektische Methode und ihr Gegensatz zur idealistischen Dialektik Hegels." I, II, *Deutsche Zeitschrift für Philosophie* 2 (1954).

Gross, L., ed. *Symposium on Sociological Theory*. Evanston, 1959.

――――. *Sociological Theory: Inquiries and Paradigms*. New York, 1967.

Grünwald, E. *Das Probleme der Soziologie des Wissens*. Vienna, 1934.

Gunnell, J. "Social Science and Political Reality: The Problem of Explanation." *Social Research* 35 (Spring 1968).

Gurwitch, G. "Wissenssoziologie" in Eisermann, ed., *Die Lehre von der Gesellschaft*.

Haber, R. H. "The End of Ideology as Ideology" in Waxman, ed., *The End of Ideology Debate*.

Hahn, E. "Zur Kritik des burgerlichen Bewusstseins" in Lenk, ed. *Ideologie: Ideologiekritik und Wissenssoziologie*.

Haimson, L. H. *The Russian Marxists and the Origins of Bolshevism*. Cambridge, Mass., 1955.

Halpern, B. " 'Myth' and 'Ideology' in Modern Usage." *History and Theory* 1, no. 2 (1961).

Hamilton, P. *Knowledge and Social Structure*. London, 1974.

Hammen, O. J. "Alienation, Communism and Revolution in the Marx-Engels *Briefwechsel*." *Journal of the History of Ideas* 33, no. 1 (1972).

Hampshire, S. *Thought and Action*. London, 1959.

Harrell, B. "Symbols, Perception, and Meaning" in Gross, ed., *Sociological Theory: Inquiries and Paradigms*.

Harris, N. *Beliefs in Society: The Problem of Ideology*. Harmondsworth, 1971.

Hart, H. L. A. *The Concept of Law*. Oxford, 1961.

Hartmann, K. *Die Marxische Theorie*. Berlin, 1970.

Hartung, F. "Problems of the Sociology of Knowledge." *Philosophy of Science* 19 (1952).

Heeger, R. "Vad är en ideologi?" *Statsvetenskaplig Tidskrift*, no. 3 (1972).

Heisenberg, W. *Philosophical Problems of Nuclear Science*. London, 1952.

――――. *Physics and Philosophy*. London, 1959.

Heiss, R. *Die grossen Dialektiker des 19. Jahrhunderts.* Cologne, 1963.

Hempel, C. *Aspects of Scientific Explanation.* New York, 1965.

――――. *Philosophy of Natural Science.* Englewood Cliffs, N.J., 1966.

Hessler, C. A., ed. *Idéer och ideologier.* Stockholm, 1969.

Heussi, K. *Die Krisis des Historismus.* Tübingen, 1932.

Hillman, G. *Marx und Hegel.* Frankfurt, 1966.

Himmelstrand, U. "A Theoretical and Empirical Approach to Depolitization and Political Involvement." *Acta Sociologica* 6 (1962).

Hinshaw, V. "The Epistemological Relevance of Mannheim's Sociology of Knowledge." *Journal of Philosophy* 40, no. 3 (1943).

――――. "Epistemological Relativism and the Sociology of Knowledge." *Philosophy of Science* 15 (1948).

Hobsbawm, E. J. "Karl Marx's Contribution to Historiography." *Marx and Contemporary Scientific Thought.*

Hodges, D. C. "The End of 'The End of Ideology' " in Waxman, ed., *The End of Ideology Debate.*

Hofer, W. *Geschichtschreibung und Weltanschauung.* Munich, 1950.

Hollitscher, W. "Der Ideologiebegriff in marxistischer Sicht." *Proceedings of the Fourteenth International Congress of Philosophy.* Vienna, 1968.

Hook, S. *From Hegel to Marx: Studies in the Intellectual Development of Marx.* New York, 1950.

――――. *Dialectical Materialism and Scientific Method.* Manchester, 1955.

――――., ed. *Philosophy and History* New York, 1963.

Horkheimer, M. "Ideologie und Handeln" in Lenk, ed., *Ideologie: Ideologiekritik und Wissenssoziologie.*

――――. "Ein neuer Ideologiebegriff?" in Lenk, ed., *Ideologie: Ideologiekrtik und Wissenssoziologie.*

Horowitz, I. L. *Philosophy, Science and the Sociology of Knowledge.* Springfield, 1961.

――――., ed. *The New Society.* London, 1964.

Hughes, H. S. "The End of Political Ideology." *Measure* 2 (Spring 1951).

――――. *Consciousness and Society.* London, 1959.

Jakubowski, F. *Der ideologische Überbau in der materialistische Geschichtsauffsaung.* Frankfurt, 1968.

Jarvie, I. C. *Concepts and Society.* London, 1972.

Johnson, H. M. "Ideology and the Social System." *International Encyclopedia of the Social Sciences* 7 (1968).

Joravsky, D. *Soviet Marxism and Natural Science, 1917-1932.* New York, 1961.

――――. "Soviet Ideology." *Soviet Studies* 18, no. 1 (1966).

Jordan, Z. A. *Philosophy and Ideology.* Dordrecht, 1963.

――――. *The Evolution of Dialectical Materialism.* New York, 1967.

Joynt, C. B. and Rescher, N. "On Explanation in History." *Mind* 68 (1959).

Kalleberg, A. L. "Concept Formation in Normative and Political Studies: Toward Reconciliation in Political Theory." *American Political Science Review* 60, no. 1 (1969).

Kamenka, E. *The Ethical Foundations of Marxism.* London, 1962.

Kaplan, A. *The Conduct of Inquiry*. San Francisco, 1964.

Kelsen, H. *Aufsätze zur Ideologiekritik*. Neuwied, 1964.

Kettler, D. "Sociology of Knowledge and Moral Philosophy: The Place of Traditional Problems in the Formation of Mannheim's Thought." *Political Science Quarterly* 82 (1967).

Knorr, K. and Rosenau, J. N., eds. *Contending Approaches to International Politics*. Princeton, 1969.

Kolakowski, L. "Karl Marx and the Classical Definition of Truth" in Labedz, ed., *Revisionism*.

Kordig, C. R. *The Justification of Scientific Change*. Dordrecht, 1971.

Kruger, M. "Sociology of Knowledge and Social Theory." *Berkeley Journal of Sociology* 14 (1969).

Kuhn, T. *The Structure of Scientific Revolution*. 2d ed. Chicago, 1970.

Köhler, H. *Gründe des dialektischen Materialismus im europäischen Denken*. Munich, 1961.

Labedz, L., ed. *Revisionism*. New York, 1962.

Lakatos, I. and Musgrave, A., eds. *Criticism and the Growth of Knowledge*. Cambridge, 1970.

Lamprecht, S. P., "Comments on the Symposium 'What Is Philosophy of History?' ". *Journal of Philosophy* 49, no. 10 (1952).

Landau, M. "Comment: On Objectivity." *American Political Science Review* 46, no. 3 (September 1972).

Lane, R. E. *Political Ideology*. New York, 1962.

———. "The Decline of Politics and Ideology in a Knowledgeable Society." *American Sociological Review* 31, no. 5 (1966).

———. "The Meanings of Ideology" in Larson and Wasburn, eds., *Power, Participation and Ideology*.

LaPalombara, J. "Decline of Ideology: A Dissent and an Interpretation." *American Political Science Review* 60, no. 1 (1966).

Larson, C. J. and Wasburn, P. C., eds. *Power, Participation and Ideology*. New York, 1969.

Larsson, R. *Theories of Revolution*. Stockholm, 1970.

Lasky, M. J. "The Prometheans: On the Imagery of Fire and Revolution." *Encounter* 31, no. 4 (October 1968).

———. "The Sweet Dream: Kant and the Revolutionary Hope for Utopia." *Encounter* 33, no. 4 (October 1969).

———. "The Birth of a Metaphor, I and II." *Encounter* 34, nos. 2, 3 (February, March 1970).

Laslett, P. and Runciman, W. G., eds. *Philosophy, Politics and Society, Third Series*. Oxford, 1969.

Laslett, P., Runciman, W. G., and Skinner, S., eds. *Philosophy, Politics and Society, Fourth Series*. Oxford, 1972.

Lavine, T. Z. "Sociological Analysis of Cognitive Norms." *Journal of Philosophy* 39 (1942).

———. "Knowledge as Interpretation: An Historical Survey, Part II." *Philosophical and Phenomenological Research* 11 (1950-1951).

——. "Reflections on the Genetic Fallacy." *Social Research* 29 (1962).

——. "Karl Mannheim and Contemporary Functionalism." *Philosophical and Phenomenological Research* 25 (1964-1965).

Lee, D. E. and Beck, R. N. "The Meaning of Historicism." *American Historical Review* 59 (1953-1954).

Lefebvre, H. *La pensée de Lénine*. Paris, 1957.

——. *The Sociology of Marx*. London, 1968.

——. *Lenins tänkande*. Stockholm, 1971.

Leff, G. *History and Social Theory*. London, 1969.

——. *The Tyranny of Concepts*. London, 1969.

Lenin, V. I. *What Is to Be Done?* Oxford, 1963.

——. *Collected Works*. Vols. 5, 14. Moscow, 1964.

——. *Selected Works*. Vol. 1. Moscow, 1967.

Lenk, K., ed. *Ideologie: Ideologiekritik und Wissenssoziologie*. Neuwied, 1967.

——. *Marx in der Wissenssoziologie*. Neuwied, 1972.

Levison, A. "Knowledge and Society." *Inquiry* 9 (1966).

Lewin, L. *Folket och eliterna*. Stockholm, 1970.

Lichtheim, G. *Marxism: An Historical Survey*. New York, 1961.

——. "Comments." *Slavic Review* 24, no. 4 (1965).

——. *The Concept of Ideology and Other Essays*. New York, 1967.

Lieber, H.-J. *Wissen und Gesellschaft*. Tübingen, 1952.

——. *Philosophie, Soziologie, Gesellschaft*. Berlin, 1965.

Lipset, S. M. *Political Man*. Garden City, 1963.

——. "Some Further Comments on the 'The End of Ideology'." *American Political Science Review* 60, no. 1 (1966).

——. *Youth and Dissent*. New York, 1971.

——. "Ideology and No End." *Encounter* 39, no. 6 (December 1972).

Livergood, N. D. *Activity in Marx's Philosophy*. The Hague, 1967.

Löwenstein, J. I. *Vision und Wirklichkeit*. Basel, 1970.

Löwith, K. *Meaning in History*. Chicago, 1949.

——. *From Hegel to Nietzsche*. New York, 1964.

Lukács, G. *Geschichte und Klassenbewusstsein*. Berlin, 1923.

——. *Der junge Hegel*. Berlin, 1954.

——. *Lenin*. Neuwied, 1967.

MacIntyre, A. *Against the Self-Images of the Age*. London, 1971.

Mackenzie, W. J. M. *Politics and Social Science*. Harmondsworth, 1967.

MacMaster, R. E. "In the Russian Manner: Thought as Incipient Action." *Harvard Slavic Studies* 24 (1957).

MacRae, D. G. *Ideology and Society*. London, 1961.

Madge, C. *Society in the Mind*. New York, 1964.

Mandelbaum, M. *The Problem of Historical Knowledge*. New York, 1938.

——. "Causal Analysis in History." *Journal of the History of Ideas* 2 (1942).

——. "Some Neglected Philosophic Problems Regarding History." *Journal of Philosophy* 49, no. 10 (1952).

——. "Comments." *Journal of Philosophy* 49, no. 10 (1952).

Mannheim, K. *Ideologie und Utopie*. Bonn, 1929.
———. *Ideology and Utopia*. London, 1936.
———. "Der Historismus" in Wolff, ed., *Karl Mannheim: Wissenssoziologie*.
Marcuse, H. *Soviet Marxism: A Critical Analysis*. 1958. Reprint. Harmondsworth, 1971.
———. *Vernunft und Revolution*. Neuwied, 1962.
Martin, D. "The Sociology of Knowledge and the Nature of Social Knowledge." *British Journal of Sociology* 19 (1968).
Marx and Contemporary Scientific Thought. The Hague, 1969.
Marx, K. *Grundrisse der Kritik der politischen Ökonomie*. London, 1963.
———. *Economic and Philosophical Manuscripts of 1844*.
Marx, K. and Engels, F. *Gesamtausgabe*. Moscow, 1927-.
———. *Werke*. Berlin, 1954-1968.
———. *Selected Works in Two Volumes*. Moscow, 1955.
———. *Die deutsche Ideologie*. Berlin, 1960.
———. *Selected Works*. Moscow, n.d.
———. *Selected Works*. New York, n.d.
McClosky, H. "Consensus and Ideology in American Politics." *American Political Science Review* 58, no. 2 (1964).
McLellan, D. *Karl Marx: His Life and Thought*. London, 1973.
Meinecke, F. *Die Enstehung des Historismus, Werke, Vol. 3*. Munich, 1959.
Mepham, J. "The Theory of Ideology in Capital." *Radical Philosophy*, no. 2 (Summer 1972).
Merelman, R. M. "The Development of Political Ideology: A Framework for the Analysis of Political Socialization." *American Political Science Review* 63, no. 3 (1969).
Merton, R. K. *Social Theory and Social Structure*. New York, 1957.
Mészáros, I. *Marx's Theory of Alienation*. London, 1972.
Meyer, A. G. *Leninism*. Cambridge, Mass., 1957.
———. "The Foundations of Ideology in the Soviet Political System." *Soviet Studies* 17, no. 3 (1966).
Meyerhoff, H., ed. *The Philosophy of History in Our Time*. New York, 1959.
Mills, C. W. *The Power Elite*. New York, 1959.
———. *Power, Politics and People*. New York, 1963.
Minar, D. W. "Ideology and Political Behavior." *Midwest Journal of Political Science* 5, no. 4 (1961).
Moore, B. *Political Power and Social Order*. Cambridge, Mass., 1958.
Mukerji, K. P. *Implications of the Ideology Concept*. Bombay, 1955.
Mullins, W. A. "On the Concept of Ideology in Political Science." *American Political Science Review* 66, no. 2 (1972).
———. "Sartori's Concept of Ideology: A Dissent and an Alternative" in Allen R. Wilcox, ed., *Public Opinion and Political Attitudes: A Reader*. New York, 1974.
Munch, P. A. "Empirical Science and Max Weber's *Verstehende Soziologie*." *American Sociological Review* 22, no. 1 (1957).

Naess, A., Christophersen, J. A., and Kvalø, N. *Democracy, Ideology and Objectivity: Studies in the Semantics and Cognitive Analysis of Ideological Controversy.* Oslo, 1956.

Naess, A. *Communication and Argument.* Oslo, 1966.

Nagel, E. *The Structure of Science.* New York, 1961.

Neisser, H. *On the Sociology of Knowledge.* New York, 1965.

Nisbet, R. A. *Social Change and History.* New York, 1969.

————. "The Nemesis of Authority." *Encounter* 39, no. 2 (August 1972).

————. *The Social Philosophers.* New York, 1973.

Oertel, H. "Zur Genesis des Ideologiebegriffs." *Deutsche Zeitung für Philosophie* 18, no. 2 (1970).

Ollman, B. *Alienation: Marx's Conception of Man in Capitalist Society.* Cambridge, 1971.

O'Malley, J. J. "History and Man's 'Nature' in Marx." *Review of Politics* 28, no. 4 (1966).

Pannekoek, A. *Lenin as Philosopher.* New York, 1948.

Parekh, B. "Social and Political Thought and the Problem of Ideology" in Benewick et al., eds., *Knowledge and Belief in Politics.* London, 1973.

Parsons, T. *Sociological Theory and Modern Society.* New York, 1967.

Partridge, P. H. "Politics, Philosophy, Ideology" in Quinton, ed., *Political Philosophy.*

Paul, G. A. "Lenin's Theory of Perception." *Analysis* 5, no. 5 (1938).

Plamenatz, J. *German Marxism and Russian Communism.* London, 1954.

————. *Man and Society.* Vol. 2. London, 1963.

————. *Ideology.* London, 1970.

Popper, K. "What Is Dialectic?" *Mind* n.s. 49 (1940).

————. *The Poverty of Historicism.* New York, 1957.

————. *The Open Society and Its Enemies.* Vol. 2. London, 1962.

————. *Conjectures and Refutations.* Rev. ed. London, 1972.

————. "*On Reason and the Open Society.*" *Encounter* 38, no. 5 (May 1972).

Putnam, R. D. "Studying Elite Political Culture: The Case of 'Ideology'." *American Political Science Review* 65, no. 2 (1971).

Quinton, A., ed. *Political Philosophy.* Oxford, 1967.

Rejai, M., ed. *Decline of Ideology?* Chicago, 1971.

————. "Political Ideology: Theoretical and Comparative Perspectives" in Rejai, ed., *Decline of Ideology?*

————. "Ideology" in Philip P. Wiener, ed., *Dictionary of the History of Ideas.* New York, 1973.

Rejai, M., Mason, W. L., and Beller, D. C. "Empirical Relevance of the Hypothesis" in Rejai, ed., *Decline of Ideology?*

Richards, I. A. *Principles of Literary Criticism.* London, 1924.

Rickert, H. *Die Grenzen der naturwissenschaftlichen Begriffsbildung.* Frieburg, 1896; Tübingen, 1929.

————. *Probleme der Geschichtsphilosophie.* Heidelberg, 1924.

Rokeach, M. *The Open and the Closed Mind: Investigations into the Nature of Belief Systems and Personality Systems.* New York, 1960.

Roucek, J. S. "A History of the Concept of Ideology." *Journal of the History of Ideas* 5 (1944).

Rudner, R. S. *Philosophy of Social Science*. Englewood Cliffs, N.J., 1966.

Runciman, W. G. *Social Science and Political Theory*. Cambridge, 1963.

———. *A Critique of Max Weber's Philosophy of Social Science*. Cambridge, 1972.

———. "Ideological and Social Science" in Benewick et al., eds., *Knowledge and Beliefs in Politics*.

Runes, D. D., ed. *Dictionary of Philosophy*. London, 1942.

Rüschemeyer, D. *Probleme der Wissenssoziologie*. Cologne, 1958.

Russell, B. *The Analysis of Matter*. London, 1954.

———. *History of Western Philosophy*. London, 1961.

Ryan, A. *The Philosophy of the Social Sciences*. London, 1970.

———. " 'Normal' Science or Political Ideology" in Laslett, Runciman, and Skinner, eds., *Philosophy, Politics and Society, Fourth Series*.

———., ed. *The Philosophy of Social Explanation*. London, 1973.

Sartori, G. "Politics, Ideology, and Belief Systems." *American Political Science Review* 63 (1969).

———. "Concept Formation in Comparative Politics." *American Political Science Review* 64 (1970).

Schapiro, L. "Lenin's Contribution to Politics." *Political Quarterly* 35 (1964).

Scheffler, I. *Science and Subjectivity*. Indianapolis, 1967.

von Schelting, A. *Max Weber's Wissenslehre*. Tübingen, 1943.

Scheler, M. *Die Wissensformen und die Gesellschaft*. Leipzig, 1926.

Schenck-Notzing, C. *Zukunftsmacher*. Stuttgart, 1968.

Schumpeter, I. A. "Science and Ideology." *American Economic Review* 39 (1949).

Seliger, M. "Fundamental and Operative Ideology: The Two Dimensions of Political Argumentation." *Policy Sciences* 1, no. 3 (1970).

———. *Ideology and Politics*. London, 1976.

———. *The Marxist Conception of Ideology*. London, 1977.

Senghaas, D. "Ideologiekritik und Gesellschaftstheorie." *Neue politische Litteratur* 10 (1965).

Shils, E. A. "The Concept and Function of Ideology." *International Encyclopedia of the Social Sciences* 7 (1968).

———. "End of Ideology." *Encounter* 5, no. 5 (November 1955).

———. "Ideology and Civility: On the Politics of the Intellectual." *Sewanee Review* 66, no. 3 (1958).

Shklar, J. N. *After Utopia: The Decline of Political Faith*. Princeton, 1957.

———., ed. *Political Theory and Ideology*. New York, 1966.

Sigmund, P. E., ed. *The Ideologies of the Developing Areas*. New York, 1967.

Simmel, G. *Die Probleme der Geschichtsphilosophie*. Munich, 1922.

Simonds, A. P. *Karl Mannheim's Sociology of Knowledge*. Oxford, 1978.

Smith, T. C. "The Writing of American History in America, from 1884 to 1934." *American Historical Review* 40, no. 3 (1935).

Stark, W. *The Sociology of Knowledge*. London, 1958.

Steiner, G. *Language and Silence*. London, 1967.

Stevenson, C. L. *Ethics and Language*. New Haven, 1944.

Tagliacozzo, G. and White, H. V., eds. *Giambattista Vico: An International Symposium*. Baltimore, 1969.

Tarschys, D. *Beyond the State*. Stockholm, 1970.

Taylor, C. "Neutrality in Political Science" in Laslett and Runciman, eds., *Philosophy, Politics and Society, Third Series*.

Thyssen, J. *Geschichte der Geschichtsphilosophie*. Bonn, 1936.

———. *Der philosophische Relativismus*. Bonn, 1941.

Tingsten, H. "Stability and Vitality in Swedish Democracy." *Political Quarterly* 26, no. 2 (1955).

Topitsch, E. "Begriff und Funktion der Ideologie," in Topitsch, ed., *Sozialphilosophie zwischen Ideologie und Wissenschaft* (Neuwied, 1966).

———., ed. *Logik der Sozialwissenschaften*. Cologne, 1965.

Toulmin, S. "Conceptual Revolutions in Science." *Boston Studies in the Philosophy of Science*. Dordrecht, 1967.

Treadgold, D. W. *Lenin and His Rivals*. New York, 1955.

Troeltsch, E. *Der Historismus und seine Probleme*. Tübingen, 1923.

Tucker, R. C. "The Deradicalization of Marxist Movements." *American Political Science Review* 61, 2 (1967).

———. *Philosophy and Myth in Marx*. Cambridge, Mass., 1969.

Tudor, H. *Political Myth*. London, 1972.

Ulam, A. B. *Lenin and the Bolsheviks*. London, 1966.

Utechin, S. V. "Philosophy and Society: Alexander Bogdanov" in Labedz, ed., *Revisionism*.

Vierkant, A., ed. *Handwörterbuch der Soziologie* (Stuttgart, 1931).

Wagner, H. L. "Mannheim's Historicism." *Social Research* 19 (1952).

Wagner, H. R. "The Scope of Mannheim's Thinking." *Social Research* 20 (1953).

Walsh, W. H. *An Introduction to Philosophy and History*. London, 1951.

———. *Philosophy of History: An Introduction*. New York, 1960.

Walter, B. "The Sociology of Knowledge and the Problem of Objectivity" in Gross, ed. *Sociological Theory: Inquiries and Paradigms*.

Watnick, M. "Relativism and Class Consciousness" in Labedz, ed., *Revisionism*.

Wax, M. L. "On Misunderstanding *Verstehen*: A Reply to Abel." *Sociology and Social Research* 51 (1966-1967).

Waxman, C. I., ed. *The End of Ideology Debate*. New York, 1968.

Wetter, G. A. *Der dialektische Materialismus*. Freiburg, 1952.

———. *Sowjetideologie heute*. Frankfurt, 1962.

Wiener, P., ed. *Dictionary of the History of Ideas*. New York, 1973.

Wilcox, A. R., ed. *Public Opinion and Political Attitudes: A Reader*. New York, 1974.

Williams, B. and Montefiori, eds. *British Analytic Philosophy*. London, 1966.

Winch, P. *The Idea of a Social Science and Its Relations to Philosophy*. London, 1958.

Wolfe, B. D. *Marxism: One Hundred Years in the Life of a Doctrine*. London, 1967.

Wolff, K. H. "The Sociology of Knowledge: Emphasis on an Empirical Attitude." *Philosophy of Science* 10 (1943).

――――. "The Unique and the General: Toward a Philosophy of Sociology." *Philosophy of Science* 15 (1948).

――――. "On the Scientific Relevance of 'Imputation'." *Ethics* 61 (1950-1951).

――――. "A Preliminary Inquiry into the Sociology of Knowledge from the Standpoint of the Study of Man." *Scritti di Sociologia e Politica in onere di Luigi Sturzo*. Vol. 3 (Bologna, 1953).

――――. "The Sociology of Knowledge and Sociological Theory" in Gross, ed., *Symposium on Sociological Theory*.

――――., ed. *Karl Mannheim: Wissenssoziologie*. Berlin, 1964.

――――. "The Sociology of Knowledge in the United States." *Current Sociology* 15, 1 (1967).

――――, ed. *From Karl Mannheim*. New York, 1971.

von Wright, G. H. *Explanation and Understanding*. London, 1971.

Zeitlin, I. M. *Marxism: A Re-Interpretation* (Princeton, 1967).

――――. *Ideology and the Development of Sociological Theory*. Englewood Cliffs, N.J., 1968.

Zeltner, H. *Ideologie und Wahreit*. Stuttgart, 1966.

Zitta, V. *Georg Lukács' Marxism: Alienation, Dialectics, Revolution*. The Hague, 1964.

Zolberg, A. "Frantz Fanon: A Gospel for the Damned." *Encounter* 27, 5 (November 1966).

INDEX

ABOUT THE AUTHOR

WALTER CARLSNAES is Research Associate at the Swedish Institute of International Affairs, Stockholm, and Assistant Professor of Government at the University of Uppsala, Sweden.